Read this book online today:

With SAP PRESS BooksOnline we offer you online access to knowledge from the leading SAP experts. Whether you use it as a beneficial supplement or as an alternative to the printed book, with SAP PRESS BooksOnline you can:

- Access your book anywhere, at any time. All you need is an Internet connection.
- Perform full text searches on your book and on the entire SAP PRESS library.
- Build your own personalized SAP library.

The SAP PRESS customer advantage:

Register this book today at *www.sap-press.com* and obtain exclusive free trial access to its online version. If you like it (and we think you will), you can choose to purchase permanent, unrestricted access to the online edition at a very special price!

Here's how to get started:

1. Visit *www.sap-press.com*.
2. Click on the link for SAP PRESS BooksOnline and login (or create an account).
3. Enter your free trial license key, shown below in the corner of the page.
4. Try out your online book with full, unrestricted access for a limited time!

Your personal free trial **license key**
for this online book is:

i6ms-25yg-aejr-nbt7

Integrating SAP® BusinessObjects™ BI Platform 4.x with SAP NetWeaver®

 PRESS

Ingo Hilgefort
Inside SAP BusinessObjects Advanced Analysis
2011, 343 pp., hardcover
978-1-59229-371-1

Ingo Hilgefort
Inside SAP BusinessObjects Explorer
2010, 307 pp., hardcover
978-1-59229-340-7

Jim Brogden, Heather Sinkwitz, Mac Holden
SAP BusinessObjects Web Intelligence
2010, 583 pp., hardcover
978-1-59229-322-3

Ingo Hilgefort
Reporting and Analytics with SAP BusinessObjects (Second Edition)
2012, app. 675 pp., hardcover
978-1-59229-387-2

Ingo Hilgefort

Integrating SAP® BusinessObjects™ BI Platform 4.x with SAP NetWeaver®

Bonn • Boston

Galileo Press is named after the Italian physicist, mathematician and philosopher Galileo Galilei (1564–1642). He is known as one of the founders of modern science and an advocate of our contemporary, heliocentric worldview. His words *Eppur si muove* (And yet it moves) have become legendary. The Galileo Press logo depicts Jupiter orbited by the four Galilean moons, which were discovered by Galileo in 1610.

Editor Kelly Grace Harris
Copyeditor Pamela Siska
Cover Design Graham Geary
Photo Credit iStockphoto/173217/Robert Kyllo
Layout Design Vera Brauner
Production Graham Geary
Typesetting Publishers' Design and Production Services, Inc.
Printed and bound in the United States of America

ISBN 978-1-59229-395-7

© 2012 by Galileo Press Inc., Boston (MA)

2nd edition 2012

Library of Congress Cataloging-in-Publication Data
Hilgefort, Ingo.
Integrating SAP BusinessObjects 4.x bi platform with SAP NetWeaver /
Ingo Hilgefort. — 1st ed.
p. cm.
ISBN-13: 978-1-59229-395-7
ISBN-10: 1-59229-395-6
1. BusinessObjects. 2. SAP NetWeaver BW. 3. Management information
systems. 4. Business intelligence—Data processing. I. Title.
HF5548.4.B875H549 2012
658.4'038028553—dc23
2011035200

Contents at a Glance

Dear Reader,

The 4.0 release of the SAP BusinessObjects BI platform was long-awaited and much anticipated—and I daresay that the same can be said of this book. Indeed, readers of the best-selling first edition may not even recognize this as a second edition, as its greatly expanded content and brand new format give it an identity all its own. Inside these pages, you will find a veritable bounty of both updated and brand new information, giving you the ammunition you need to effectively integrate the SAP BusinessObjects BI platform with your SAP NetWeaver system.

Ingo Hilgefort is a well-known name in the SAP BusinessObjects community. He is also one of SAP PRESS' most prolific authors: He wrote his first title back in April of 2009, and produced three additional titles in the next year and a half. The book that you are reading now is the second edition of his first book…making it his fifth book overall. I hope you will find, as I did, that this fifth book reflects the quality of content of his four other titles. (This I say as his third—and most annoying, I trust he would tell you—editor.)

We at SAP PRESS are always eager to hear reader feedback, as your comments and suggestions are the most useful tools to help us make our books the best they can be. We encourage you to visit our website at *www.sap-press.com* and share your feedback about this work.

Thank you for purchasing a book from SAP PRESS!

Kelly Grace Harris
Editor, SAP PRESS

Galileo Press
Boston, MA

kelly.harris@galileo-press.com
www.sap-press.com

Contents

Introduction

SAP® BusinessObjects™ (and former companies Crystal Decisions and Seagate Software) has been delivering an integration with SAP Enterprise Resource Planning (ERP) (R/3, R/3 Enterprise) and SAP NetWeaver® Business Warehouse (SAP NetWeaver BW) for over 10 years. When SAP acquired SAP BusinessObjects in 2008, the software started to reach a much greater number of customers because SAP positioned SAP BusinessObjects as its business information solution on top of SAP NetWeaver BW. The demand for good instructions on how to leverage the SAP BusinessObjects products in an SAP landscape increased, and customers were looking for simple product documentation explaining the usage and deployment of the SAP BusinessObjects software with a focus on SAP NetWeaver BW and SAP ERP. Customers were seeking instruction on how to bring their existing knowledge of SAP NetWeaver BW into the SAP BusinessObjects world, and this is what I am aiming to teach here. You are holding the updated version of my very first book in your hands—revised to show how customers can leverage the 4.x release of the SAP BusinessObjects Business Intelligence (BI) platform in combination with their SAP landscape.

Release 4.x of SAP BusinessObjects BI Platform

The official name of the 4.x release of the SAP BusinessObjects BI software is "SAP BusinessObjects Business Intelligence platform," and was previously referred to as "SAP BusinessObjects Enterprise." Hereafter, we will refer to it simply as "SAP BusinessObjects BI platform." The instructions and guidelines shown in the book are based on the 4.x release of the software.

Please note that all mentions of 4.x refer to the 4.0 release and the release immediately following the 4.0 release.

I hope this book gives you a simple but sufficiently technically detailed overview of what you can do today with the latest SAP BusinessObjects 4.x software in combination with your SAP landscape. I wrote this book from an SAP angle to show you how to leverage the existing knowledge and investment in your SAP system with SAP BusinessObjects 4.x on top.

Target Group

The book is written for those who are looking for simple instructions on how to use and deploy the SAP BusinessObjects software in combination with an SAP landscape. The book focuses on putting you in a position to leverage an SAP BusinessObjects 4.x system on top of your SAP system, to install and configure the software, and to create your first reports with tools such as SAP Crystal Reports®, SAP Business-Objects Web Intelligence, SAP BusinessObjects Live Office, SAP BusinessObjects Explorer, SAP BusinessObjects Analysis, and SAP BusinessObjects Dashboards (formerly Xcelsius) software. It is not the goal of this book to make you an SAP BusinessObjects expert or to explain every detailed aspect of the SAP Business-Objects software, because several other resources already fulfill such a need.

As a reader of this book, you should have some previous knowledge of SAP NetWeaver BW and SAP ERP. On the SAP BusinessObjects side, I tried to keep the need for previous knowledge as minimal as possible. You should be able to follow this book even without any SAP BusinessObjects knowledge, but you should consider further product documentation and training.

Technical Prerequisites

All steps and examples in this book are based on the SAP BusinessObjects 4.x release in combination with an SAP NetWeaver BW 7.x and SAP ERP 2005 system, but you can use previous releases from SAP NetWeaver BW and SAP ERP as long as they are supported by the SAP BusinessObjects 4.x release.

You can download the SAP BusinessObjects software from the SAP Service Marketplace or from the *Downloads* section of the Software Developer Network (SDN). The book is very practical, so I highly recommend that you download the following components so you can follow all outlined steps:

- SAP BusinessObjects BI platform 4.x

- SAP Crystal Reports for Enterprise 4.x

- SAP BusinessObjects Dashboards 4.x

- SAP BusinessObjects Live Office 4.x

- SAP BusinessObjects Analysis, edition for Microsoft® Office® 4.x

- SAP BusinessObjects Analysis, OLAP edition 4.x

You will notice that the version of the products specifies 4.1, which is the first enhancement package for the SAP BusinessObjects 4.0 release. During the installation steps we will show how to install the SAP BusinessObjects 4.0 software, as the 4.1 release is an enhancement package and otherwise you would miss several steps of the original installation.

From the previous edition of this book and your previous experience of the integration of SAP ERP and SAP NetWeaver BW with SAP BusinessObjects, you might recall a product called SAP BusinessObjects Integration for SAP Solutions, sometimes also referred to as the SAP Integration Kit. The SAP Integration Kit is part of the core product release starting with SAP BusinessObjects 4.0 and therefore is not listed as its own product anymore.

You should ensure that you have access to an SAP NetWeaver BW and SAP ERP system so that you can follow the examples. If you can't get access to an existing system, you can download a trial version from SAP NetWeaver via the *Downloads* section of SDN.

Structure of the Book

When this project started, I wasn't sure whether I would be able to explain the topic in enough detail and yet still keep this a simple book that doesn't overwhelm the reader. In each chapter, I try to give you a very practical and step-by-step approach to using the software so you'll have very quick and early success with it.

Here is an overview of the content of the chapters.

▶ **Chapter 1 — SAP BusinessObjects 4.x and SAP NetWeaver**
This chapter introduces you to the 4.x release of the SAP BusinessObjects BI platform and the SAP BusinessObjects suite of BI client tools that you will use in the following chapters. You'll get a brief overview of the main parts of the SAP BusinessObjects BI platform components and take a quick look at the purpose of each of the SAP BusinessObjects 4.x client tools.

▶ **Chapter 2 — Installation and Configuration**
In Chapter 2 you'll learn how to install and configure the 4.x release of the SAP BusinessObjects BI platform server and client components. You'll receive step-by-step instructions on the installation of the software, the configuration steps

on the SAP BusinessObjects BI platform side, and the configuration steps on the SAP NetWeaver side.

▶ **Chapter 3—Semantic Layer and Data Connectivity**
In Chapter 3 you'll learn about the role of the semantic layer from SAP Business-Objects as part of your overall BI landscape and get details on how you can establish data connections to your SAP systems with the SAP BusinessObjects 4.x client tools.

▶ **Chapters 4 to 10—SAP BusinessObjects client tools chapters**
In Chapters 4 to 10 you'll receive an overview of how each of the SAP Business-Objects client tools is able to connect to your SAP system and what the supported elements are for each of the client tools. In addition, each of these chapters includes step-by-step instructions on how you can use the client tool to create your first report, ad-hoc analysis, or dashboard on top of your SAP data.

▶ **Chapter 11—Publications with SAP Data Level Security**
Publications are the SAP BusinessObjects counterpart to the information broad-casting capabilities of SAP NetWeaver. In this chapter you'll receive details on how to configure your SAP and SAP BusinessObjects system to leverage publica-tions with your configured SAP authorizations and distribute reports and analyt-ics to a large number of recipients.

▶ **Chapter 12—Integration with SAP NetWeaver Portal**
In this chapter you'll learn the necessary steps to integrate your SAP Business-Objects system into the SAP NetWeaver Portal. You'll learn how to create iViews based on SAP BusinessObjects templates and how to integrate your SAP Business-Objects system with the Knowledge Management component of your SAP NetWeaver Portal.

▶ **Chapter 13—Troubleshooting and Tips**
In this chapter you'll receive additional details on how to trace and troubleshoot your SAP BusinessObjects deployment. You'll also receive tips on performance-related questions.

▶ **Chapter 14—Outlook**
This chapter offers a brief outlook on topics that might be of interest for you and your deployment. These topics are part of the integration roadmap given out by SAP and SAP BusinessObjects but were technically not finalized at the time this book was written.

> **Lifecycle Management Console**
>
> At the time of this writing (September 2011), the steps for SAP NetWeaver integration with the lifecycle management console for the SAP BusinessObjects BI platform has not been finalized. An online chapter devoted to the lifecycle management console will be added to the book's website at *www.sap-press.com* by January 2012.

Acknowledgments

There are a few people who have helped me over the years to become who I am today, and without them this book would have not been possible. I feel honored to work with these people and to be part of such a great team: Jacob Klein, Ty Miller, Whye Seng Hum, Peter Di Giulio, Grant Oltmann, Henrik Areskoug, Eric Schemer, Alexander Peter, Philipp Hassler, Gavin Olle, Ian McAlpine, Mike Seblani, Boris Kovacevic, Juergen Lindner, Isabell Petzelt, and Elvira Wallis.

Special thanks go to the team from SAP PRESS, who made it possible for me to focus on the writing and not to worry about style, layout, or publishing a book. Thank you, Kelly Harris—without you this would not have happened. I cannot forget to mention the SAP community here, which always provides excellent feedback and input.

In addition, I would like to thank the following people for providing their valuable feedback during the updating of this book:

- Tammy Powlas, Fairfax Water & ASUG BI Community
- Joyce Butler, Cameron International & ASUG BI Community
- Helle Knudsen, Vestas Wind Systems A/S
- Rajeev Kapur, Newell Rubbermaid & ASUG BI Community
- Yatkwai Kee, Newell Rubbermaid & ASUG BI Community
- Lee Bishop, Coca-Cola Refreshments

Finally, many thanks to Gaby, Ronja, and Sally for giving me the time to write, but more importantly, for giving me great writing breaks even while writing my fifth book.

Understanding the architecture of the SAP BusinessObjects BI platform is essential to understanding the components that are part of the installation.

1 SAP BusinessObjects 4.x and SAP NetWeaver

In this chapter, we take a quick look at the SAP BusinessObjects BI platform and the SAP BusinessObjects client tools that we discuss throughout the book. In the second half of the chapter, you'll receive an overview of the main components relevant for integration with your SAP landscape.

The purpose of this chapter is not to give an in-depth overview of the SAP Business-Objects architecture; the intention is to provide an overview of the architecture with enough details such that you can install, deploy, and configure the software. Figure 1.1 outlines the different tiers of SAP BusinessObjects BI platform.

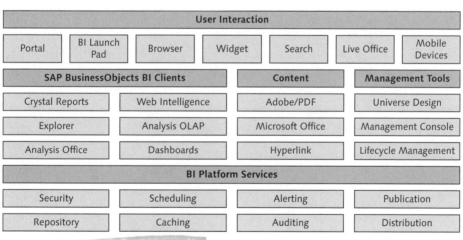

Figure 1.1 SAP BusinessObjects BI Platform

1.1 User Interaction

For user interaction, the SAP BusinessObjects BI platform includes a large set of tools and options. The most common user interface is the BI launch pad (formerly InfoView). The BI launch pad provides the user with a complete set of capabilities to leverage all of the features and functions of the BI client tools, and delivers functionality such as viewing, scheduling, and broadcasting of reports and analytics to the end user.

SAP BusinessObjects Live Office is a plug-in for the Microsoft Office environment that allows the user to use the BI client tools inside Microsoft Excel®, Word®, PowerPoint®, and Outlook®.

Part of the user interaction layer is also the integration into the different portal environments–including SAP NetWeaver Portal. We discuss the different options and required steps to integrate the SAP BusinessObjects BI platform into the SAP NetWeaver Portal in Chapter 11.

1.2 BI Tools and Clients

On the BI tools front, the platform supports all the different content types from SAP BusinessObjects, such as SAP Crystal Reports, SAP BusinessObjects Web Intelligence, SAP BusinessObjects Analysis, SAP BusinessObjects Explorer, SAP BusinessObjects Dashboards, and so on. All of the BI client tools are integrated with the platform to allow you to share your BI content in a secure and scalable platform. In addition, the platform also allows you to share content from other systems such as Microsoft Office or Adobe® Acrobat®, and gives you the opportunity to use your BI platform to share different types of content in the same platform.

We go into more detail on the BI client tools in Chapters 4-10.

1.3 Management Tools

In the area of the management tools, the BI platform delivers several options to manage the system itself and manage the integration with other system landscapes. We discuss these next.

1.3.1 Central Management Console

The Central Management Console (CMC) is a web-based tool that allows you to administer and configure your SAP BusinessObjects solutions. The following list represents some of the main tasks you can perform using the Central Management Console:

▶ Create, configure, and manage users and user groups

▶ Create, configure, and manage services of your platform

▶ Integrate with other user authentication providers, such as Lightweight Directory Access Protocol, Microsoft Active Directory, and SAP

▶ Assign object security to users and user groups

▶ Set up and configure scheduling and publications

▶ Administer and manage your BI content and content categories

1.3.2 Central Configuration Manager

The Central Configuration Manager (CCM) provides the administrative functionality to configure and manage the services of your SAP BusinessObjects system. You can use the Central Configuration Manager to start, stop, enable, or disable services and to perform configuration steps on those services. In contrast to the Central Management Console, which is available as a web client, the Central Configuration Manager is available as a Windows client only.

1.3.3 Lifecycle Management Tool

SAP BusinessObjects delivers a lifecycle management console for SAP Business-Objects BI platform 4.0 that allows you to move content and dependent objects from your development environment to your test and quality environment and finally to your production environment. You can manage different versions, data connectivity, content dependencies, and the promotion of content objects between different systems. A chapter on lifecycle management and integration with SAP CTS+ will be available at the book's website at *www.sap-press.com* by January 2012.

1.4   Platform Service

The platform services deliver the core BI platform functionality to the end user and system administrator. The following is a brief explanation of the main components of the platform services.

1.4.1   Central Management Server

The Central Management Server (CMS) is the "heart" of the system; it manages and controls all of the other services. In addition, the Central Management Server manages access to the system database. The system database contains all information about the users, groups, server configurations, available content, available services, and so on. The main tasks of the Central Management Server are:

▶ Maintaining security by managing users and user groups and the associated groups configured in the SAP BusinessObjects platform.

▶ Managing objects by keeping track of all objects hosted in the platform and managing the physical location of those objects and the object definition by using the system database.

▶ Managing services by constantly validating the status of each service and the overall list of available services. In addition, the Central Management Server is able to handle load balancing to allow for enhanced scalability and better usage of hardware.

▶ Auditing by keeping track of any event inside the platform and thus allowing the administrator to base further deployment considerations on actual information from the usage of the system.

1.4.2   File Repository Services

Each deployment of the SAP BusinessObjects platform has an input and an output file repository service. The input service is responsible for storing the content available in the platform, except instances (scheduled reports), which are managed by the output file repository service.

1.4.3 Processing Tier

The processing tier of the SAP BusinessObjects platform includes (along with other components) the following main components:

► **Job processing services**
The job processing services are responsible for fulfilling requests from the Central Management Server to execute a prescheduled job for a specific report. To be able to run the job successfully, these services require access to the underlying data sources.

► **Cache services**
The cache services are used in combination with the processing services. When a request from a user can be fulfilled with cached information, there is no need to use the processing service. Otherwise, the cache services hand over the request to the processing services.

► **Viewing processing services**
The viewing processing services are responsible for retrieving the content objects from the file repository services, executing the content against the data source, and showing the actual content to the end user via the different viewer types.

1.4.4 Server Intelligence Agent

The Server Intelligence Agent (SIA) allows you to simplify some administrative tasks such as adding or removing services or starting and stopping services. For example, you could assign all of the processing services to a specific SIA, which then allows you to start and stop all those service with a single command.

1.4.5 Publication and Publishing Services

Part of the 4.x release of the SAP BusinessObjects BI platform is the ability to create a publication for SAP Crystal Reports or SAP BusinessObjects Web Intelligence. Publication on the SAP BusinessObjects platform is the counterpart to information broadcasting on the SAP NetWeaver platform. It allows you to set up a scheduling process for document types that will send out the personalized result set to a large set of users. We take a closer look at this functionality in combination with your configured SAP data-level security in Chapter 11.

1.5   SAP BusinessObjects BI Client Tools

In this section we briefly cover the BI client tools that you can use in combination with your SAP system. The main purpose of this section is to give you a brief introduction to each of the tools and to explain the main use for each of the tools.

1.5.1   SAP Crystal Reports

SAP Crystal Reports is a tool that allows you to create a broad range of reports. You can create legal or form-based reports such as an actual tax report or a customer invoice. SAP Crystal Reports also provides you the flexibility to create very complex reports; for example, financial reports involving hierarchies.

By using features like crosstabs and the strong formatting capabilities, you can easily create financial reports, as shown in Figure 1.2.

Actual vs Budget with Variances
12/18/2008 6:24:55PM

Actual vs Budget with Variances
For the Months Ending 03/31/2005

	March					YTD				
	Actual	Budget	Act vs Bud Variance	Last Year	Curr vs Last Year	Actual	Budget	Act vs Bud Variance	Last Year	Curr vs Last Year Variance
Revenue										
Sales Revenue										
Bke Sales - Competitin	$183,342.03	$141,284.73	($42,057.30)	$94,572.06	$88,769.97	$530,577.42	$466,006.26	($64,571.16)	$444,161.41	$86,416.01
Bke Sales - Hybrid	$35,268.67	$25,972.11	($9,286.56)	$15,799.35	$19,459.32	$58,835.00	$27,717.17	($31,117.83)	$54,999.16	$3,835.84
Bke Sales - Kds	$10,575.30	$7,449.72	($3,125.58)	$5,020.80	$5,554.50	$13,483.19	$15,896.47	$2,413.28	$11,690.43	$1,792.76
Bke Sales - Mountain	$117,392.84	$81,079.78	($36,313.06)	$62,599.69	$54,793.15	$127,030.57	$144,175.75	$17,145.18	$108,284.54	$18,745.93
Sales Gloves	$1,101.50	$990.77	($110.73)	$442.21	$659.29	$2,046.05	$1,667.94	($378.11)	$2,036.64	$9.41
Sales Helmets	$5,347.12	$6,054.00	$706.88	$1,634.82	$3,712.30	$9,600.78	$14,840.39	$5,239.61	$7,831.41	$1,769.37
Sales Locks	$531.75	$107.99	($623.76)	$366.83	$264.92	$1,435.23	$2,118.56	$683.33	$1,220.53	$214.70
Sales Returns	$5,351.02	$3,504.21	($1,846.81)	$5,351.02	$0.00	$17,757.85	$7,645.52	($14,263.64)	$15,416.63	($2,341.22)
Sales Saddles	$1,116.13	$204.78	($911.35)	$532.13	$584.00	$2,263.16	$1,351.67	($911.49)	$2,375.62	($112.46)
Net Sales	$349,414.32	$259,639.68	($89,774.64)	$175,616.87	$173,797.45	$727,513.55	$666,128.70	($61,384.85)	$617,183.21	$110,330.34

Figure 1.2   Crystal Reports Sample Financial Report

In Figure 1.3 you can see that SAP Crystal Reports also provides the functionality to create reports with charts and other visualization elements, and includes user interactivity such as drill-down and interactive filtering.

Overall, SAP Crystal Reports is the industry leader for enterprise reporting, allowing you to create highly formatted reports but also to provide interactive reports to your end users.

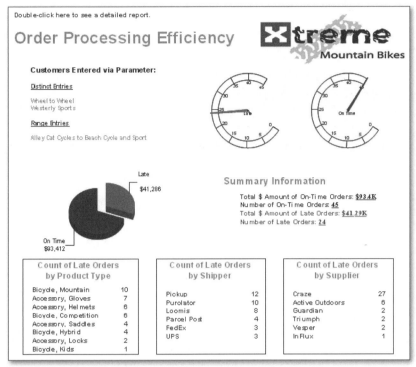

Figure 1.3 SAP Crystal Reports Sample Report

In the SAP BusinessObjects 4.x suite, you will notice that there are two versions of the SAP Crystal Reports Designer. SAP Crystal Reports 2011 is an enhanced version of the SAP Crystal Reports 2008 designer environment, and SAP Crystal Reports for Enterprise 4.x is a new, purely Java-based report design environment. For the purposes of this book, we focus on the SAP Crystal Reports for Enterprise 4.x version of Crystal Reports, as this is the one that will be leveraged for integration with SAP landscapes.

1.5.2 SAP BusinessObjects Web Intelligence

SAP BusinessObjects Web Intelligence is a BI tool focusing on the concept of self-service reporting and providing the end user the ability to create ad-hoc new reports or to change existing reports based on new business requirements. SAP BusinessObjects Web Intelligence empowers the end user to answer business questions using a very simple and intuitive user interface (UI) and typically providing access to a broader range of data.

SAP BusinessObjects Web Intelligence allows the end user to dynamically create data-relevant queries; apply filters to the data; sort, slice, and dice through data; drill down; find exceptions; and create calculations.

Using SAP BusinessObjects Web Intelligence, you can easily create a simple sales report showing revenue broken down according to several dimensions, as shown in Figure 1.4.

Sales Report

Year	Quarter	State	City	Sales revenue	Quantity sold
2004	Q1	California	Los Angeles	$308,928	2,094
2004	Q1	California	San Francisco	$210,292	1,415
2004	Q1	Colorado	Colorado Springs	$131,797	921
2004	Q1	DC	Washington	$208,324	1,467
2004	Q1	Florida	Miami	$137,530	924
2004	Q1	Illinois	Chicago	$256,454	1,711
2004	Q1	Massachusetts	Boston	$92,596	609
2004	Q1	New York	New York	$555,983	3,717

Figure 1.4 Simple SAP BusinessObjects Web Intelligence Report

More importantly, with a few clicks you'll be able to change the report to a sales report showing the top 10 states based on revenue with a chart showing the top 10 cities based on revenue (see Figure 1.5).

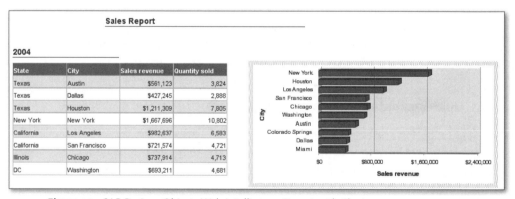

Figure 1.5 SAP BusinessObjects Web Intelligence Report with Chart

SAP BusinessObjects Web Intelligence allows you to reduce your IT department's workload of creating or changing reports and to provide your end users with a real self-service reporting environment.

1.5.3 SAP BusinessObjects Dashboards (formerly Xcelsius)

SAP BusinessObjects Dashboards (formerly Xcelsius) is a product that allows you to transform your data into stunning visualization models that will allow your end users to monitor key performance indicators (KPIs) and identify critical data in a very simple and intuitive way. SAP BusinessObjects Dashboards provides the ability to create a simple dashboard such as a single gauge or a complex what-if scenario based on a broad range of data. SAP BusinessObjects Dashboards is designed to put you in a position to develop simple to complex dashboards in days instead of months. You can share the dashboards with your end users via Microsoft Office, Adobe PDF, or a page in your corporate portal.

Figure 1.6 shows a simple SAP BusinessObjects Dashboards dashboard providing you access to three different views in the form of charts, and allowing you to use a slider as a navigation element to change the value of the sales growth for your forecast.

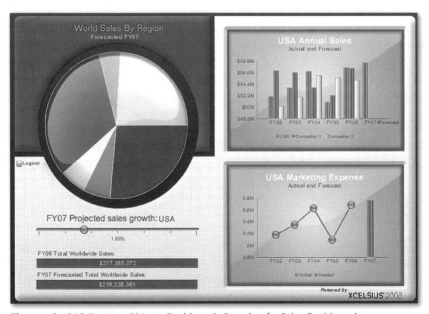

Figure 1.6 SAP BusinessObjects Dashboards Sample of a Sales Dashboard

Figure 1.7 shows a more complex dashboard that allows you to perform a complete profitability analysis by changing multiple factors such as growth rate and expenses. The SAP BusinessObjects Dashboards dashboard immediately shows the impact on overall net income.

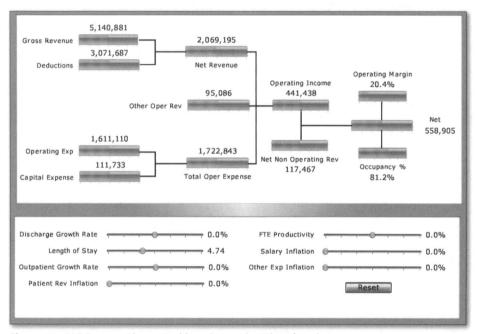

Figure 1.7 SAP BusinessObjects Dashboards Sample: What-if Analysis

1.5.4 SAP BusinessObjects Analysis

SAP BusinessObjects Analysis is an effective new addition to the overall BI client portfolio as part of the SAP BusinessObjects 4.x suite. SAP BusinessObjects Analysis is available in two versions. SAP BusinessObjects Analysis, edition for Microsoft Office (see Figure 1.8) is the premium successor to the SAP BusinessExplorer (BEx) Analyzer, and allows you to use analytical capabilities inside Microsoft Excel and Microsoft PowerPoint.

SAP BusinessObjects Analysis, edition for OLAP is the counterpart to the Microsoft Office edition of SAP BusinessObjects Analysis, but for a web-based deployment (see Figure 1.9).

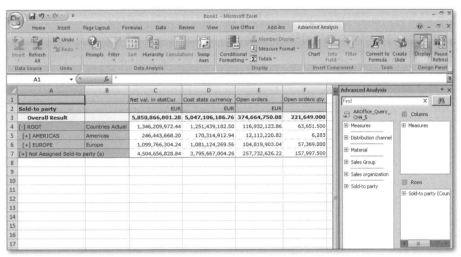

Figure 1.8 SAP BusinessObjects Analysis, Edition for Microsoft Office

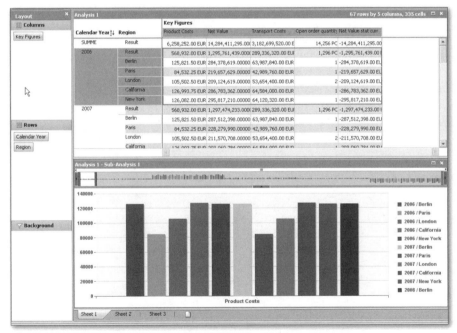

Figure 1.9 SAP BusinessObjects Analysis, Edition for OLAP

Both versions of SAP BusinessObjects Analysis provide you with a BI client tool that enables your typical business analyst to conduct analytical driven workflows.

1.5.5 SAP BusinessObjects Explorer

SAP BusinessObjects Explorer provides your users with a unique user experience. The client tool itself leverages search as much as possible (see Figure 1.10) to help the user find answers to questions quickly and easily.

Figure 1.10 SAP BusinessObjects Explore: Search Dialog

The user is able to search across several so-called *information spaces* (see Figure 1.11), and SAP BusinessObjects Explorer then leverages the index information and provides a best guess of the information, which can be used by the user to further analyze the data.

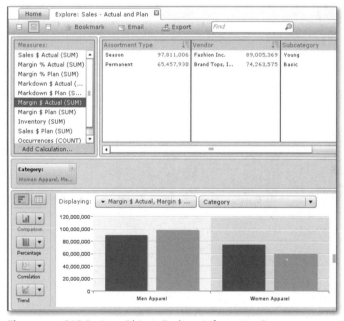

Figure 1.11 SAP BusinessObjects Explorer Information Space

SAP BusinessObjects Explorer is very easy to use and available on-premise, on-demand, and on-device—such as with the iPad and iPhone. These features have been factors in the success of this unique product.

1.5.6 Semantic Layer

The Information Design Tool allows you to create connections to your data sources and to create universes that you can then provide to business users to analyze data in a more user-friendly way. A universe provides an easy to understand and nontechnical interface for your users so they can focus on analyzing and sharing the data by using common business terms.

The Information Design Tool provides you with a graphical interface allowing you to define connections to relational databases management systems (RDBMS) and multidimensional data structures (online analytical processing [OLAP]), and to define the business semantics on top of the data source. We discuss further details and the role of the semantic layer as part of your overall BI landscape in Chapter 3.

1.6 Components for Integration with SAP Landscapes

In the previous release of the SAP BusinessObjects suite, a product called SAP BusinessObjects Integration for SAP Solutions was part of the overall integrated solution with your SAP landscape. As of the SAP BusinessObjects 4.0 suite release, this product has been fully integrated into the core products of the SAP BusinessObjects stack; there is no longer any separate installation. However, the configuration steps must still be performed as part of the configuration of your SAP BusinessObjects system. In the following chapters we look at the components that are relevant for integration between SAP systems and your SAP BusinessObjects system.

1.6.1 Data Connectivity

You can use a broad range of data connectivity in combination with your SAP system. Table 1.1 provides you with an overview of the available options.

Data Connectivity	Usage
BW MDX driver	You can use this connectivity with SAP Crystal Reports 2011 only, and can connect to your SAP NetWeaver BW system.
ODS	You can use this connectivity to connect SAP Crystal Reports 2011 directly (without the need for an SAP BW query) to the operational data store (ODS) layer in your SAP NetWeaver BW system.
InfoSet	You can use this connectivity with SAP Crystal Reports 2011 and use classic InfoSets (not to be confused with InfoSets from SAP NetWeaver BW) and SAP queries from your SAP ERP system.
ABAP functions	You can use this connectivity with SAP Crystal Reports 2011 to connect to Advanced Business Application Programming (ABAP) functions.
Table, function, cluster (Open SQL)	You can use this connectivity with SAP Crystal Reports 2011 to connect to tables, ABAP functions, and data clusters in the ABAP Dictionary.
BI Consumer Services (BICS)/ transient universes	Direct BICS connectivity—also referred to as transient universes—allows you to connect all SAP BusinessObjects BI client tools to BEx queries or InfoProviders in your SAP NetWeaver BW system.
Relational universes	As part of the SAP BusinessObjects 4.x release you are able to connect with a universe using SQL to the SAP NetWeaver BW system and create a relational universe. You are also able to create a universe based on classic InfoSets and ABAP functions from your SAP ERP system.

Table 1.1 Data Connectivity Options

1.6.2 SAP Authentication

The SAP authentication component allows you to integrate your SAP roles and users with your SAP BusinessObjects BI platform system. You can import the SAP roles and users and use them as standard user groups and users in your SAP Business-Objects server. In addition, the component allows you to use single sign-on (SSO) functionality.

1.6.3   BW Publisher

The BW Publisher allows you to take an SAP Crystal Reports 2011 object from the SAP NetWeaver BW system and publish it (save it) to the SAP BusinessObjects BI platform system. This integration is still available as part of the SAP BusinessObjects 4.x suite, but given the new lifecycle management integration with SAP CTS+, the publishing integration for SAP Crystal Reports 2011 becomes less relevant.

1.6.4   Content Administration Workbench

The Content Administration Workbench gives you the functionality to set up, configure, and administer the integration of your SAP BusinessObjects BI platform system with your SAP NetWeaver BW system. The tool is available as a standard SAP transaction, and it allows you to publish, delete, and synchronize your SAP Crystal Reports content in the SAP NetWeaver BW system with your SAP BusinessObjects BI platform system.

This integration is still available as part of the SAP BusinessObjects 4.x suite, but given the new lifecycle management integration with SAP CTS+, it becomes less relevant.

1.6.5   SAP NetWeaver Portal — Knowledge Management

You can integrate the complete repository of your SAP BusinessObjects system into the SAP NetWeaver Portal and provide functionality such as feedback, ranking, and collaboration on top of your SAP BusinessObjects system by using the features from the Knowledge Management component.

1.6.6   SAP NetWeaver Portal — iView Templates and Sample iViews

The 4.x release of the SAP BusinessObjects BI platform also delivers a specific iView template that you can use to integrate BI content into SAP NetWeaver Portal for viewing specific reports or for integration of the BI launch pad into SAP NetWeaver Portal. The iView template offers functionalities such as defining a viewer or selecting between a last instance and on-demand reporting of a particular report. In addition to the iView template for viewing a report, you can leverage the option to integrate the BI launch pad from the SAP BusinessObjects BI platform into the SAP NetWeaver Portal environment.

1.6.7 Lifecycle Management with CTS+

As of the SAP BusinessObjects 4.0 suite release, the lifecycle management console from the SAP BusinessObjects environment is able to integrate with the SAP CTS+ environment, and thus provide you an integrated solution for lifecycle management of your BI content. This integration is discussed in further detail in an online chapter on *www.sap-press.com*, which will be available by January 2012.

1.7 Summary

In this chapter, you received an overview of the different BI client tools that are part of the overall SAP BusinessObjects 4.x suite, and you learned about the relevant components for integration with your SAP systems. In the next chapter, we start with the installation and configuration of the SAP BusinessObjects 4.0 environment.

In this chapter you'll learn the necessary steps to install and deploy the SAP BusinessObjects server and client components in combination with required components to leverage the corporate assets from your SAP landscape.

2   Installation and Configuration

SAP BusinessObjects Menu Structure

The following chapters are based on SAP BusinessObjects release 4.1 (release 4, enhancement package 01). In this release, the menu structure for SAP BusinessObjects products on a Windows operating system is START • PROGRAMS • SAP BUSINESSOBJECTS BI PLATFORM 4 • SAP BUSINESSOBJECTS PLATFORM. If you are using SAP BusinessObjects 4.0 products, the menu structure is START • PROGRAMS • SAP BUSINESSOBJECTS ENTERPRISE XI 4.0 • SAP BUSINESSOBJECTS ENTERPRISE. The changes outlined here in regards to the menu structure are introduced with SAP BusinessObjects 4.0 Service Pack 2.

The installation and configuration of the SAP BusinessObjects Enterprise server and client components consists of several main areas:

1. Verifying the minimum versions of your SAP landscape.

2. Installing the server-side components of SAP BusinessObjects BI platform (see Section 2.2).

3. Installing the client-side components from the BI client tools (SAP Crystal Reports, SAP BusinessObjects Dashboards, and Universe Designer) (see Section 2.3).

4. Preparing the SAP server landscape to work in combination with the SAP BusinessObjects software (see Section 2.4).

5. Configuring the integration between SAP NetWeaver and the SAP BusinessObjects solutions (see Section 2.5).

6. Configuring the SAP and SAP BusinessObjects landscape to enable the hosting of BEx web applications in the SAP BusinessObjects BI platform (see Section 2.5.5).

7. Configuring the new SSO Token Service as part of the SAP BusinessObjects landscape (see Section 2.5.6).

In the following sections, the installation and configuration is broken down into the installation of the server-side software and the client-side software. If you follow all of these steps with a single hardware system available to you, you can install the server and client components from SAP BusinessObjects on a single system.

The recommended approach for this situation is to install the software in the following order:

▶ SAP BusinessObjects BI platform

▶ SAP BusinessObjects client tools

You will notice that the installation steps do not explicitly include a section on the installation of the SAP BusinessObjects Integration for SAP Solutions. Starting with the release of SAP BusinessObjects 4.0, the required components are part of the standard installation routines of the SAP BusinessObjects server and client components, and therefore there is no need for a separate installation routine section.

> **SAP BusinessObjects Re-Branding**
>
> Depending on the exact release of your SAP BusinessObjects 4.x version, the products and some of the related UI components may use different names.
>
> ▶ Up to SAP BusinessObjects 4.0 Service Pack 01, the menu APPLICATIONS in the BI launch pad calls for INTERACTIVE ANALYSIS. Starting with Service Pack 02 and later, this has been renamed Web Intelligence.
>
> ▶ Up to SAP BusinessObjects 4.0 Service Pack 01, the menu structure for your programs was PROGRAMS • SAP BUSINESSOBJECTS ENTERPRISE XI 4.0 • SAP BUSINESSOBJECTS ENTERPRISE. Starting with Service Pack 02 and later, this menu structure has been changed to PROGRAMS • SAP BUSINESSOBJECTS BI PLATFORM 4 • SAP BUSINESSOBJECTS BI PLATFORM.
>
> In this book, we use the SAP BusinessObjects 4.x structure and names.

2.1   Verifying Your SAP Landscape

Before you start the installation and configuration of your SAP BusinessObjects system in combination with your SAP landscape, you should ensure that your SAP landscape is a so-called "supported platform."

SAP BusinessObjects 4.x supports the following SAP-related platforms (at the time of the writing of this book—September 2011):

▸ SAP NetWeaver J2EE v 7.2 SP03 is supported as Java Application Server for SAP BusinessObjects Enterprise.

▸ SAP BusinessObjects BI platform can be integrated with SAP NetWeaver Portal 7.x.

▸ SAP GUI 7.10 and SAP GUI 7.20 are supported as part of the integration with the SAP BusinessObjects client tools.

▸ SAP BusinessObjects Analysis, edition for Microsoft Office supports SAP NetWeaver BW 7.0 and higher.

▸ SAP BusinessObjects Analysis, edition for OLAP supports SAP NetWeaver BW 7.0 SP23 and higher, SAP NetWeaver BW 7.01 SP05 and higher, and SAP NetWeaver BW 7.3.

▸ SAP BusinessObjects Web Intelligence, SAP Crystal Reports for Enterprise, and SAP BusinessObjects Dashboards support SAP NetWeaver BW 7.01 SP06 and higher using the direct access method with the BI Consumer Services (BICS) and the relational universe approach.

▸ Hosting BEx web applications as part of your SAP BusinessObjects BI platform requires SAP NetWeaver BW 7.01 SP08 at a minimum. Please see SAP Notes 1541365 and 1476156 for further details.

> **Supported Platforms at the Service Marketplace**
>
> You can always check the most recent list of supported platforms for all the products on the Service Marketplace at *http://service.sap.com/bosap-support*.

2.2   SAP BusinessObjects—Server-Side Installation

In this section we concentrate on the server side of the landscape. First we provide an overview of the SAP BusinessObjects BI platform. We then install the server landscape and configure our SAP BusinessObjects BI platform environment to work in combination with our SAP landscape.

> **SAP BusinessObjects Software Download**
>
> All available software from SAP BusinessObjects can be downloaded from the Service Marketplace at *http://service.sap.com/swdc*.
>
> In the INSTALLATIONS AND UPGRADES category, you can find the software listed alphabetically, or you can use the BROWSE OUR DOWNLOAD CATALOG item and navigate to the SAP BUSINESSOBJECTS PORTFOLIO.
>
> Temporary license key codes can be obtained from the Service Marketplace at *http:// service.sap.com/licensekeys*.

The focus here is to enable you to deploy a simple SAP BusinessObjects platform scenario. The SAP BusinessObjects BI platform is a BI platform that can be deployed and scaled to fit your requirements. Further details on complex deployment scenarios and detailed installation material can be downloaded from *http://service.sap. com/bosap-instguides* (to access the Service Marketplace you need a logon account, which can be requested on the main page, *http://service.sap.com*).

The default installation of the SAP BusinessObjects BI platform includes Tomcat, the Java application server, and Microsoft SQL Server Express for your system database. For details on how to deploy the software using a different database system or a different supported application server, including SAP J2EE, you can download the following documentation at *http://service.sap.com/bosap-instguides:*

▶ SAP BusinessObjects BI Platform Planning Guide

▶ SAP BusinessObjects BI Platform Master Guide

▶ SAP BusinessObjects BI Platform Installation Guide for Windows

▶ SAP BusinessObjects BI Platform Installation Guide for UNIX

▶ Web Application Deployment Guide for Windows

▶ Web Application Deployment Guide for UNIX

2.2.1 Technical Prerequisites

Before you start the actual installation of the SAP BusinessObjects BI platform, please ensure that the following requirements are met:

▶ Validate the exact details of the supported platforms and ensure that these match your environment. You can review the list of supported platforms at *http://service. sap.com/bosap-support*.

- ▶ Check that your account for the operating system has administrative privileges.

- ▶ If you plan to deploy on a distributed system, you need to have access to all machines via TCP/IP.

- ▶ You must have administrative access to the application server. Supported application servers are Jboss, Tomcat, Oracle, WebLogic, WebSphere, and SAP J2EE.

- ▶ You must have access to a database system to install the system database for SAP BusinessObjects. Supported database systems are IBM DB2, MySQL, Microsoft SQL Server, Oracle, SAP MaxDB, and Sybase ASE.

2.2.2 Installation Routine

For the installation routine, we assume a single-server deployment scenario and use Tomcat as the Java application server and Microsoft SQL Express for the system database. Table 2.1 shows the information for the environment that we'll use, as well as the example values we will use for the configuration screens.

Description	Value
SAP BusinessObjects BI platform server name	BOEXI4
SAP NetWeaver BW application server	IHILGEFORT.DYNDNS.ORG
SAP system ID	IH1
SAP client number	800
SAP system number	00

Table 2.1 System Information

If you want to leverage a logon group for your SAP system, you need to have the details of the message server and the logon group of your system, which then replace the values for the application server and the system number shown in Table 2.1.

Technical Prerequisites

- ▶ SAP BusinessObjects is 64-bit software, so please ensure that your server operating system is a 64-bit system.
- ▶ Windows .NET Framework version 3.5 Service Pack 01 is a prerequisite for installation on Windows operating systems.

> ▸ Windows Installation Program version 4.5 is a prerequisite for installation on Windows operating systems.
>
> ▸ The account being used for the installation should have administrative rights on the system.

Based on the fact that you are performing a single-server deployment, the server name (BOEXI4) will also become the name for your SAP BusinessObjects BI platform system.

1. After you download the software, you start the installation routine by starting `Setup.exe`.

2. After you start the installation routine, you are asked to select a language for the installation routine itself. This does not influence the language for the actual deployment of the software. In our example, we select ENGLISH as the setup language.

3. After accepting the setup language, you are presented with the prerequisites check (see Figure 2.1). You cannot install the SAP BusinessObjects BI platform unless all of those listed prerequisites are met.

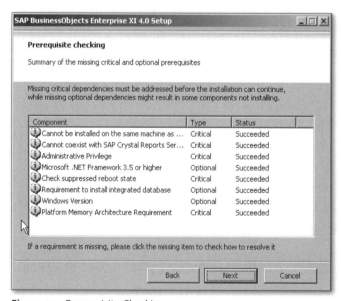

Figure 2.1 Prerequisite Checking

4. After the prerequisites have been verified, you are shown the start of the Installation Wizard (see Figure 2.2). Click NEXT to start the actual installation process.

Figure 2.2 Installation Wizard

5. In the next two screens, you are asked to accept the license agreement and enter the license key code that you obtained. After this step, you have a choice of language packs (Figure 2.3). This time, the selection influences the availability of the software in different languages. For our installation, we select ENGLISH.

6. The next screen allows you to select the installation type. You can select a FULL installation, a CUSTOM installation, or an installation option for the WEB TIER (see Figure 2.4).

Figure 2.3 Language Packs

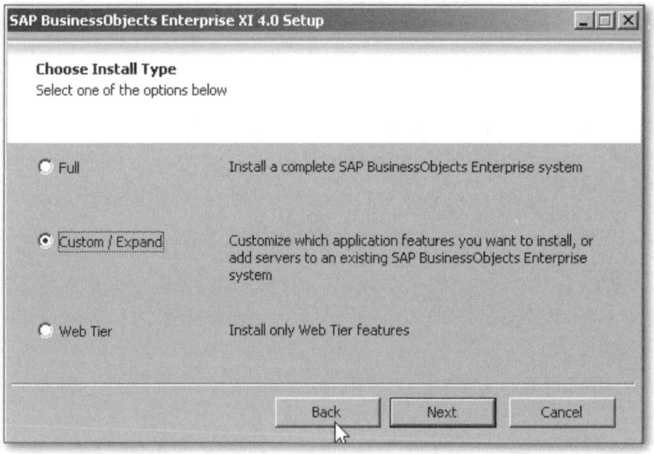

Figure 2.4 Installation Type

In our example, we use the CUSTOM/EXPAND option so that we are presented with all detailed options during the installation process.

7. Next, you select the base folder for your SAP BusinessObjects BI platform system. After configuring the folder location you can decide which components you would like to install as part of your overall SAP BusinessObjects BI platform system (see Figure 2.5).

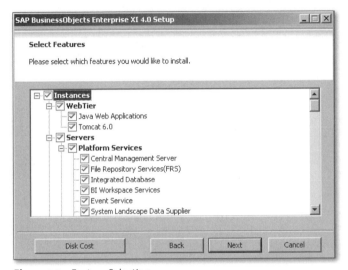

Figure 2.5 Feature Selection

SAP NetWeaver BW Publishing Service

If you plan to leverage the BW publishing integration in combination with SAP Crystal Reports 2011, make sure BW PUBLISHER SERVER in the INTEGRATION SERVERS area is selected.

---

8. After you select the components you are asked to select whether the installation is a new SAP BusinessObjects system, or whether you are planning to expand an existing deployment (see Figure 2.6). In our example, we select the option to start a new installation.

Figure 2.6 New or Expand Installation

9. In the next step, you need to enter the name for the SERVER INTELLIGENT AGENT. In our example, we use the value BOEXI4 (see Figure 2.7).

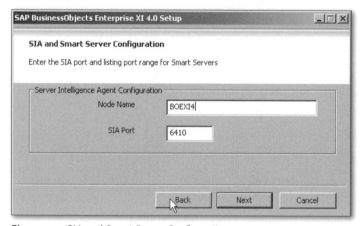

Figure 2.7 SIA and Smart Server Configuration

10. In the next step, you are asked to configure the port for the Central Management Server (CMS). The default value is 6400 (see Figure 2.8).

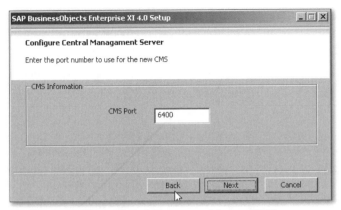

Figure 2.8 Configure Central Management Server (CMS)

11. As part of the installation of the SAP BusinessObjects BI platform system, you also need to set up default passwords (see Figure 2.9). The installation routine creates an administrator account, and you need to set up the default password.

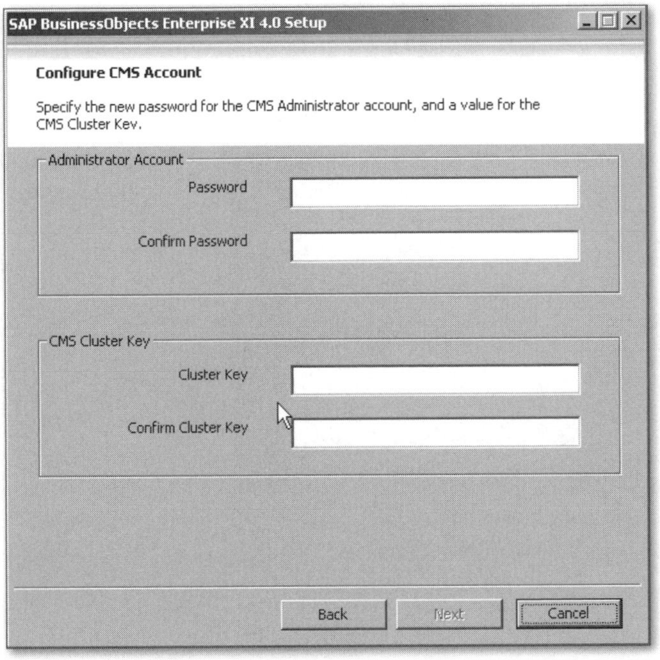

Figure 2.9 Configure CMS Account

12. After configuring the default passwords for the administrator account, you also need to set up passwords for the Microsoft SQL Server 2008 Express installation. We select the default database installation, which is Microsoft SQL Server 2008 Express (see Figure 2.10). The installation routine sets up an administrator account and a specific account that is used by the SAP BusinessObjects BI platform system.

Password Requirements

As part of a new installation, you are asked to enter the password for the administrator account as well as for your underlying system database. The default configuration for passwords enforces a mixed-case password and requires you to use at least six characters. An example of a valid password is "Password1."

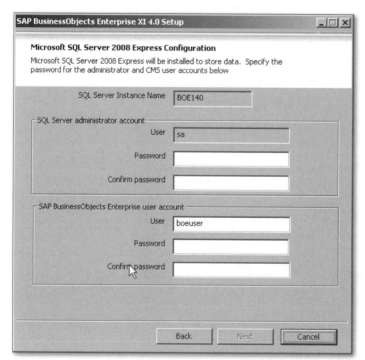

Figure 2.10 Microsoft SQL Server 2008 Express Configuration

13. In the next step, you choose to activate all servers after the installation has finished (see Figure 2.11).

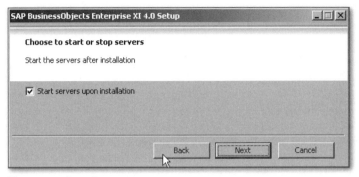

Figure 2.11 Start Servers

14. In the next step (see Figure 2.12), you need to configure the ports of the Java Application Server. In our example, we select to install Tomcat as part of the default installation. If you prefer to install using another Java Application Server, you have to manually deploy the applications.

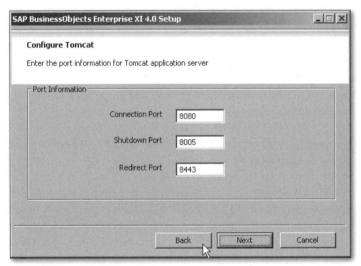

Figure 2.12 Configure Tomcat

In our example, we accept the default ports for the Tomcat application server that the installation process recommends, and continue to the next screen.

15. In the next step, you need to configure the password for the SUBVERSION repository as part of the lifecycle management configuration (see Figure 2.13).

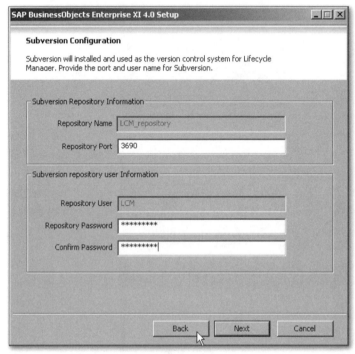

Figure 2.13 Subversion Configuration

16. In the next screen, you are asked whether you would like to configure the integration with SOLUTION MANAGER (see Figure 2.14). For our example, we will not configure it.

17. As the next option, you can configure an integration into INTROSCOPE ENTER-PRISE MANAGER (see Figure 2.15) if you are not using Solution Manager for the tracing and monitoring of your SAP BusinessObjects BI platform system. For our example, we will not configure it.

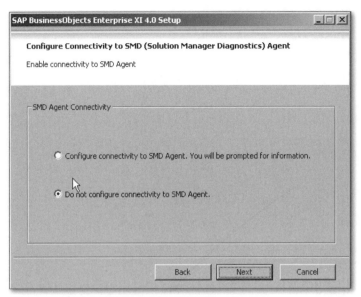

Figure 2.14 Solution Manager Agent Configuration

Figure 2.15 Introscope Integration

18. Finally, you can start the actual installation of your new SAP BusinessObjects BI platform system (see Figure 2.16).

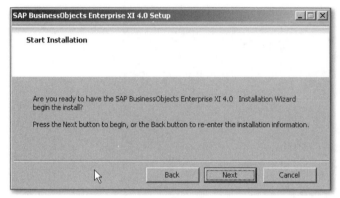

Figure 2.16 Start of the Installation

You have now installed your first SAP BusinessObjects BI platform 4.0 environment. We can continue with the client part of the installation and configuration.

SAP BusinessObjects Explorer

SAP BusinessObjects Explorer is not part of the core installation of the SAP BusinessObjects BI platform, and needs to be downloaded and installed separately. The installation of the product is very similar to the steps involved in the installation of the SAP BusinessObjects BI platform server, and therefore the installation will not be described in full detail in this book.

2.3   SAP BusinessObjects—Client-Side Installation

In this section we cover the installation of the SAP BusinessObjects client products. A more detailed technical overview of how each of these client tools can be used in combination with your SAP system is provided in the following chapters.

When we refer to SAP BusinessObjects client products, we mean the following:

▶ SAP BusinessObjects Analysis, edition for Microsoft Office
▶ SAP BusinessObjects BI platform client tools

- SAP Crystal Reports 2011
- SAP Crystal Reports for Enterprise
- SAP BusinessObjects Live Office
- SAP BusinessObjects Dashboards

Products such as the new Information Design Tool and the Universe Designer are part of the SAP BusinessObjects BI platform client tools installation.

SAP BusinessObjects Web Intelligence and SAP BusinessObjects Analysis, edition for OLAP are part of your core server deployment of SAP BusinessObjects Enterprise. For the purpose of this book, we go through the installation routines of Crystal Reports for Enterprise, SAP BusinessObjects Live Office, SAP BusinessObjects BI platform client tools, SAP BusinessObjects Dashboards, and SAP BusinessObjects Analysis, edition for Microsoft Office.

> **Requirement for SAP GUI—Or Not?**
>
> In the SAP BusinessObjects 4.x release, only two of the client products have a mandatory requirement for an SAP GUI with BI/BEx add-ons installed on the client computer: SAP Crystal Reports 2011 and SAP BusinessObjects Dashboards (formerly Xcelsius). SAP Crystal Reports 2011 requires the SAP GUI when the SAP toolbar and the connectivity towards the SAP landscape is being leveraged, and SAP BusinessObjects Dashboards requires the SAP GUI when the direct BI Consumer Service (BICS) connectivity as part of the SAP NetWeaver BW stack is being leveraged (not as part of the SAP Business-Objects BI platform stack).
>
> SAP BusinessObjects Analysis, edition for Microsoft Office does not require a complete SAP GUI installed; instead the `saplogon.ini` file with the system entries is sufficient. Alternatively, you can configure the connection as part of the SAP BusinessObjects system.

In this section we go through the installation of the client tools: SAP Crystal Reports for Enterprise, SAP BusinessObjects Dashboards, SAP BusinessObjects BI platform client tools, SAP BusinessObjects Analysis, edition for Microsoft Office, and SAP BusinessObjects Live Office. In an actual production environment, it is not necessary to deploy the client tools on the server environment, but for now we are working on the assumption that this is a single-server deployment. If you have separate hardware available to you, you should have no problem following the steps to install the client tools on the additional system.

2.3.1 SAP Crystal Reports for Enterprise

To install SAP Crystal Reports for Enterprise, follow the steps below.

1. After you download the software, you can start the installation routine by starting `Setup.exe`.

2. Just as in the installation routine for SAP BusinessObjects, you first select the setup language for the installation routine.

3. After you select the language for the setup routine, you are presented with the results of the prerequisites check (see Figure 2.17). You will not be able to continue the installation until all of the prerequisites have been met.

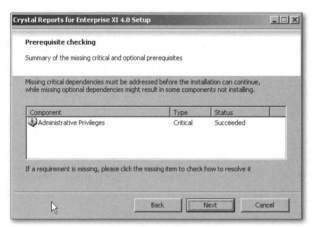

Figure 2.17 Crystal Reports for Enterprise Setup

4. You are then presented with the welcome screen for the installation routine. After clicking the NEXT button, you are asked to accept the license agreement. After you accept the agreement, you are presented with the option to configure the location for the files (see Figure 2.18).

   Given that SAP Crystal Reports for Enterprise is not the first SAP BusinessObjects products, the location points to the folder location of the SAP BusinessObjects system.

Figure 2.18   Destination Folder

5. After configuring the installation folder, you need to enter your license key code. In the next screen you can then configure the list of language packs that are installed for the product. This time, the selection of languages will influence the product itself (see Figure 2.19).

Figure 2.19   Language Packs

6. In the next screen (see Figure 2.20), you can select the installation type. The TYPICAL option installs SAP Crystal Reports for Enterprise with the most common elements, and the CUSTOM option allows you to select the components you want to install. If you're not sure which option to select, we recommend selecting CUSTOM.

Figure 2.20 Installation Type

7. For the CUSTOM installation type (see Figure 2.21), you can select the exact components that you want to install on your client.

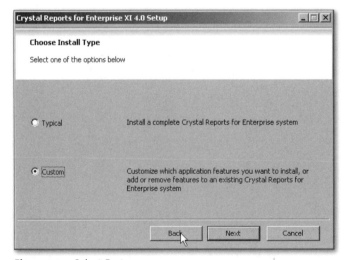

Figure 2.21 Select Features

As you will notice, SAP Crystal Reports for Enterprise lists the actual SAP Crystal Reports Designer as well as a variety of data access options as a component. SAP Crystal Reports for Enterprise in release 4.x leverages the data connectivity from the SAP BusinessObjects BI platform environment and is also able to leverage local data connectivity.

8. In the next step of the installation process, you can configure the option to automatically update your SAP Crystal Reports for Enterprise installation.

9. In the final step, you can start the actual installation routine for SAP Crystal Reports for Enterprise.

10. Next the installation of SAP Crystal Reports for Enterprise will start. You should be able to use SAP Crystal Reports for Enterprise after a short time.

2.3.2 SAP BusinessObjects Dashboards

Technical Prerequisites

- Microsoft Excel 2003 or higher needs to be installed on the client system.
- The account being used for the installation should have administrative rights on the system.
- Adobe FlashPlayer with Active X v 9.0 or later is required on the client system.
- Your client system operating system needs to be one of the supported platforms, which can be reviewed at *http://service.sap.com/bosap-support*.

1. After you download the software, you can start the installation routine by starting `Setup.exe`.

2. Just as in the installation routine for SAP Crystal Reports for Enterprise, you are first asked to select a setup language.

3. In the next step, you are presented with the installation welcome screen and shown the result of the prerequisite check (see Figure 2.22).

   Remember that you will not be able to continue the installation unless all the prerequisites have been met.

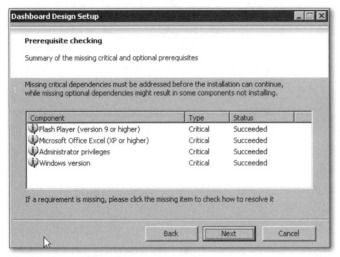

Figure 2.22 Dashboard Design Setup

4. In the next step, you need to accept the license agreement. After doing so, you can define the location for the installation files from SAP BusinessObjects Dashboards (see Figure 2.23).

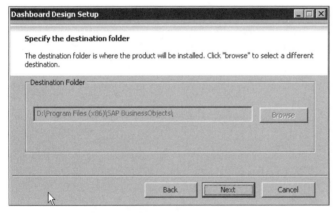

Figure 2.23 Destination Folder

As before, the installation folder points to the location of the SAP BusinessObjects system, as SAP BusinessObjects Dashboards is not the first product being installed.

5. After defining the destination folder, enter the license key code in the next step. Then you can select the language packs that will be installed for SAP Business-Objects Dashboards. The list of language packs does influence the list of available languages for the product.

6. In the next step, you can select between a TYPICAL installation or a CUSTOM installation type (see Figure 2.24). In our example, we select CUSTOM.

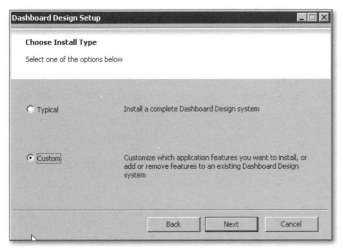

Figure 2.24 Installation Type

7. The next step (see Figure 2.25) shows the components that are available for installation. In our example, we select all available components.

Figure 2.25 Selected Features

8. After you have selected the components to be installed, you can move to the next screen, which allows you to start the actual installation routine. After this screen, the installation will start, and you can use SAP BusinessObjects Dashboards after a short period of time.

SAP BusinessObjects Dashboards and SAP BusinessObjects Live Office

If you install SAP BusinessObjects Live Office and SAP BusinessObjects Dashboards on the same system, SAP BusinessObjects Dashboards will ask you to configure the SAP BusinessObjects Live Office compatibility on the first start of SAP BusinessObjects Dashboards. You can configure the compatibility in the menu path FILE • PREFERENCES • EXCEL OPTIONS.

If you prefer to work with SAP BusinessObjects Live Office inside SAP BusinessObjects Dashboards, you need to activate the compatibility mode. If you disable the compatibility mode, you'll need to work with SAP BusinessObjects Live Office outside SAP Business-Objects Dashboards in a separate Microsoft Excel spreadsheet.

2.3.3 SAP BusinessObjects Live Office

Technical Prerequisites

▶ Microsoft Office needs to be installed on the client system. To see a list of supported Microsoft Office versions, you can refer to the list of supported platforms on *http://service.sap.com/bosap-support*.

▶ If you plan to use Microsoft Office 2003, you need to ensure that the patch for Microsoft Office 2003 (KB907417) is installed.

▶ The account being used for the installation should have administrative rights on the system.

▶ Microsoft .NET Framework v 3.5 or higher needs to be installed on the client system.

---

1. After you download the software, you can start the installation routine by starting `Setup.exe`.

2. Just like the previous installation routines, begin by selecting the setup language.

3. Next, you will get an overview of the technical prerequisites (see Figure 2.26).

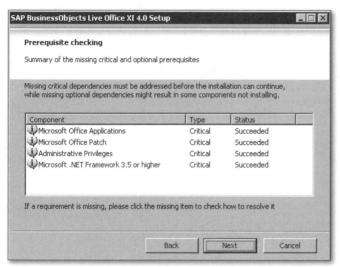

Figure 2.26   Live Office Prerequisites

SAP BusinessObjects Live Office Prerequisites

The following is a list of technical prerequisites for the installation of SAP Business-Objects Live Office:

▶ Microsoft Office 2003 or 2007 should be installed.

▶ Microsoft .NET Framework v 3.5 or higher should be installed.

▶ The user used for the installation needs administrative rights on the client computer.

4. You are then presented with the welcome screen of the installation for SAP BusinessObjects Live Office. In the next screen, you can accept the license agreement.

5. After accepting the license agreement you can select the destination folder for the installation of SAP BusinessObjects Live Office.

6. After you have configured the destination folder, you can select the language packs for your SAP BusinessObjects Live Office deployment. In our installation, we select ENGLISH.

7. After you select the language packs for your installation, you can select the type of installation. You can choose between a TYPICAL or a CUSTOM installation. In our example, we select the CUSTOM option.

8. In the next screen, you can the select the components you would like to install (see Figure 2.27).

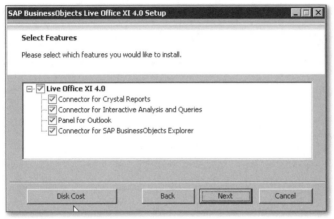

Figure 2.27 Selected Features

After this step, you can start the actual installation process. You should be able to use the SAP BusinessObjects Live Office functionality in Microsoft Excel, Power-Point, Outlook, and Word as soon as the installation is finished.

SAP BusinessObjects Live Office License Keys

Notice that the client-side installation routine of SAP BusinessObjects Live Office does not ask for a license key. The reason is that the license key has to be entered on the SAP BusinessObjects system. To do so, you can log on to the Central Management Console, navigate to the LICENSE KEYS area, and enter the key code for SAP BusinessObjects Live Office.

2.3.4 SAP BusinessObjects BI Platform Client Tools

The following is a list of SAP BusinessObjects client tools that are delivered as part of the SAP BusinessObjects BI platform client tools installation:

▶ Interactive Analysis Desktop (formerly Web Intelligence Rich Client)

▶ Report Conversion Tool

▶ Information Design Tool

▶ Translation Management Tool

- Query as a Web Service
- Business View Manager
- Universe Designer
- Widgets

Technical Prerequisites

- The account used for the installation should have administrative rights on the system.
- Microsoft .NET Framework v 3.5 or higher needs to be installed on the client system.

Different from release XI 3.1, the SAP BusinessObjects BI platform client tools for the SAP BusinessObjects 4.x release are not included as part of the server installation; instead, they are part of a separate download and installation routine.

1. After you download the software, you can start the installation routine by starting `Setup.exe`.

2. As the first step in the installation process for the SAP BusinessObjects BI platform client tools, you need to select the language for the installation process.

3. After you select the language—in our example, ENGLISH—you are presented with the technical prerequisites check (see Figure 2.28).

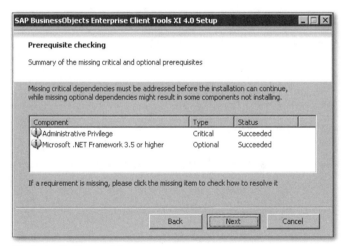

Figure 2.28 Prerequisites

4. In the next steps, you are shown the installation welcome screen and you can accept the license agreement.

5. After accepting the license agreement, select the language packs for the SAP BusinessObjects client tools installation. You are asked to configure the destination folder.

6. As part of the next step, you can select the components that should be installed (see Figure 2.29).

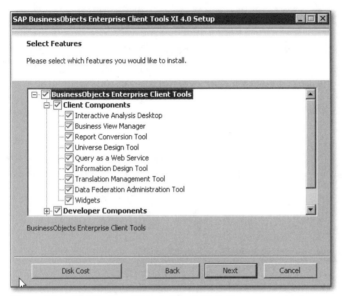

Figure 2.29 SAP BusinessObjects Client Features

7. After you select the components to be installed, you can start the installation process.

2.3.5 SAP BusinessObjects Analysis, Edition for Microsoft Office

As the last step of the client-side installation process, you need to install SAP BusinessObjects Analysis, edition for Microsoft Office.

Technical Prerequisites

▶ Microsoft Office needs to be installed on the client system. To see a list of supported Microsoft Office versions, you can refer to the list of supported platforms on *http://service.sap.com/bosap-support*.

▶ Microsoft .NET Framework 2.0 Redistributable Package is required.

▶ Primary Interop Assemblies for Microsoft Office are required.

▶ The account used for the installation should have administrative rights on the system.

1. After you download the software, you can start the installation routine by starting `SapAaoSetup.exe`.

2. You are presented with the welcome screen for the installation of SAP Business-Objects Analysis, edition for Microsoft Office.

3. Next, you can select the components for the installation (see Figure 2.30).

Figure 2.30 SAP NetWeaver Frontend Installer

4. In the next step, you can configure the destination folder for the installation (see Figure 2.31).

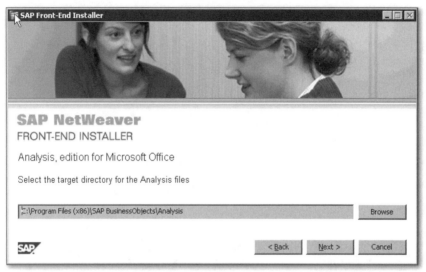

Figure 2.31 Destination Folder

5. After these steps, the actual installation process starts; you should be able to use SAP BusinessObjects Analysis, edition for Microsoft Office, shortly after this.

This concludes the installation of the client components. In the next section, we configure the SAP server side for integration with the SAP BusinessObjects landscape.

2.4   SAP NetWeaver—Server-Side Configuration

In the previous sections, we installed and configured the SAP BusinessObjects BI platform and the BI client tools. In the next couple of sections, we configure the SAP NetWeaver system to work in combination with the SAP BusinessObjects system. The following is a set of activities that need to be performed on the SAP system server side to ensure that you can move forward with the installation and configuration of the two systems.

2.4.1 Server Patch Level

The integration of SAP BusinessObjects with your SAP landscape requires a minimum version and patch level for your SAP NetWeaver BW and SAP ERP system. You need to ensure that your SAP system meets those requirements. You can verify the patch level of your SAP system by logging on to your SAP system and following the menu path System • Status (see Figure 2.32).

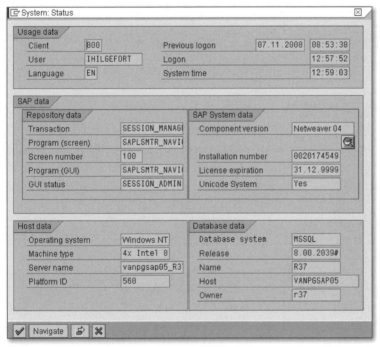

Figure 2.32 System Status

Selecting the magnifying glass next to the component version takes you to a detailed list of patch levels of your SAP system (see Figure 2.33). You can compare the patch level and version of your system with the supported systems for the SAP Business-Objects products. You can find the most recent list of supported versions for the SAP BusinessObjects portfolio at *http://service.sap.com/bosap-support*. Navigate on the left-hand side to the Documentation menu item and then to the Supported Platforms submenu.

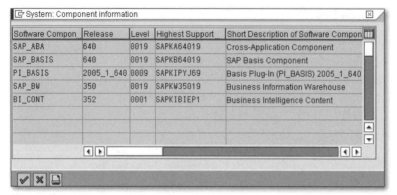

Figure 2.33 Component Information

2.4.2 Supported Platforms

The list of supported platforms for the SAP BusinessObjects 4.0 release can be viewed at *http://service.sap.com/bosap-support*. After you open the URL on the Service Marketplace, navigate on the left-hand side to the DOCUMENTATION menu item and the SUPPORTED PLATFORMS submenu item, where you will find the needed information broken down by product. For integration with your SAP landscape, the list of supported versions of data sources, Java Application Server, and SAP NetWeaver Portal are part of the supported platform details for the SAP Business-Objects BI platform.

Ensure that you pay attention to the additional notes in the list of supported platforms because SAP BusinessObjects also mentions very recent SAP Notes that will help you improve the overall solution or fix known issues.

2.4.3 ABAP Transport

Parts of the integration of SAP Crystal Reports 2011 and the SAP landscape are a set of ABAP transports that must be imported into the SAP system. These ABAP transports enable the functionality required to use SAP Crystal Reports 2011 in combination with your SAP landscape. You can find the ABAP transports directly on the source media (download from the Service Marketplace or DVD) in the sub-folder called \collaterals\Add-Ons\SAP\Transports. The following list specifies the components that require an ABAP transport to be imported into the SAP system.

▸ Open SQL connectivity

▸ InfoSet connectivity

- BW MDX driver connectivity
- BW ODS connectivity
- Row-level Security Definition Editor
- Cluster Definition Editor
- Content Administration Workbench
- BW query parameter personalization

ABAP Transports

You can find details on the ABAP transports and the objects that are created in the "Supplementary Configurations for ERP Environments" chapter of the SAP Business-Objects Enterprise Administrator's Guide. The installation guide can be downloaded from *http://help.sap.com*.

Ensure that you also verify whether future service packs for the SAP BusinessObjects software do contain updates to those transports.

2.4.4 Single Sign-On

To be able to use SSO between the SAP NetWeaver system and SAP BusinessObjects, you need to configure the SAP system to accept SSO logon tickets and to create them. This configuring involves setting parameter values in the profile (see Table 2.2) of your SAP system via Transaction RZ10; setting or changing those values requires a restart of the system.

Profile Parameter	Value	Comment
`login/create_sso2_ticket`	1 or 2	Use the value 1 if the server possesses a public key certificate signed by the SAP CA (*SAP Certification Authority*). Use the value 2 if the certificate is self-signed. If you are not sure, then use the value 2.
`login/accept_sso2_ticket`	1	Use the value 1 so that the system will also accept logon tickets.

Table 2.2 Single Sign-On Profile Parameters

2.4.5   User Authorization

Depending on the SAP BusinessObjects client tool and the connectivity you use for your SAP system, SAP users will require specific authorizations to be able to create, edit, or simply view the content created with the SAP BusinessObjects tools.

A detailed list of required authorizations is available in the "Authorizations" section of the "Supplementary Configurations for ERP Environments" chapter of the SAP BusinessObjects Enterprise Administrator's Guide, which is available for download at *http://help.sap.com.*

In addition to the standard authorizations to perform tasks such as viewing a BW query in the case of an SAP NetWeaver BW system, the integration of SAP Crystal Reports 2011 with your SAP system also includes a specific authorization class: ZSSI. This class includes authorization objects that allow you to specify authorizations for specific tasks, such as creating a new report or changing a server definition in the Content Administration Workbench.

2.5   Integrating SAP BusinessObjects and SAP NetWeaver

In this section we focus on configuring the integration between the SAP Business-Objects server landscape and the SAP NetWeaver system. The main tasks we cover are:

▶ Configuring the SAP authentication for SAP BusinessObjects (see Section 2.5.1).

▶ Setting up the publishing process for SAP Crystal Reports (see Section 2.5.2).

▶ Configuring the viewing of reports as part of the SAP system frontend (see Section 2.5.3).

▶ Configuring the hosting of BEx web applications (see Section 2.5.5).

2.5.1   Configuration of SAP Authentication

After installing SAP BusinessObjects, you need to configure the SAP authentication so that you can import the SAP users and roles into your SAP BusinessObjects system and allow them to use their SAP credentials to get access to their BI assets.

1. To start the configuration of the SAP authentication, you need to log on to the Central Management Console with an administrative account. You can use the Enterprise authentication method and the administrator account that was created during the installation. To reach the Central Management Console (CMC), open the URL *http://localhost:8080/BOE/CMC* in your browser (see Figure 2.34).

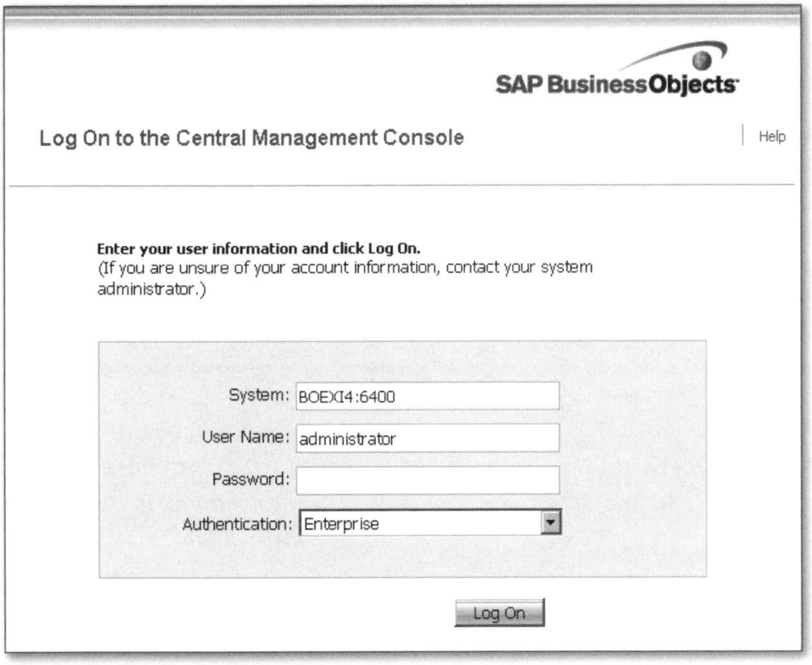

Figure 2.34 Central Management Console

2. After a successful authentication you are presented with the main screen (see Figure 2.35) of the Central Management Console, which provides two main navigation elements. On the top is a dropdown box that you can use to navigate directly to the configuration areas. In addition, you can use the toolbar on the left-hand side.

Figure 2.35 Central Management Console Start Screen

3. To configure the SAP authentication details, select AUTHENTICATION, and the system then presents the list of available authentication providers (see Figure 2.36).

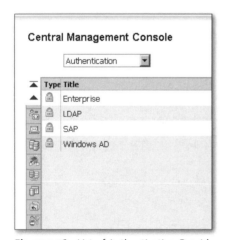

Figure 2.36 List of Authentication Providers

4. You can now double-click the SAP authentication provider, and the system will present you with the screen shown in Figure 2.37 so that you can create a new SAP system entry.

In this first part of the configuration, you can identify the SAP systems that you want to use in combination with the SAP BusinessObjects system. Only systems that are configured during this step can use the full functionality of the SAP Business-Objects landscape.

The configuration screen allows you to configure your system based on an application server with a system number, or a message server with a logon group.

1. Start by entering the system ID of your SAP system and the client number; then enter either a combination of message server with a logon group or application server with a system number (see Figure 2.37). When you finish with the configuration, your system will appear in the LOGICAL SYSTEM NAME field so that you can select any of the configured systems later on.

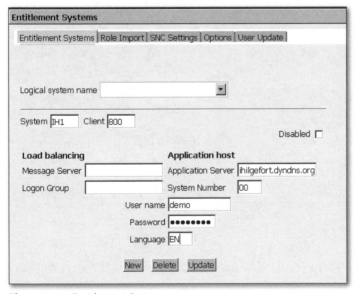

Figure 2.37 Entitlement System

The user account that is requested here is used only for administrative tasks, such as reading the users and roles from the SAP system or validating role membership of users authenticating against the system. The user account requires only a bare minimum of authorizations on the SAP side (see Table 2.3 for details).

2. Enter the user credentials from the SAP account that you created based on those authorizations and the language code, and click the UPDATE button to save your entries.

Table 2.3 lists all necessary authorization objects and authorization values that need to be assigned to the user credentials that are leveraged in the SAP authentication configuration dialog.

Authorization Object	Authorization Field	Value
S_DATASET	ACTVT	33,34
	FILENAME	*
	PROGRAM	*
S_RFC	ACTVT	16
	RFC_NAME	BDCH, STPA, SUSO, SUUS, SU_USER, SYST, SUNI, PRGN_J2EE, /CRYSTAL/SECURITY
	RFC_TYPE	FUGR
S_USER_GROUP	ACTVT	3
	CLASS	* For security reasons you can also list user groups that have access to SAP BusinessObjects.

Table 2.3 Authorizations for SAP Authentication Configuration

To configure further options for the SAP authentication, follow the steps below:

1. Navigate to the OPTIONS tab of the SAP authentication (see Figure 2.38). This dialog allows you to configure the behavior of the SAP authentication for your SAP BusinessObjects server. All configurations you perform in this step will apply to all of the SAP entitlement systems. A detailed explanation of all possible options is shown in Table 2.4.

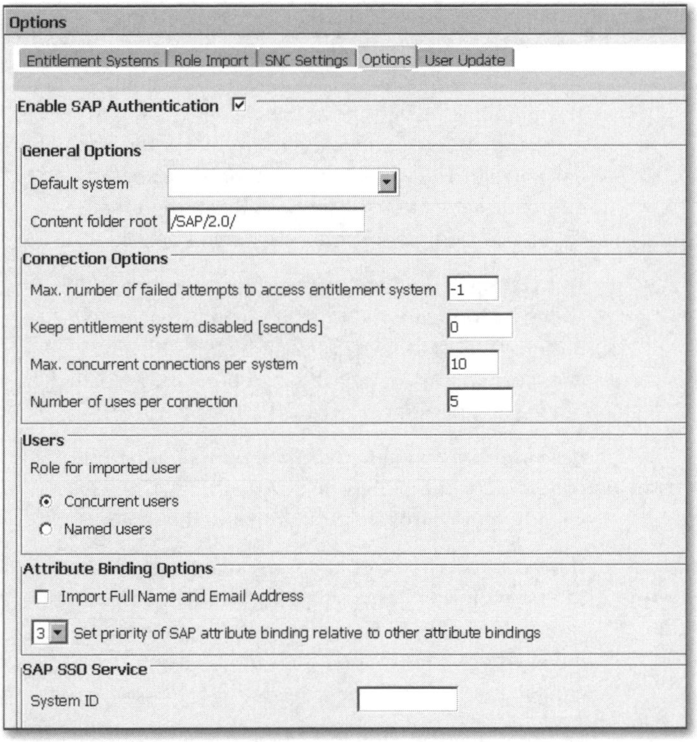

Figure 2.38 Authentication Options

Configuration Option	Description
ENABLE SAP AUTHENTICATION	You can use this checkbox to disable SAP authentication for the SAP BusinessObjects system. If you want to disable only a single entitlement SAP system, you can do that on the ENTITLEMENT SYSTEMS tab.
DEFAULT SYSTEM	The default system is used when a user is trying to authenticate SAP credentials without specifying the SAP system. A common scenario is a user navigating from the SAP NetWeaver Portal to the SAP Business-Objects system without specifying for which SAP system the authentication should be performed. In such a scenario, the default system will be used as a fallback, and the SAP BusinessObjects system will try to authenticate the user against the default system.

Table 2.4 Available Configuration Options

Configuration Option	Description
MAX. NUMBER OF FAILED ATTEMPTS TO ACCESS ENTITLEMENT SYSTEM	You can use this setting to configure how many attempts the SAP BusinessObjects server should make to connect to an SAP system that is temporarily unavailable. The value -1 is used for an unlimited number; the value 0 is used for one attempt; values larger than 0 represent the actual numeric value.
KEEP ENTITLEMENT SYSTEM DISABLED (SECONDS)	This setting is used in combination with the option above to configure the time in seconds that the SAP BusinessObjects server will wait before trying to re-access an SAP system that had previously reached the maximum number of failed attempts.
MAX. CONCURRENT CONNECTIONS PER SYSTEM	Here you can configure the maximum number of concurrent connections that SAP BusinessObjects can keep open towards the SAP entitlement system.
NUMBER OF USES PER CONNECTION	Here you can specify the number of operations that can be performed on a single connection. For example, setting the value to 5 will result in the connection being closed after 5 operations or logons on this connection.
ROLE FOR IMPORTED USER	This option allows you to configure whether the imported SAP users should be marked for a concurrent or named user license.
CONTENT FOLDER ROOT	This setting is used for the publishing process for SAP Crystal Reports objects. The path entered here specifies the starting folder for replicating the SAP role structure during the publishing process. This value has to be identical to the value entered in the Content Administration Workbench.
IMPORT FULL NAME AND EMAIL ADDRESS	Select this option if you want to import the full names and descriptions used in the SAP accounts into the user objects in SAP BusinessObjects.
SET PRIORITY OF SAP ATTRIBUTE BINDING RELATIVE TO OTHER ATTRIBUTE BINDINGS	Specifies a priority for binding SAP user attributes. Value 1: SAP attributes take priority in scenarios where SAP and other plugins (Windows AD and LDAP) are enabled. Value 3: Attributes from other enabled plugins will take priority

Table 2.4 Available Configuration Options (Cont.)

76

We discuss the SSO service shown as part of the Options tab and the necessary configuration steps in Section 2.5.6.

2. After configuring the options for SAP authentication, you can navigate to the Role Import tab (see Figure 2.39) to use the SAP roles and users for your SAP BusinessObjects system. The screen allows you to select one system from the list of SAP entitlement systems you created and provides a list of available SAP roles. Each of these roles can be imported by adding it to the Imported Roles field. As soon as you click the Update button, each of the SAP roles becomes a user group in your SAP BusinessObjects system and, if you configured it to automatically import the users, the assigned users become users in your system.

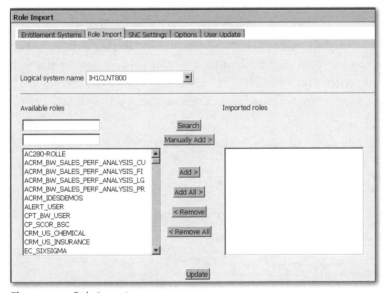

Figure 2.39   Role Import

For each of the imported SAP roles, the system generates an SAP BusinessObjects user group based on the following logic:

```
[SAP System ID] ~ [SAP client number]@[SAP role]
```

Example:

```
CIM~003@BUSINESSOBJECTS_CONTENT_ROLE
```

Each imported user follows the syntax:

```
[SAP System ID] ~ [SAP client number]/[SAP user]
```

Example:

```
CIM~003/DEMO_USER
```

Role Import and Authentication with SAP Credentials

The ROLE IMPORT option offers only those SAP roles that have users assigned to them. SAP roles with no user assignment will not be shown as available roles for the import.

After you import the SAP roles, each of the generated user groups has no assigned rights in the SAP BusinessObjects system. Those resulting user groups are assigned only to the standard SAP BusinessObjects user group *Everyone*.

If you want to continue in a very simple way and configure the correct rights assignment of all of your user groups later on, you can add those user groups to the *Administrator* group for now by navigating to the USER AND GROUPS area, selecting the imported roles, and right-clicking to select JOIN GROUP. Then join them to the user group *Administrators*.

After you import the SAP roles and users from your entitlement system, you should be able to use your SAP credentials and authenticate against the SAP BusinessObjects server. You should also be able to log on with those credentials to InfoView or the Central Management Console using the SAP authentication.

3. After importing the roles, navigate to the USER UPDATE tab (see Figure 2.40). Here you can establish a regular update of the imported SAP roles and users simply by setting up a schedule.

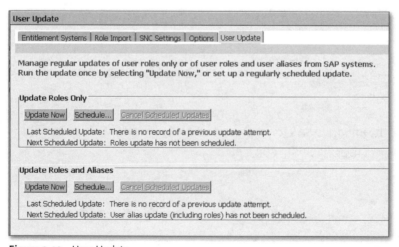

Figure 2.40 User Update

At this point you have configured the SAP authentication and imported your SAP users and roles as part of your SAP BusinessObjects system. Next we integrate the publishing process for SAP Crystal Reports 2011with SAP NetWeaver BW.

2.5.2 Setting up the Publishing Process for SAP Crystal Reports 2011

The publishing process for SAP Crystal Reports 2011 allows the storage of SAP Crystal Reports 2011 objects into the SAP NetWeaver BW repository, and then the synchronization of them with your SAP BusinessObjects system. Please note that this integration is for SAP Crystal Reports 2011 only, and not for Crystal Reports for Enterprise, which is part of the generic integration between the SAP Business-Objects lifecycle management console and SAP CTS+. This task can be done from within the SAP Crystal Reports Designer tool or via the Content Administration Workbench as an administrative task. The main benefit of the publishing integration with SAP NetWeaver BW is the integration of the SAP Crystal Reports 2011 objects into the lifecycle management console and translation integration with your SAP system. When stored in the SAP NetWeaver BW system, the SAP Crystal Reports 2011 object becomes an object that can be transported between SAP systems. In addition, all translation-relevant objects are pushed into the translation-relevant tables as part of the publishing process.

> **Crystal Reports Publishing**
>
> The publishing integration with the SAP NetWeaver BW system described here is available only for SAP Crystal Reports 2011 and cannot be used with SAP Crystal Reports for Enterprise. Overall, the recommendation for customers connecting SAP Crystal Reports with SAP NetWeaver BW is to use SAP Crystal Reports for Enterprise. SAP Crystal Reports 2011 might be an alternative for reporting on top of your SAP ECC landscape. We discuss these details later, in Chapter 4.

The actual publishing process consists of multiple steps (see Figure 2.41):

❶ If the user creates a new report object with the SAP Crystal Reports Designer 2011 and then saves this report into the SAP NetWeaver BW repository, the publishing process identifies the SAP BusinessObjects system that is assigned to the SAP role used as the location for the report object. During this step, the configuration details, such as the actual TCP/IP destination configured in Transaction SM59 and the assigned languages, are read from the configuration details set in the Content Administration Workbench.

❷ The SAP NetWeaver BW system then sends the SAP Crystal Reports 2011 content object (rpt file), the name of the Central Management Server, the translated strings, and the actual publishing command via RFC to the SAP NetWeaver BW publishing service.

❸ In the last step, the SAP Crystal Reports 2011 object is added to the repository of the SAP BusinessObjects system. Each language configured in the Content Administration Workbench results in a single report object.

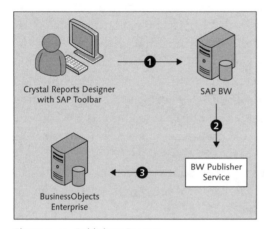

Figure 2.41 Publishing Process

The actual location of the SAP Crystal Reports 2011 content can be configured based on a base folder in the Content Administration Workbench. Below the base folder the SAP Crystal Reports 2011 objects are stored in a folder structure based on the following logic (see also Figure 2.42):

▸ Below the configured based folder, a folder with the logical system name of your SAP system is created (for example, CIMCLNT003 for the system ID CIM and client 003).

▸ Below the folder for the logical system name, a folder for each of the roles containing SAP Crystal Reports 2011 content is created. The folder is created based on the technical name and description of the SAP role.

▸ For each language configured in the Content Administration Workbench, an SAP Crystal Reports 2011 object is stored in the role folder.

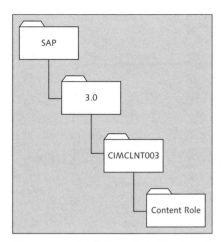

Figure 2.42 Publishing—Role Structure Example

The overall configuration of the publishing process consists of five main steps that will be explained in detail in the following sections:

1. Configuring the publishing service.

2. Creating an RFC destination.

3. Creating an SAP BusinessObjects server entry in the Content Administration Workbench.

4. Configuring the BW source parameters for the publishing process.

5. Configuring the necessary rights for the SAP BusinessObjects user groups and users.

Configuring the Publishing Service

On a Windows installation, the BW publishing service is configured via settings in the Central Configuration Manager.

1. Start the Central Configuration Manager from START • PROGRAM • SAP BUSINESS-OBJECTS BI PLATFORM 4 • SAP BUSINESSOBJECTS BI PLATFORM.

2. Select BW PUBLISHING SERVICE from the list and open the PROPERTIES.

3. Navigate to the CONFIGURATION tab (see Figure 2.43).

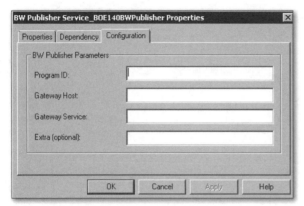

Figure 2.43 BW Publishing Service Configuration

4. Enter the details based on the descriptions shown in Table 2.5.

Parameter Name	Description
PROGRAM ID	Enter a name for the BW report publishing service. This program ID identifies the service. You cannot enter any spaces in the name, and the name is case sensitive. Example: BW_PUBLISHING
GATEWAY HOST	Enter the fully qualified name of your SAP server. If you are using an SAP cluster environment, enter the name of the central instance here. Example: IHILGEFORT.DYNDNS.ORG
GATEWAY SERVICE	Enter the port number on which the gateway host is listening. Example: 3300

Table 2.5 Parameter Options for the BW Report Publishing Service

5. After you configure the values, you can restart the BW publishing service via the Central Configuration Manager.

On a UNIX deployment you can run the following script to start a publishing service instance:

```
SAP BusinessObjects/bwcepub.sh num -aPROGID -gGWHOST—Xgwservice
```

▶ SAP BusinessObjects is the root directory of your SAP BusinessObjects Enterprise installation.

- ▶ num is the number of publishing service instances to start.

- ▶ Regarding PROGID, GWHOST, and GWSERVICE, refer to Table 2.5 for further details.

Creation of an RFC Destination

The second step is to set up an RFC destination that will use the BW publishing service. This RFC destination is used for the SAP NetWeaver BW system to communicate with the BW publishing service. If you're looking to set up multiple BW publishing services for fault tolerance or you're looking to configure a single SAP NetWeaver BW system to publish content to multiple SAP BusinessObjects systems, you need to create separate RFC destinations for each BW publishing service.

1. To create the new RFC destination, log on to the SAP NetWeaver BW system and start Transaction SM59 (see Figure 2.44).

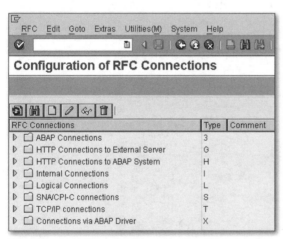

Figure 2.44 RFC Destination

2. Follow the menu path EDIT • CREATE to start a new RFC destination. You need to enter a name for the RFC destination and select a type (see Figure 2.45). For our configuration, we use the name BI_PUBLISHING and the type TCP/IP for the RFC destination.

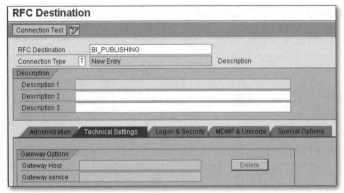

Figure 2.45 RFC Destination—Connection Type

3. Click SAVE (🖫) (alternatively, you can follow the menu path CONNECTION • SAVE), and the screen will get updated (see Figure 2.46). You can now enter the details from the previously configured publishing service.

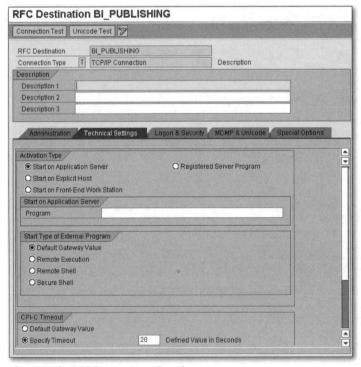

Figure 2.46 RFC Destination—Details

In Table 2.6 you can see the configuration values you need to enter for your RFC destination.

Value	Description
APPLICATION TYPE	Registered server program
PROGRAM	The program ID you entered for the BW publishing service (case sensitive) Example: BW_PUBLISHING
START TYPE OF EXTERNAL PROGRAM	Default gateway value
CPI-C TIMEOUT	Default gateway value
GATEWAY HOST	Enter the fully qualified name of your SAP server. If you're using an SAP cluster environment, enter the name of the central instance here. Example: IHIGEFORT.DYNDNS.ORG
GATEWAY SERVICE	Enter the port number on which the gateway host is listening. Example: 3300

Table 2.6 Values for the RFC Destination

If you plan to use SAP Gateway instead of the BW publishing service, then you need to configure your RFC destination according to Table 2.7.

Value	Description
APPLICATION TYPE	Start on explicit host
PROGRAM	Enter the full path to the executable BWCEPUB.exe. The path needs to be entered in an MS-DOS style.
TARGET HOST	Enter the full qualified name of the server that contains the executable. Example: BOEXI4.DYNDNS.ORG
GATEWAY HOST	Enter the fully qualified name of your SAP server. If you're using an SAP cluster environment, enter the name of the central instance here. Example: IHILGEFORT.DYNDNS.ORG
GATEWAY SERVICE	Enter the port number on which the gateway host is listening. Example: 3300

Table 2.7 Values for the RFC Destination (SAP Gateway)

4. You can now save your newly created RFC destination and test the connection. If you're using the BW publishing service, ensure that the service is up and running (via the Central Configuration Manager) before testing the connection. If the RFC destination works well, you should receive an overview on the response time (see Figure 2.47).

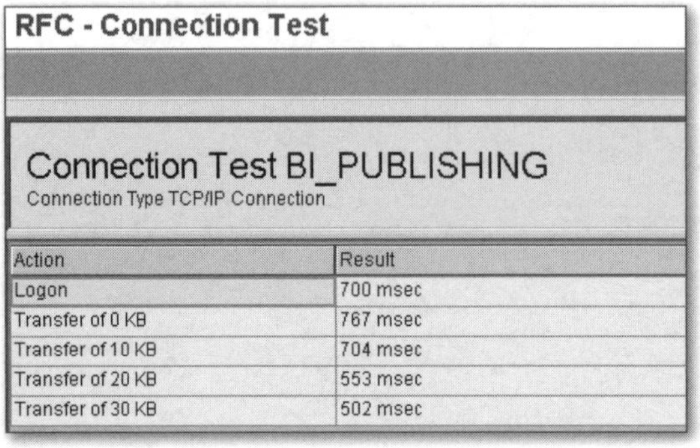

RFC - Connection Test

Connection Test BI_PUBLISHING
Connection Type TCP/IP Connection

Action	Result
Logon	700 msec
Transfer of 0 KB	767 msec
Transfer of 10 KB	704 msec
Transfer of 20 KB	553 msec
Transfer of 30 KB	502 msec

Figure 2.47 RFC Destination—Connection Test

SAP BusinessObjects Server Definition

After you have configured the BW publishing service and the RFC destination, you can define your SAP BusinessObjects system and put the separate parts together into your server definition. The Content Administration Workbench is part of the ABAP transports for the integration with your SAP landscape, and allows you to define and administer the SAP BusinessObjects systems that you want to use in combination with the SAP NetWeaver BW system. Follow the steps below.

1. Before accessing the Content Administration Workbench, ensure that the SAP account you'll be using has the authorization objects listed in Table 2.8.

Authorization Object	Authorization Field	Value
S_RFC	RFC_TYPE	FUGR
	RFC_NAME	/CRYSTAL/CE_SYNCH, SH3A, SUNI
	ACTVT	16

Table 2.8 Authorizations for Content Administration Workbench

Authorization Object	Authorization Field	Value
S_TCODE	TCD	/CRYSTAL/RPTADMIN, RSCR_MAINT_PUBLISH
S_TABU_CLI	CLIIDMAINT	X
S_TABU_DIS	ACTVT	02, 03
	DICBERCLS	&NC&
S_BTCH_JOB	JOBACTION	DELE, RELE
	JOBGROUP	' '
S_RS_ADMWB	ACTVT	16
	RSADMWBOBJ	WORKBENCH
ZCNTADMCES	ACTVT	01, 02, 03, 06
ZCNTADMJOB	ACTVT	01, 06
ZCNTADMRPT	ACTVT	02, 03, 06, 07, 23, 39

Table 2.8 Authorizations for Content Administration Workbench (Cont.)

Detailed Authorizations

The authorizations listed in Table 2.8 are authorizations for an administrative user. You can find a detailed list of authorization for administrators, publishers, and consumers in the Administrator's Guide for the SAP BusinessObjects Enterprise BI platform, which is available at *http://help.sap.com*.

2. Access the Content Administration Workbench by starting Transaction /CRYSTAL/ RPTADMIN (see Figure 2.48).

3. Double-click the item ADD NEW SYSTEM to start the process of creating your own SAP BusinessObjects server definition. First, you are shown the SYSTEM tab of your server definition (see Figure 2.49).

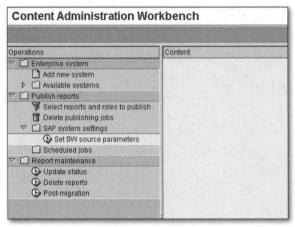

Figure 2.48 Content Administration Workbench

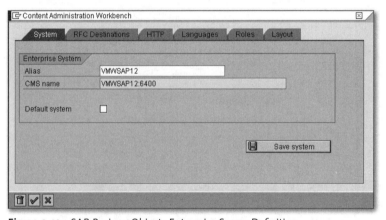

Figure 2.49 SAP BusinessObjects Enterprise Server Definition

4. You can enter an alias for your system and then enter the full qualified name of the Central Management Server of your SAP BusinessObjects system. If you're using the default port (6400), then there's no need to enter it in addition to the name of your Central Management Server, but if you configured a different port, you need to enter the port as part of your Central Management Server name. The DEFAULT SYSTEM checkbox allows you to set up one SAP BusinessObjects system as the default system for your SAP NetWeaver BW system. Those reports

stored in SAP roles that have not been assigned explicitly to an SAP Business-Objects system will then be published to the default system.

5. You can now move to the RFC DESTINATIONS tab (see Figure 2.50). Here you can add the RFC destination that you created in the previous section. If you created multiple destinations to use fault tolerance, you can add all of them here.

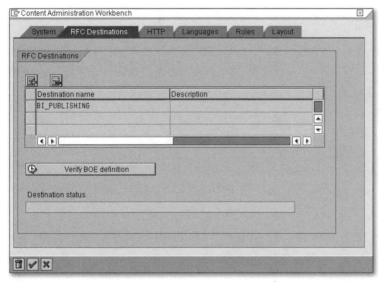

Figure 2.50 SAP BusinessObjects Enterprise System Definition—RFC Destination

As soon as you have finished the configurations, the VERIFY BOE DEFINITION button allows you to verify that all of the communication between the SAP NetWeaver BW system and your SAP BusinessObjects Enterprise system is working. This function does not run an actual publishing process; it validates all communication steps between all involved components.

The HTTP tab (see Figure 2.51) allows you to configure the necessary entries so that your end users will be able to view SAP Crystal Reports 2011 objects from the SAP GUI.

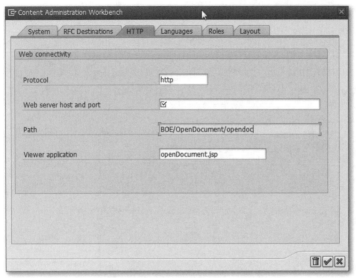

Figure 2.51 SAP BusinessObjects System Definition: HTTP

You can use Table 2.9 to see the values that you need to enter in this dialog.

Value	Description
PROTOCOL	Enter either "http" or "https" as the protocol for viewing reports here.
WEB SERVER HOST AND PORT	Enter the fully qualified name of the server that hosts the web applications of your SAP BusinessObjects system. If you're using a Java application server, include the port for the application server. Example: BOEXI4:8080
PATH	Enter the virtual path from your application server that contains the viewing application. For the default installation, this value is "BOE/OpenDocument/opendoc." There is no need to include a forward slash in the dialog.
VIEWER APPLICATION	Enter the name of the actual application being used to open the report. The default value is "openDocument.jsp."

Table 2.9 SAP BusinessObjects System Definition: HTTP Values

On the Languages tab (see Figure 2.52) you can configure the list of languages that will be used for the translation of SAP Crystal Reports 2011 objects. For each language configured in this screen, the publishing process will create one SAP Crystal Reports 2011 object so that you can, after translating the strings, view a report in multiple languages. With the Add All Languages button you can add all of the languages configured for your SAP NetWeaver BW system to the list.

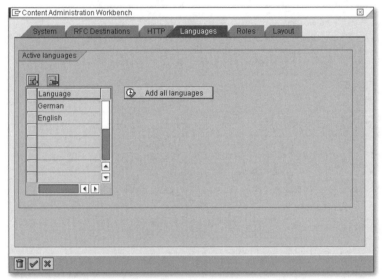

Figure 2.52 SAP BusinessObjects System Definition: Languages

Publishing and Translation

Part of the actual publishing process is the extraction of strings into the translation system. The list of languages you configure here (see Figure 2.52) also represents the list of available languages for the report. When saving SAP Crystal Report 2011 into the SAP system, you can decide to prepare the report object for translation, which results in the strings being pushed into the translation system, and you can use Transaction SE63 for translation purposes.

On the Roles tab (see Figure 2.53) you need to select those roles that will be assigned to your SAP BusinessObjects system. Any SAP Crystal Reports 2011 object stored in the assigned roles will then be published to your SAP BusinessObjects system. With the Insert row icon (🖻) you can select roles from your SAP NetWeaver BW system and assign them to your SAP BusinessObjects server definition. Click the

REASSIGN ROLES button to select roles that have already been assigned to another SAP BusinessObjects system definition. Those roles will then be removed from their current assigned server definition and will be assigned to your SAP Business-Objects system.

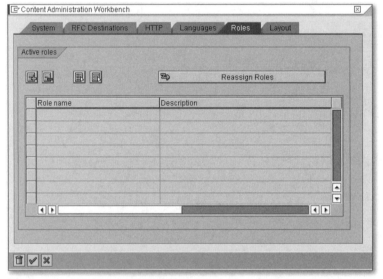

Figure 2.53 SAP BusinessObjects System Definition: Roles

SAP BusinessObjects—Role Assignment

Based on the ability to assign an SAP BusinessObjects system to a subset of SAP NetWeaver BW roles, you can easily connect a single SAP NetWeaver BW system to multiple SAP BusinessObjects systems; for example, by using one SAP BusinessObjects system for your HR department and another system for all other departments.

On the LAYOUT tab (see Figure 2.54) you can configure the base folder that will be used for the publishing. The role replication occurs underneath the base folder (see Figure 2.42).

Two additional options allow you to specify a default security setting for the role folders and the SAP Crystal Reports 2011 objects that will be created as a result of the publishing process. You can accept the default settings for now because we discuss the security assignment later in this chapter.

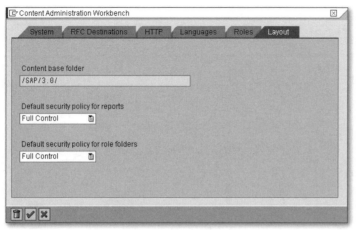

Figure 2.54 SAP BusinessObjects System Definition: Layout

<table>
<tr><td>

Content Base Folder

The folder listed as part of the SAP BusinessObjects BI platform definition (see Figure 2.54) needs to match the CONTENT BASE FOLDER configured in the OPTIONS tab of the SAP authentication (see Figure 2.38).

</td></tr>
</table>

After you have finished all of the settings, you can confirm your SAP BusinessObjects BI platform system. You should now reopen your system definition (by double-clicking it) and navigate to the RFC DESTINATION tab. You can use the VERIFY BOE DESTINATION button to validate that all involved components can communicate with each other. Keep in mind that this test is not performing an actual publishing; it is only testing the communication.

Configuring BW Source Parameters

During the publishing process the SAP NetWeaver BW system creates SAP Crystal Reports 2011 objects in the SAP BusinessObjects BI platform system. Part of this process is the configuration of the connection to the underlying SAP system, and you need to configure those values inside the Content Administration Workbench:

1. Log onto the SAP server and start Transaction /CRYSTAL/RPTADMIN for the Content Administration Workbench.

2. Follow the menu path PUBLISH REPORTS • SAP SYSTEM SETTINGS (see Figure 2.55).

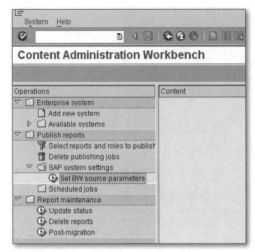

Figure 2.55 SAP NetWeaver BW Source Parameters

3. Double-click the SET BW SOURCE PARAMETERS entry to bring up the screen shown in Figure 2.56.

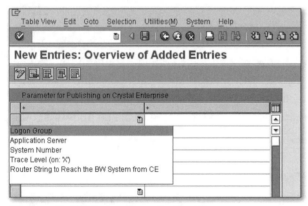

Figure 2.56 BW Source Parameter Start Screen

4. Click the CHANGE icon () to allow changes to the table (or you can follow the menu path TABLE VIEW • DISPLAY • CHANGE).

5. You can now click the NEW ENTRIES button to create new entries. Depending on your system landscape, you need to enter either a combination of application server and system number or a combination of application server (which then

represents a message server) and logon group. In our example, we enter the values shown in Table 2.10.

Property	Value
APPLICATION SERVER	IHILGEFORT.DYNDNS.ORG
SYSTEM NUMBER	00

Table 2.10 Values for SAP NetWeaver BW Source Parameters

Assignment of Necessary Rights

So far you've configured your SAP BusinessObjects BI platform and SAP system to be able to publish SAP Crystal Reports 2011 objects. The only step missing to complete the configuration is the assignment of security rights to those user groups in SAP BusinessObjects BI platform—in our scenario the imported SAP roles—that will view or publish content.

The following is only a recommendation for dividing users based on the functional aspects. There are many different ways to implement the user and user group rights, and the following is only meant to convey the concepts.

It is recommended that you split up the SAP users into three main roles:

▸ **SAP BusinessObjects administrators**
Users with this role will be able to configure the publishing and perform administrative tasks in your SAP BusinessObjects system such as importing other SAP roles and users or assigning security rights to folders and objects.

▸ **SAP BusinessObjects content publishers**
Users with this role will be able to publish content in the assigned roles. These users can create, edit, and publish content. The reason for explicitly creating such a role is to be able to differentiate these users from the next group of users—role members.

▸ **Role members**
A role member is a user assigned to a role in the SAP system that has been imported into your SAP BusinessObjects BI platform system. These members have the necessary security rights to view the content that is assigned to their role, but they cannot create, edit, or publish the content.

The overall recommendation is to set up these role definitions and the user assignments in your SAP system. You can then use those configurations by importing the SAP roles and users into the SAP BusinessObjects BI platform during the configuration of the SAP authentication.

Assigning the necessary rights is possible in two main areas. You can use the Content Administration Workbench to assign a set of default rights to the role members, and you need to use the Central Management Console to assign the necessary rights to the content publisher roles in the SAP BusinessObjects user group area.

Content Administration Workbench

To configure the default security settings for role members, follow the steps below:

1. Log on to your SAP system and start Transaction /CRYSTAL/RPTADMIN for the Content Administration Workbench.

2. Open the list of SAP BusinessObjects BI platform systems and select your previously defined system.

3. Navigate to the LAYOUT tab. Here you can configure the recommended default security values for the role members. It is recommended that you use VIEW for the default policy for the report objects and use the VIEW ON DEMAND value for the default policy on the folder level. These settings represent the standard definitions available in your SAP BusinessObjects BI platform systems and will allow these users to view the published reports on demand. If you also want to allow your role members to schedule reports, you can set the default policy to the SCHEDULE option.

Central Management Console

For our example we assume that we have the following SAP roles:

▶ **CONTENT_ADMINISTRATOR**
We use this role to configure users that are able to publish and administer content for our configured entitlement system, CIM.

▶ **SAP_BUSINESSOBJECTS_CONTENT_ROLE**
This is the role that contains the actual content. Users with this role will be able to view the content but not publish new or change existing content.

The following steps outline how to assign the necessary rights in the SAP Business-Objects BI platform system to the imported SAP roles:

1. Log on to the Central Management Console to configure the necessary rights for the content publisher role. Ensure that you log on with an administrator account and that the content publisher role you want to use is imported into your SAP BusinessObjects BI platform system using the configuration of the SAP authentication.

2. Select the FOLDERS area in the top left of the Central Management Console (see Figure 2.57).

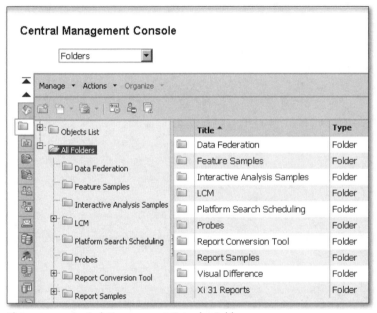

Figure 2.57   Central Management Console: Folders

3. You can now open the list of folders from your SAP BusinessObjects system and navigate down to the folder structure for your SAP system. In our example—based on the default configuration—you should see an SAP folder, and, underneath it, a 3.0 folder. Below that you will see a folder named for your SAP system ID and the client number (see Figure 2.58). This folder structure

represents the default configuration that you created in the previous steps during the configuration of the publishing.

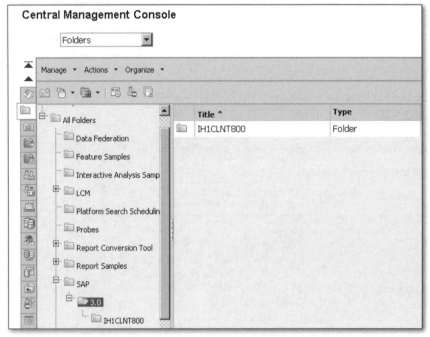

Figure 2.58 Central Management Console: Folder Structure

4. Now select the folder and open the menu MANAGE • USER SECURITY (see Figure 2.59).

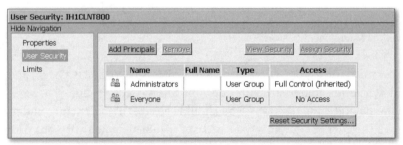

Figure 2.59 User Security

You can use the ADD PRINCIPALS function and select the groups you want to use for the assignment of security rights on this folder. In our example, we add the role IH1~800@CONTENT_ADMINISTRATOR. After you add the role to the list of selected users/groups, click the ADD AND ASSIGN SECURITY button.

1. Navigate to the ADVANCED tab and click the ADD/REMOVE RIGHTS link to see a detailed list of security rights that you can assign to the role.

2. By using the ADD/REMOVE RIGHTS option you can now grant the following rights to the selected role:

   ▶ Add objects to the folder that the user owns

   ▶ Add objects to the folder

   ▶ Copy objects to another folder that the user owns

   ▶ Copy objects to another folder

   ▶ Delete objects that the user owns

   ▶ Delete objects

   ▶ Edit objects

   ▶ Edit objects that the user owns

   ▶ Modify the rights users have to objects

   ▶ View objects

   ▶ View objects that the user owns

   You can use the three columns to grant, deny, or inherit the security authorization for the role. In our example, we explicitly grant the rights listed above.

   Based on the listed security rights, the user role is able to publish, update, and delete content in the folder. Based on the level that you selected to assign the security rights, this can mean that the role is able to perform those tasks only for a single role, for all roles for a single entitled SAP system, for multiple entitled SAP systems, or even for all entitled SAP systems.

3. Confirm the changes and confirm the assignments in the next screen.

After you confirm the assigned security, navigate to the USERS AND GROUPS area in the Central Management Console (see Figure 2.60) and follow the steps below:

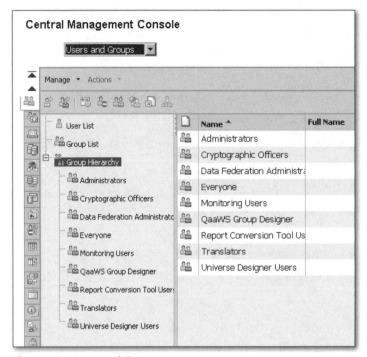

Figure 2.60 Users and Groups

1. Select the content-containing role—in our example, IH1~800@SAP_BUSINES-SOBJECTS_CONTENT_ROLE—and select the menu MANAGE • USER SECURITY (see Figure 2.61).

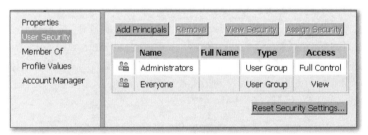

Figure 2.61 User Security

2. Click the ADD PRINCIPALS button and add the content administrator role—in our example, IH1~800@CONTENT_ADMINISTRATOR—as principal to the role.

3. Click the ADD AND ASSIGN SECURITY button to assign the list of rights:

- Add objects to the folder that the user owns
- Add objects to the folder
- Copy objects to another folder that the user owns
- Copy objects to another folder
- Delete objects that the user owns
- Delete objects
- Edit objects
- Edit objects that the user owns
- Modify the rights users have to objects
- View objects
- View objects that the user owns

You can use the three columns to grant, deny, or inherit the security authorization for the role. In our example, we explicitly grant the rights listed above.

Based on the listed security rights, the content administrator role will be able to add, edit, or change the assignment of rights for the content-containing role.

4. Confirm your changes and the assignment of the content administrator role as principal for the content containing role.

After you confirm the changes, navigate to the ACCESS LEVELS area in the Central Management Console (see Figure 2.62) and follow the steps below:

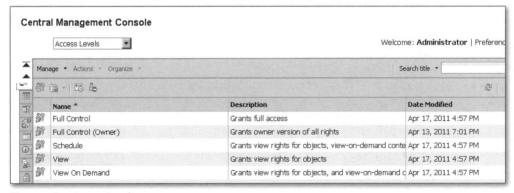

Figure 2.62 Access Levels

1. Follow the menu path MANAGE • TOP-LEVEL SECURITY • ALL ACCESS LEVELS.

2. Select ADD PRINCIPALS and add the content administrator role (IH1~800@ CONTENT_ADMINISTRATOR).

3. Use the functionality ADD AND ASSIGN SECURITY to specify the rights for the role. Add the following rights:

   ▶ View objects

   ▶ View objects that the user owns

   ▶ Edit objects

   ▶ Edit objects that the user owns

   ▶ Use access level for security assignment

4. Confirm the changes.

> **Assigned Security for the Content Administrator**
>
> The need for the content administrator to be able to modify the role and folder assigned rights is based on the content administrator role needing to be able to use the settings from the LAYOUT tab (see Figure 2.54) to specify the security according to those settings.

2.5.3 Viewing Reports within the SAP System Frontend

Because you can store SAP Crystal Reports objects in the SAP role menu, your users can also view these objects directly from their role menu. During the process of storing the SAP Crystal Reports object in the SAP system, a role entry is created that can be used to view the SAP Crystal Reports object on demand. To enable viewing of reports via the role menu, you need to configure an http request handler that is included as part of the Crystal Content Administration Workbench transport. Follow the steps below:

1. Log on to your SAP system and start Transaction SICF (see Figure 2.63).

2. Navigate to the *default_host/SAP/BW* folder and open the *ce_url* entry. From there, navigate to the HANDLER LIST tab (see Figure 2.64).

   The /CRYSTAL/CL_BW_HTTP_HANDLER entry, as shown in Figure 2.64, must be your top entry in the handler list.

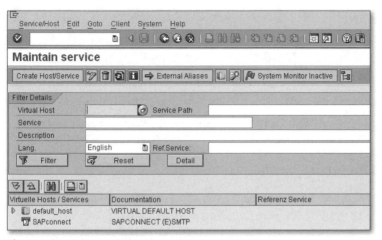

Figure 2.63 Maintain Services

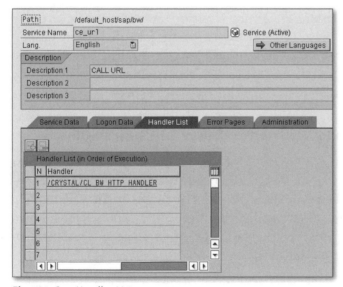

Figure 2.64 Handler List

2.5.4 Publishing Summary

At this point, as part of the publishing configuration, you have:

▶ Configured the SAP authentication and imported SAP roles and users in the Central Management Console.

▸ Configured the publishing service on your SAP BusinessObjects system.

▸ Created an RFC destination in Transaction SM59 for communication between your SAP system and your SAP BusinessObjects publishing service.

▸ Created an SAP BusinessObjects server definition in Transaction /CRYSTAL/ RPTADMIN and assigned SAP roles to your SAP BusinessObjects system.

▸ Assigned the necessary rights to the SAP roles in your SAP BusinessObjects system.

Based on those steps you are now able to:

▸ Publish an SAP Crystal Reports object from the SAP Crystal Reports Designer via an SAP role to your SAP BusinessObjects system.

▸ View an SAP Crystal Reports object via the role menu of your SAP system frontend.

Please note that the publishing integration is relevant only when you plan to use SAP Crystal Reports 2011 instead of SAP Crystal Reports for Enterprise. In Chapter 4, we make recommendations about which edition of SAP Crystal Reports is best under which circumstances. In the next section, we explain how to configure the SAP BusinessObjects system to be able to host BEx web applications.

2.5.5   Hosting SAP BEx Web Applications in SAP BusinessObjects

As part of the SAP BusinessObjects 4.x release, customers are now able to host their SAP BEx Web Application Designer applications and their BEx Web Reporting documents inside their SAP BusinessObjects landscape. In this case, hosting means that the application is rendered as part of the SAP BusinessObjects system instead of the SAP NetWeaver stack, but the physical storage of the application stays within the SAP NetWeaver stack.

As shown in Figure 2.65, the development and change of the BEx Web Application Designer applications and the BEx web templates is done using the BEx Web Application Designer, and the storage is in SAP NetWeaver BW. You can then configure the hosting of these templates and applications as part of your SAP BusinessObjects BI platform, and users can launch the templates and applications as part of the BI launch pad.

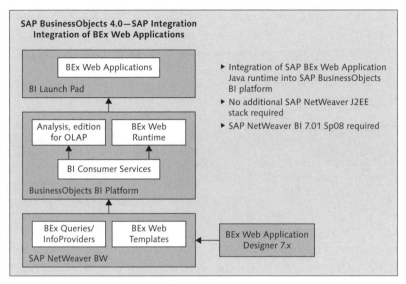

Figure 2.65 Hosting BEx Web Applications

The benefits for you as a customer using SAP NetWeaver BW and SAP Business-Objects 4.x with hosted BEx web applications are:

▶ There is no mandatory requirement for an SAP BI Java component as part of your SAP NetWeaver stack when hosting your BEx web applications in the SAP BusinessObjects environment.

▶ Your end users will be able to access all BI assets from a single environment.

The current limitations of the integration of your BEx web applications into the SAP BusinessObjects environment are:

▶ Because of the missing SAP BI Java component, the following components are not supported unless you install the SAP BI Java component as part of the SAP NetWeaver BW stack:

  ▶ Information Broadcasting

  ▶ Adobe Document Services (ADS)

  ▶ SAP NetWeaver Portal Knowledge Management

▶ The BEx web applications integrated into the SAP BusinessObjects environment can contain only data sources that are available in the SAP NetWeaver master BW system. The master system is configured as part of the SAP BusinessObjects administration.

▶ Only one SAP NetWeaver BW system is supported per SAP BusinessObjects system.

▶ Report-report interface from and to BEx web applications is not supported.

▶ SSO between SAP BusinessObjects and the hosted BEx web application is not enabled yet.

Technical Prerequisites

To be able to host your BEx web applications as part of your SAP BusinessObjects system, you will need SAP NetWeaver BW 7.01 SP08 or higher. You can find further details in SAP Notes 1541365 and 1471463.

The configuration to host your BEx web applications with the SAP BusinessObjects environment includes configuration steps for the SAP NetWeaver BW backend and for the SAP BusinessObjects system. We start by configuring the SAP NetWeaver BW system.

1. Log on via SAP GUI to your SAP NetWeaver BW system.

2. Start Transaction SM59.

3. Use the menu EDIT • CREATE to create a new RFC destination.

4. Enter a name for the RFC destination and select the T connection type for TCP/IP connections (see Figure 2.66). You will need the configured name later on as part of the configuration on the SAP BusinessObjects system.

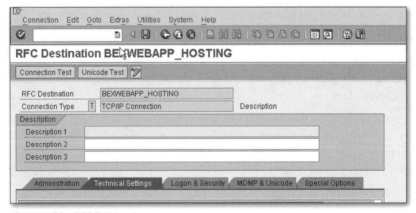

Figure 2.66 RFC Destination

5. Save the changes using the SAVE icon (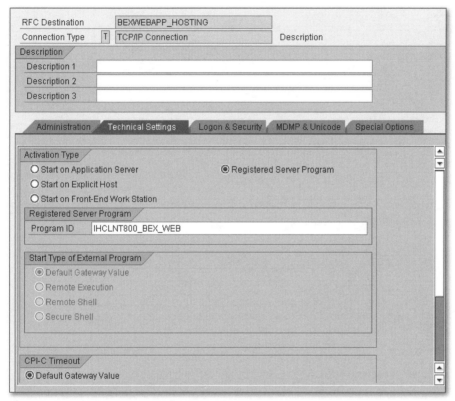) in the toolbar or the menu CONNEC-
TION • SAVE.

6. Select the REGISTERED SERVER PROGRAM option and enter a program ID (see
Figure 2.67). The program ID is case sensitive; in our example, it is: IH1CLNT800_
BEX_WEB.

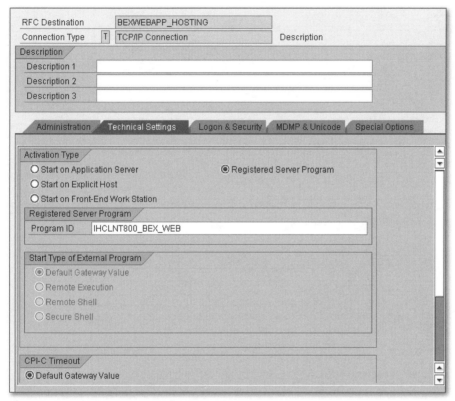

Figure 2.67 RFC Destination Configuration: Part 1

7. In the GATEWAY HOST field, enter the full qualified name of your SAP NetWeaver
BW server; for GATEWAY SERVICE enter the number 33## where "##" is replaced
with the instance number of the SAP NetWeaver BW server (see Figure 2.68).

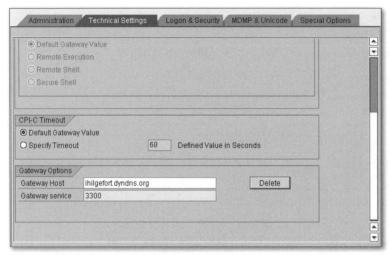

Figure 2.68 RFC Destination Configuration: Part 2

8. Navigate to the LOGON & SECURITY tab.

9. Activate the SEND ASSERTION TICKETS option and enter the details for the TARGET SYSTEM and TARGET CLIENT (see Figure 2.69).

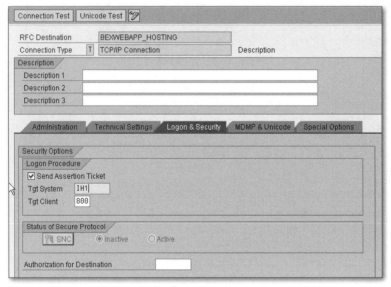

Figure 2.69 Logon & Security Configuration

10. Save your changes using the menu CONNECTION • SAVE and close the transaction.

11. Start Transaction SM30.

12. Enter RSPOR_T_PORTAL into the TABLE/VIEW field.

13. Click the MAINTAIN button (see Figure 2.70).

Change View "Connected Portals": Overview							
💱 ☖ New Entries 🗐 🗐 🗐 🗐 🗐 🗐							
Connected Portals							
RFC Destination	Name of System	Standard Portal	Portal URL Prefix	P	KM Metadata Repository Manager Prefix	BI CM Repository Prefix fo	
BI_STANDARD_J2EE	SAP_BW	☐	http://portal-dmb.wdf.sap.corp:50100		/bi_metadata		▲
IH1_IHILGEFORT_IH1	SAP_BW	☑	http://ihilgefort.dyndns.org:50000		/bw_metadata		▼

Figure 2.70 Maintain Table Entries

14. Click NEW ENTRIES.

15. Enter the following details (see Figure 2.71):

   ▶ DESTINATION: Enter the name of the RFC destination you created previously. In our example: BEXWEBAPP_HOSTING.

   ▶ NAME OF SYSTEM: Enter a name for the system. In our example: Hosting on BI4.

   ▶ Select the STANDARD PORTAL option.

   ▶ URL PREFIX: Enter the base URL for your SAP BusinessObjects system. In our example: *http://boexi4.dyndns.org:8080.*

   ▶ PLATFORM: Select BOE for this option.

   ▶ Activate the USE SAP EXPORT LIBRARY (PDF) option if you want to be able to export the BEx web applications to a PDF file.

   ▶ STANDARD PORTAL: This option is activated only if all your BEx web applications are going to be hosted as part of your SAP BusinessObjects system.

16. Save your changes using the menu TABLE VIEW • SAVE.

17. Close the session with the SAP NetWeaver BW system.

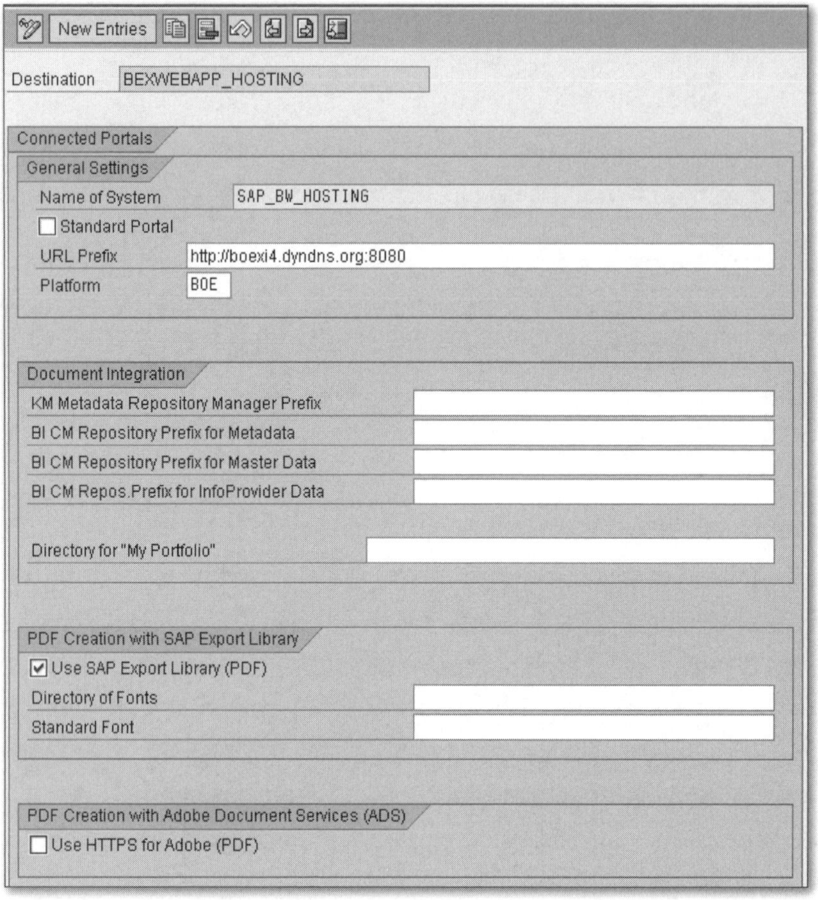

Figure 2.71 New Table Entries

In the next couple of steps, we configure the SAP BusinessObjects system to allow for the hosting of the BEx web applications.

1. Log on to the Central Management Console (CMC) of your SAP BusinessObjects system using the URL *http://localhost:8080/BOE/CMC*.

2. Navigate to the OLAP CONNECTIONS area (see Figure 2.72).

3. Use the NEW CONNECTION icon (⬆) to create a new OLAP connection (see Figure 2.73).

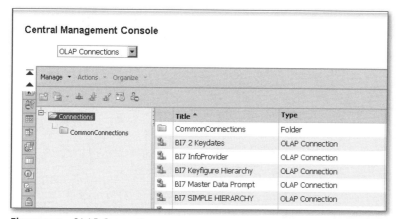

Figure 2.72 OLAP Connections

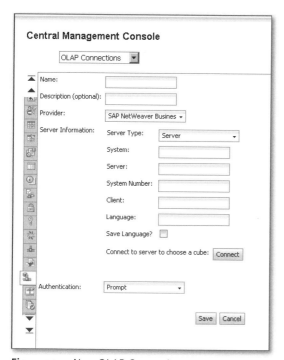

Figure 2.73 New OLAP Connection

4. Enter the details according to Table 2.11:

Value	Description
NAME	Enter a name for the connection. You will need the name later on, as part of the configuration. Example: SAP_BW_HOSTING
DESCRIPTION (OPTIONAL)	Enter a description.
PROVIDER	Select SAP NETWEAVER BUSINESSWAREHOUSE from the list.
SERVER TYPE	Select between SERVER for a connection to an application server and GROUP for a connection to a message server with a logon group.
SYSTEM	Enter the 3-digit system ID of your SAP system. Example: IH1
SERVER	Enter the full qualified name of the application server or the message server. Example: ihilgefort.dyndns.org
SYSTEM NUMBER	Enter the system number of your SAP system. Example: 00
CLIENT	Enter the client number you want to use. Example: 800
LANGUAGE	Enter the two-digit language code for the connection. Example: EN
SAVE LANGUAGE	Decide whether the language code should be saved or if the user profile will overwrite this setting. For the described usage, select the option to save the language code.

Table 2.11 OLAP Connection Details

5. Set AUTHENTICATION to the PRE-DEFINED value.

6. Enter the SAP user credentials of an administrative account.

7. Click SAVE to save the connection.

SAP Account for BEx Web App Hosting

The SAP credentials leveraged as part of the configuration for the OLAP connection need to have the SAP role SAP_BC_JSF_COMMUNICATION_RO assigned.

8. Navigate to the SERVERS area in the Central Management Console (see Figure 2.74).

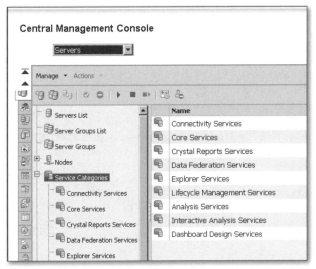

Figure 2.74 Servers

9. Select the menu MANAGE • NEW • NEW SERVER.

10. Select the service CATEGORY ANALYSIS SERVICES and the service BEX WEB APPLI-CATIONS SERVICE (see Figure 2.75).

Figure 2.75 Create New Server

11. Click NEXT. Do not select any additional options in the next screen, as it is recommended that you have a dedicated server for the hosting of the BEx web applications.

12. Click Next.

13. You can now select the SAP BusinessObjects node and enter a name for your newly created server (see Figure 2.76).

Figure 2.76   Server Name

As this server is meant to host BEx web applications, you can also enter a name indicating that, such as "<Node>.BexWebHosting".

14. Click Create.

15. Select the Analysis Services server category (see Figure 2.77).

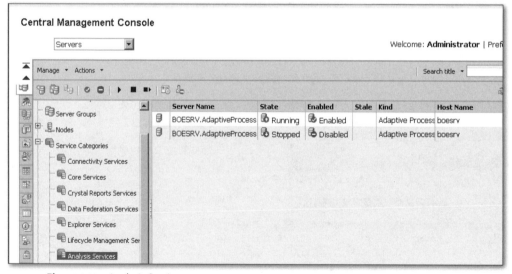

Figure 2.77   Analysis Services

16. Select your newly created server from the list.

17. Select the menu ACTIONS • ENABLE SERVER.

18. Select the menu ACTIONS • START SERVER.

19. Select your newly created server and open the context menu with a right-click.

20. Select the PROPERTIES menu entry and scroll down to the BEx WEB APPLICATION SERVICE area (see Figure 2.78).

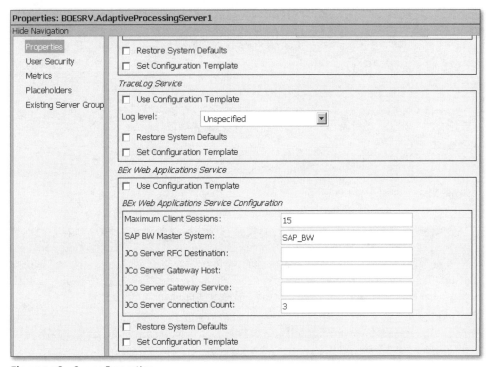

Figure 2.78 Server Properties

21. Configure the details as outlined in Table 2.12.

22. Click SAVE & CLOSE.

23. Select your configured server and use the menu ACTIONS • RE-START SERVER.

Value	Description
MAXIMUM CLIENT SESSIONS	The default value is 15.
SAP BW MASTER SYSTEM	Enter the name of the OLAP connection you created as part of the Central Management Console. In our example: SAP_BW_HOSTING
JCO SERVER RFC DESTINATION	Enter the program ID that you configured as part of the RFC destination you created as part of your SAP NetWeaver BW system. In our example: IH1CLNT800_BEX_WEB Please note that the description refers to the RFC destination but you need to enter the program ID.
JCO SERVER GATEWAY HOST	This value should match the value for the Gateway host that was entered in the RFC destination.
JCO SERVER GATEWAY SERVICE	This value should match the value for the Gateway service that was entered in the RFC destination.
JCO SERVER CONNECTION COUNT	Enter the maximum number of concurrent JCo connections.

Table 2.12 Server Properties Details

BEx Web Application Services
If you used the default installation of SAP BusinessObjects 4.x, then you should make sure that your default adaptive processing server in the analysis services category is not also configured to act as a server for the BEx Web Application hosting.

At this point you have configured your system. Now you can set up an SAP Business-Objects user group and assign this group the necessary rights on the SAP Business-Objects system so that you can add new members to the group. All members will then be able to leverage the BEx Web Applications as part of the SAP Business-Objects environment.

1. Navigate to the USERS AND GROUPS area in the Central Management Console.

2. Select the menu MANAGE • NEW • NEW GROUP.

3. Enter "BExWeb User" in the GROUP NAME field.

4. Click OK.

5. Navigate to the APPLICATIONS area in the Central Management Console (see Figure 2.79).

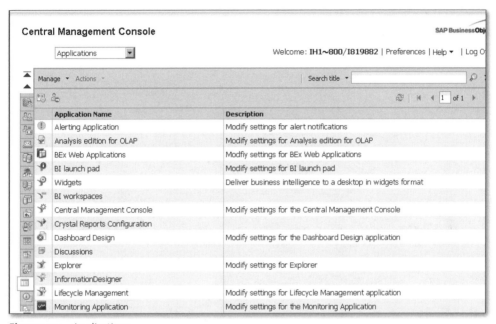

Figure 2.79 Applications

6. Select the BEx WEB APPLICATIONS entry.

7. Select the menu MANAGE • USER SECURITY (see Figure 2.80).

Figure 2.80 User Security

8. Click ADD PRINCIPALS.

9. Navigate to GROUP LIST.

10. Select the newly created BExWeb user group and add it to the list of selected user groups (see Figure 2.81).

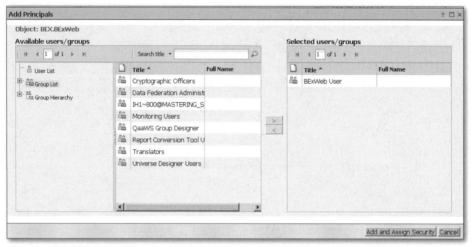

Figure 2.81 Add Principals

11. Click ADD AND ASSIGN SECURITY.

12. Select the ACCESS LEVEL VIEW and add it to the list of ASSIGNED LEVELS (see Figure 2.82).

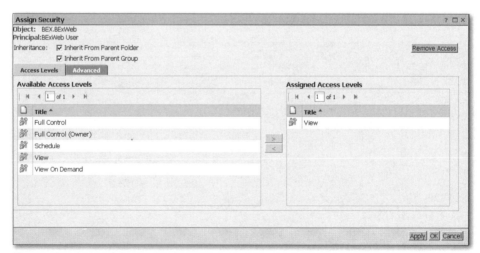

Figure 2.82 Assigned Access Levels

13. Click OK.

14. Click CLOSE.

The configuration is now complete, and you should be able to host your BEx Web Applications as part of your SAP BusinessObjects system. Your users can now open the BEx Web applications as part of the BI launch pad.

1. Start the BI launch pad by opening the URL *http://localhost:8080/BOE/BI* in your browser.

2. Use your SAP credentials and the SAP authentication to log on to your SAP BusinessObjects system.

3. Use the menu APPLICATIONS • BEx WEB APPLICATIONS in the BI launch pad (see Figure 2.83).

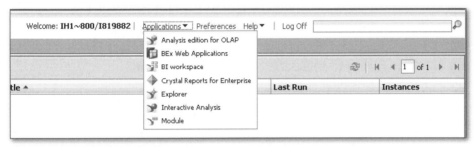

Figure 2.83   BEx Web Applications

4. The user will be asked to log on again, as single sign-on (SSO) is not part of this integration yet at the point in time writing this book. This functionality is planned to be delivered with a later Service Pack.

5. The user can now view existing BEx web applications and BEx web templates (see Figure 2.84).

In this section, you learned how you can leverage SAP BusinessObjects as a single BI platform, not only for your SAP BusinessObjects BI tools but also for your BEx web applications. In the next section we review the new single sign-on (SSO) token service.

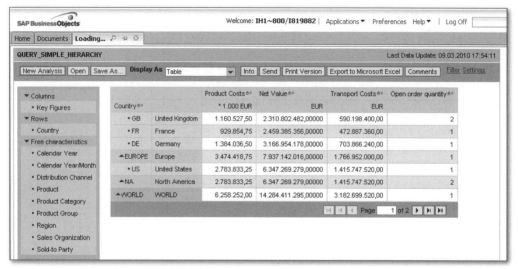

Figure 2.84 BEx Web Application

2.5.6 Configuring the SSO Token Service as Part of SAP BusinessObjects

Starting with SAP BusinessObjects 4.0, the SAP BusinessObjects BI platform provides you with an SSO token service capable of generating assertion tickets. The generated assertion tickets can help you achieve an SSO to the SAP system in several scenarios:

▸ You can leverage this new service to enable scheduling of BI content with SSO.

▸ You can leverage this new service to enable publications (report bursting) of BI content with SSO.

▸ You can leverage this new service to enable SSO to the SAP system for cases where multiple user aliases are involved.

▸ You can leverage this new service to enable SSO for scenarios where SAP credentials are not involved as part of the initial user authentication; for example, using Windows AD credentials to authenticate against the SAP BusinessObjects system and still achieve SSO in the SAP system.

▸ You can leverage this service to achieve SSO for thick client products like SAP Crystal Reports for Enterprise.

For example, you could have an SAP BusinessObjects user "User A" with a user alias configured where the alias is the SAP account for "User A" — let's call the alias "User B." The user will then be able to log on to the SAP BusinessObjects system or to a thick client like Crystal Reports for Enterprise using the SAP BusinessObjects enterprise authentication and the credentials "User A," but based on the SSO token service still achieve SSO towards the SAP server with "User B."

You might think that this new SSO service replaces what was known as *server-side trust* as part of the SAP BusinessObjects XI 3.1 integration with SAP, and that is correct. You can use SAP authentication without the SSO token service for all the standard viewing experiences with SSO to the SAP systems, but for the scenarios described above, it is required that you do leverage the new SSO token service. You can use the server-side trust configuration and the configuration is still supported. This new SSO token service simply provides you with an alternative.

SAP Aliases

The new SSO token service allows you to cover several scenarios where the new service will generate an assertion token to achieve SSO to the SAP system. The most important prerequisite for this service to work is the fact that the involved users will need an SAP alias as part of the SAP BusinessObjects system.

The configuration for the SSO token service includes several steps:

▸ Generating a keystore file and certificate for the SAP BusinessObjects system.

▸ Importing the certificate to the SAP system.

▸ Setting up SSO in the SAP BusinessObjects BI platform Central Management Console (CMC).

▸ Adding the SSO token service to your SAP BusinessObjects BI platform system.

Next, we configure the SSO token service as part of the SAP BusinessObjects BI Platform system.

Generating Keystore File and Certificate

As a first step in the overall configuration, you need to generate a keystore file and a certificate for your SAP BusinessObjects BI platform system.

To generate the keystore file, you will use the PKCS12 tool. You can locate the necessary files in the following locations:

▶ For Windows installations: *<INSTALLDIR>\SAP BusinessObjects Enterprise XI 4.0\ java\lib*

▶ For UNIX installations: *<INSTALLDIR>/sap_bobj/enterprise_xi40/java/lib*

Then follow the steps below:

1. Open a command prompt with an administrative account on your SAP Business-Objects system.

2. Navigate to the above listed location for the PKCS12 tool.

3. You can execute the tool with the parameters shown in Table 2.13.

Parameter	Description and Default Value
keystore	Define the filename for the certificate. Default Value: `Keystore.p12`
alias	Define the alias for your server. Default Value: `Myalias`
storepass	Define the password. Default Value: `123456`
dname	Define the distinguished name for your system. Default Value: `CN=CA`
validity	Define the validity for the certificate. Default Value: `365`
cert	`Cert.der`

Table 2.13 Default Values for PKCS12

4. Run the following command:
   ```
   java -jar PKCS12Tool.jar -keystore BOEServer.p12 -alias BOEServer
   -storepass 1111 -dname CN=BOESERVER,OU=PM,O=SAP,C=CA -validity 365
   ```
   (see Figure 2.85).

Figure 2.85 PKCS12Tool

5. The .p12 file is generated at the location where you start the tool.

6. You now need to export the .p12 file to a certificate. The key tool is located in the folder: *<INSTALLDIR>/SAP BusinessObjects Enterprise XI 4.0\win64_x64\sapjvm\bin.*

7. Open a command prompt with an administrative user.

8. Run the following command:

   ```
   "<INSTALLDIR>\SAP BusinessObjects Enterprise XI 4.0\win64_x64\sapjvm\
   bin\keytool" -exportcert -keystore BOEServer.p12 -storetype pkcs12
   -file BOEServer.cert -alias BOEServer
   ```

   You need to replace the <INSTALLDIR> placeholder with the path to your installation folder. The command above shows the command used with the values from our previous steps.

9. Enter the password you previously configured via the parameter storepass; in our example, 12345. The certificate is stored in the folder.

So far you have created a keystore file and a certificate for your SAP BusinessObjects system. In the next step, you will import the certificate into your SAP system.

Importing the Certificate into the SAP System

In the next steps, you will import the certificate from the SAP BusinessObjects system into the SAP system.

1. Log on to your SAP system using the SAP GUI.

2. Start Transaction STRUSTSSO2 (see Figure 2.86).

3. Open the System PSE folder.

4. Double-click the entry for your server.

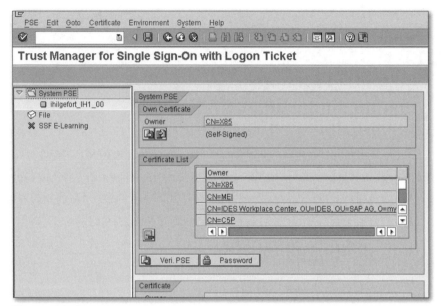

Figure 2.86 Trust Manager

5. Select the menu CERTIFICATE • IMPORT (see Figure 2.87).

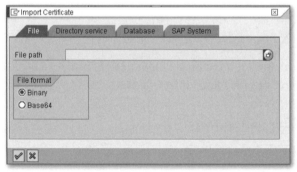

Figure 2.87 Import Certificate

6. Ensure that the BINARY option is set.

7. Select the certificate file that you created previously.

8. Use the CONTINUE icon (✓) to confirm the settings and import the certificate (see Figure 2.88).

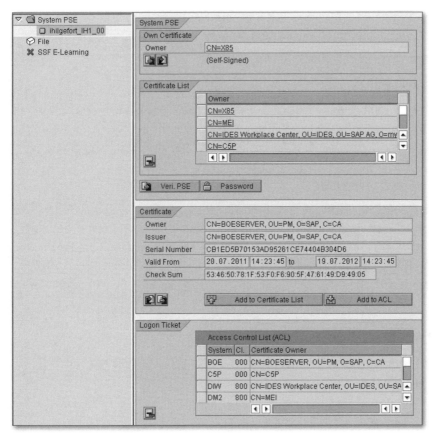

Figure 2.88 Trust Manager

9. Click ADD TO CERTIFICATE LIST.

10. Click ADD TO ACL (see Figure 2.89).

Figure 2.89 Add Entry

11. Enter a System ID for your SAP BusinessObjects system. This system ID will also be used later on in the Central Management Console.

12. For the CLIENT field, enter "000".

13. Save your settings.

You have now imported the certificate from your SAP BusinessObjects server into your SAP system. In the next step, you will configure the necessary settings in the Central Management Console (CMC) of your SAP BusinessObjects system.

Setting Up SSO in the CMC

After generating the certificate and importing it into the SAP system, you can now set up the necessary steps in the Central Management Console. Before configuring the following steps, ensure that you followed the steps in Section 2.5.1 for the SAP authentication configuration.

1. To reach the Central Management Console (CMC), open the URL *http://local-host:8080/BOE/CMC* in your browser.

2. Navigate to the AUTHENTICATION area.

3. Double-click the SAP entry.

4. Navigate to the OPTIONS tab (see Figure 2.90).

5. Click BROWSE.

6. Select your keystore file; in our example, BOEServer.p12.

7. Enter the configured KEY STORE PASSWORD. Here you enter the password you configured in the previous section.

8. Enter the configured private key password. Here you enter the password you configured in the previous section.

9. Enter the configured alias for your SAP BusinessObjects system into the PRIVATE KEY ALIAS field; in our example, BOEServer.

10. In the SYSTEM ID field, enter the system ID you configured as part of the Trust Manager for your SAP BusinessObjects server; in our example, BOE1.

11. Click UPDATE.

After you configured the details in the CMC, you can add the service to your SAP BusinessObjects server.

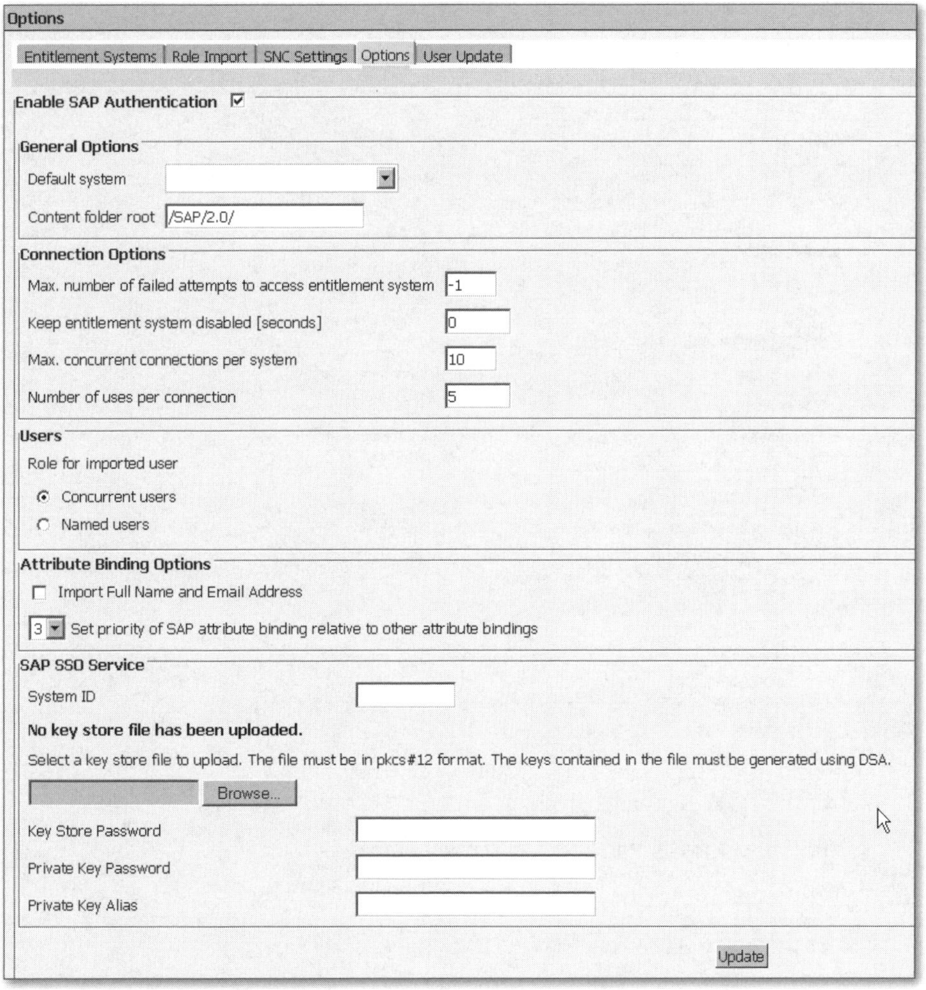

Figure 2.90 Authentication Options

Adding SSO Token Service to the SAP BusinessObjects System

In this section you will add and configure the necessary services to your SAP BusinessObjects server environment:

1. To reach the Central Management Console (CMC) open the URL *http://local-host:8080/BOE/CMC* in your browser.

2. Navigate to the SERVERS area (see Figure 2.91).

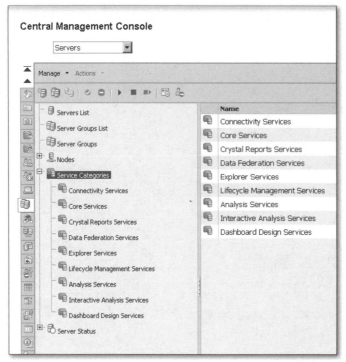

Figure 2.91 Servers

3. Select the Core Services entry.

4. Select the Adaptive Processing Server entry.

5. Select the menu Action • Stop Server.

6. Select the entry Adaptive Processing Server.

7. Select the menu Action • Select Services.

8. Add Security Token Service to the list of configured services (see Figure 2.92).

9. Click OK.

10. Select the Adaptive Processing Server entry.

11. Select the menu Action • Start Server.

You have now configured the adaptive processing server to leverage your configuration and offer the SSO token service as part of your SAP BusinessObjects platform.

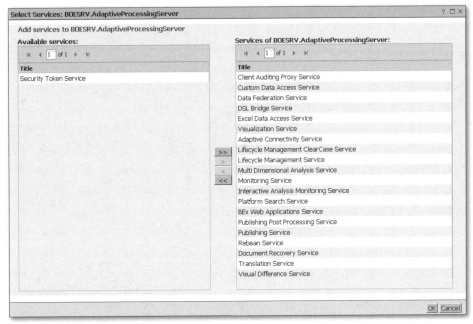

Figure 2.92 Select Services

2.6 Summary

In this chapter you installed your SAP BusinessObjects server environment and you installed the necessary client tools, such as SAP Crystal Reports for Enterprise and SAP BusinessObjects Dashboards. In addition, you configured the SAP authentication, the publishing for SAP Crystal Reports 2011, the hosting of your BEx web applications, and the new SSO token service as part of your BI platform. In the next chapter you will get an overview of the semantic layer and its role as part of your SAP landscape.

In the following sections we review the different options for leveraging the semantic layer technology as part of the SAP BusinessObjects stack to connect to your SAP system.

3 Semantic Layer and Data Connectivity

The goal of this chapter is to review the different options for connecting the corporate data in your SAP systems and explain the role the semantic layer plays in the overall SAP BusinessObjects stack. It does not review the actual steps for creating the different connections in this chapter, as these are discussed in the BI client chapters.

3.1 Semantic Layer Technology

Before we discuss the details of the data connectivity for your SAP system, we should clarify some key terms that are used not only in this book but also in other published materials.

▶ The *semantic layer* is a technology that is part of the SAP BusinessObjects stack. It allows you to expose a given data source to your end users using more user-friendly business terms.

▶ *Universes* are artifacts created using the Information Design Tool (as part of the SAP BusinessObjects 4.x release) or the Universe Designer (as part of the SAP BusinessObjects XI 3.x release). Universes represent a model using a data connection and business term and can be leveraged by the BI client tools to expose the information to your end users.

▶ *Dimensional universes* are one form of universes, focusing on multi-dimensional capabilities such as hierarchies.

▶ *Relational universes* are another form of universes, presenting the business terms in a flat view to your end users.

▶ *Multi-source universes* allow users to combine multiple data sources into a single universe, presenting a single logical view to your end users.

▶ *BI Consumer Services (BICS)* is a direct access option provided by the semantic layer. The BICS connectivity option allows the semantic layer to expose a BEx query directly to the BI client tool without the need to create a universe.

▶ The *Information Design Tool* is the client tool that allows you to establish data connections to data sources and expose them in the form of business layers to your end users.

▶ *Universe Designer* is the previous version of the Information Design Tool for the SAP BusinessObjects XI 3.1 release.

All of the above are elements and components of the overall semantic layer as part of the SAP BusinessObjects 4.x environment. In this chapter, we explain more about the different options for leveraging the semantic layer in combination with your SAP system.

3.2 SAP BusinessObjects Semantic Layer Terms

You will notice that as part of the SAP BusinessObjects 4.x release, all the BI client products try to remain consistent in the terms they use. It is important to acknowledge that all the SAP BusinessObjects BI client products are moving away from using the terms specific to SAP NetWeaver BW and are instead focusing on common terminology.

Table 3.1 shows the terms previously used by SAP NetWeaver BW and the matching terms for the 4.x release of the SAP BusinessObjects BI platform. You can use this table to make yourself familiar with the new terms of SAP BusinessObjects 4.x.

BEx Query Terms	SAP BusinessObjects 4.x Terms
Key figure	Measure
Characteristic	Dimension
Variable	Prompt
Characteristic values	Member
Condition	Filter by measure
Exception	Conditional formatting

Table 3.1 Terms Used in SAP BusinessObjects 4.x

3.3 Data Connectivity for SAP Landscapes

In this section we review the overall options that you can leverage to connect from your SAP BusinessObjects BI client tools to the different SAP landscapes. We will look at the data connectivity options for SAP NetWeaver BW, SAP ECC, and SAP HANA. SAP HANA is SAP's new in-memory database allowing you to process large amount of data in a high-performing environment.

As shown in Figure 3.1, you have two options for connecting to the SAP NetWeaver BW system. You can leverage a direct access method, which leverages the BI Consumer Services (BICS) to expose a BEx query to the BI client tools. The alternative is to create a universe as part of the semantic layer on top of the relational schema of SAP NetWeaver BW.

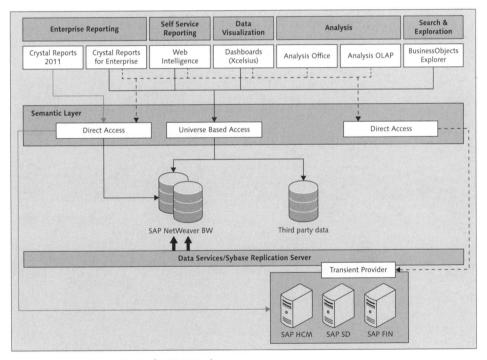

Figure 3.1 Data Connectivity for SAP Landscapes

With regard to data connectivity towards SAP HANA, you can leverage a direct access method or you can leverage universe-based access. SAP BusinessObjects Analysis, edition for Microsoft Office; SAP BusinessObjects Analysis, OLAP edition; and SAP

BusinessObjects Explorer are able to establish a direct link to SAP HANA, whereas the other BI client products leverage the universe-based approach.

In regards to the connectivity to your SAP ECC system, you can see that SAP Crystal Reports 2011 is able to connect directly to the SAP ECC system and that all other BI client products, with the exception of SAP BusinessObjects Explorer, leverage the transient provider as an entry point to the SAP ECC system. In addition to the transient provider, SAP Crystal Reports for Enterprise, SAP BusinessObjects Web Intelligence, SAP BusinessObjects Explorer, and SAP BusinessObjects Dashboards are able to leverage the connection towards SAP ECC via the universe, which is an exciting new option as part of the SAP BusinessObjects 4.x release.

Figure 3.2 shows not only which tool is able to link to which underlying data source but also the leveraged technology. You can see that all the BI client products, with the exception of SAP BusinessObjects Explorer, use the BI Consumer Service to connect to the SAP NetWeaver BW system and to the transient provider in the SAP ECC system.

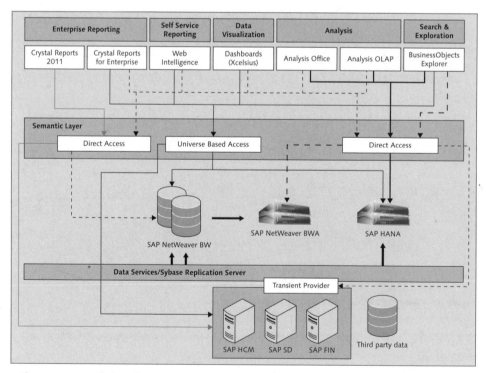

Figure 3.2 Detailed Data Connectivity

For connectivity to SAP HANA, you can see that SAP BusinessObjects Analysis, edition for Microsoft Office and SAP BusinessObjects Analysis, edition for OLAP use BICS connectivity; SAP BusinessObjects Explorer uses a SQL-based direct link to SAP HANA; and all other BI clients use a universe-based approach with an ODBC-based or a JDBC-based connection.

The above outline provides an overview of all technically available options. In the next sections we look into the details of connectivity to SAP NetWeaver BW and SAP ECC.

3.3.1 Direct Access to SAP NetWeaver BW using BICS

SAP BusinessObjects 4.x provides you with the option to expose a BEx query directly to the BI client tools such as SAP BusinessObjects Analysis, edition for Microsoft Office or SAP Crystal Reports for Enterprise. This direct connectivity to the SAP NetWeaver BW system is based on the BI Consumer Services (BICS) and exposes all the necessary metadata to the SAP BusinessObjects software.

The following are the advantages of direct access to SAP NetWeaver BW:

▶ Re-use of existing BEx queries.

▶ Shared connectivity across all BI client tools.

▶ Provides true hierarchical metadata and data.

▶ Allows for a single connection to point to multiple BEx queries.

▶ Supports advanced BEx query elements, such as restricted and calculated key figures, formulas, and custom structures.

The following are the disadvantages of direct access to SAP NetWeaver BW:

▶ Does not allow for customization of the metadata.

▶ Does not allow for the creation of custom objects.

▶ Does not allow for administrative limits such as a connection timeout on the SAP BusinessObjects stack.

▶ Does not allow for the creation of universe-based parameters. All parameters need either to be based on variables in the BEx query or to be created as parameters on a report level.

▶ Does not allow for changing the aggregation functionality of key figures. All key figures are treated as a database delegated key figure and ask for the aggregated values from SAP NetWeaver BW. The exception are key figures that are defined as a standard summary in SAP NetWeaver BW; these key figures are treated as a standard summary aggregation key figure in the BI client tools as well.

As you can see in Figure 3.3, direct access towards the SAP NetWeaver BW system can be leveraged by all the BI client tools, except SAP Crystal Reports 2011 and SAP BusinessObjects Explorer. In addition to access to SAP NetWeaver BW, access to your SAP ECC system is also possible using direct access (in combination with the transient provider of the SAP ECC system).

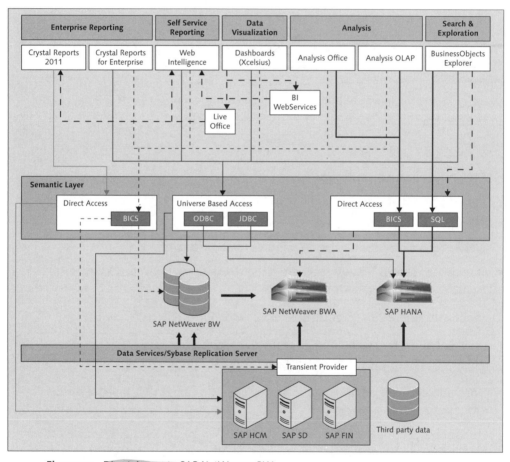

Figure 3.3 Direct Access to SAP NetWeaver BW

Leveraging direct access to SAP NetWeaver BW requires a connection to be established in the Central Management Console of your SAP BusinessObjects system, which we demonstrate in a step-by-step fashion in the BI client chapters later in this book.

> **Direct Access Connections to BEx Queries or InfoProviders**
>
> SAP BusinessObjects 4.x allows you to configure connections to your SAP NetWeaver BW system as part of the Central Management Console (CMC) and to share those connections among the different BI client products. All of the BI client products are able to use a single connection pointing to the InfoProvider and to provide a list of available BEx queries at report design time.

3.3.2 Relational Access to SAP NetWeaver BW

In addition to direct access to the SAP NetWeaver BW system, the semantic layer also offers you the option to create a relational or multi-source universe on top of SAP NetWeaver BW. The relational interface on top of SAP NetWeaver BW provides you the option to create a universe on top of the SAP NetWeaver BW system and also to combine data coming from SAP NetWeaver BW with other data sources using a multi-source universe.

The following are advantages of relational access to SAP NetWeaver BW:

▶ Direct access to the InfoProvider level.

▶ Allows combining multiple data sources into a single logical view.

▶ Allows customization of the metadata.

▶ Allows creation of custom objects.

The following are disadvantages of relational access to SAP NetWeaver BW:

▶ No support for external SAP NetWeaver BW hierarchies.

▶ No support for restricted and calculated key figures.

▶ No support for custom structures.

▶ No support for SAP variables.

As you can see, relational access provides access to the bare minimum of information about the necessary InfoProvider. The items listed as disadvantages are not impossible to solve, but those components need to be recreated as part of the universe and cannot be leveraged as pre-existing objects in SAP NetWeaver BW.

Table 3.2 shows possible workarounds for the most important metadata from your SAP NetWeaver BW system, and how you might be able to recreate them as part of the universe.

BEx Query Elements	Relational Universe
Calculated/restricted key figures	Define calculated measures as part of the universe.
Variables	Define prompts as part of the universes or Web Intelligence query panel. Not possible for EXIT variables or variables filled through authorizations.
Currency and unit conversion	Possible with manual modeling of tables with conversion rates in the SAP BusinessObjects Universe Designer and joins in Data Federator.
Display attributes	Possible with joins from InfoProvider to the master data tables in the universe.
External BW hierarchies	No workaround.
Conditions	Use filters on measures.

Table 3.2 Possible Workarounds

Further Details

You can find further details on the relational interface for SAP NetWeaver BW at this URL :

http://help.sap.com/saphelp_nw70ehp2/helpdata/en/e3/e60138fede083de10000009b38f8cf/frameset.htm

The relational access approach using a universe can be leveraged in combination with SAP Crystal Reports for Enterprise, SAP BusinessObjects Web Intelligence, SAP BusinessObjects Dashboards, and SAP BusinessObjects Explorer. In the following sections, the focus is on data connectivity using the direct BI Consumer Services (BICS) approach, because it provides the richest set of metadata support for SAP NetWeaver BW. In the next section, we provide more background information for this recommendation.

3.3.3 Recommendation for SAP NetWeaver BW Data Connectivity

Now that we have provided you with an overview of the two options for connecting to the SAP NetWeaver BW system, we compare these two options in more detail.

Figure 3.4 shows the different level of support for the elements from your SAP NetWeaver BW system across the different tools. The columns shown for the separate products assume a direct connectivity to SAP NetWeaver BW using the direct BICS data connectivity. The two columns on the right—SAP BusinessObjects Explorer and Universe (Relational)—assume a data connectivity using the relational universe option on top of SAP NetWeaver BW. In addition to these two options, SAP BusinessObjects Explorer is also able to leverage a direct connectivity to SAP NetWeaver BW Accelerator (BWA) and to leverage the pre-existing indexes.

As shown in Figure 3.4, you can see that support for the most common metadata elements is relatively identical, with the exception of support for compounded characteristics and defaults in the BEx query.

BEx Query Element	Crystal Reports for Enterprise (BICS)	Web Intelligence (BICS)	Dashboards (formerly Xcelsius)	Analysis, edition for MS Office	Analysis, OLAP Edition	SAP Business-Objects Explorer	Universe (Relational)
InfoProvider Dimension	✓	✓	✗	✓	✓	✗	✓
Characteristic	✓	✓	✓	✓	✓	✓	✓
Characteristic with Hierarchy	✓	✓	✓	✓	✓	✓	✗
Structure based on Characteristics	✓	✓	✓	✓	✓	✗	✗
Navigational Attributes	✓	✓	✓	✓	✓	✓	✓
Display Attributes	✓	✓	✗	✓	✓ (4.x)	✗	✗
Key Figure	✓	✓	✓	✓	✓	✓	✓
Unit/Currency	✓	✓	✓	✓	✓	✓	✓
Calculated Key Figure	✓	✓	✓	✓	✓	✓	✗
Restricted Key Figure	✓	✓	✓	✓	✓	✓	✗
Compounded Characteristics	✓ (!)	✓ (!)	✓ (!)	✓	✓	✗	✓
Defaults in the BEx Query	✗	✗	✓	✓	✓	✗	✗
Constant Selection	✓	✓	✓	✓	✓	✗	✗

Figure 3.4 Metadata Support Part 1

Compounded characteristics are supported by the BI client tools, but the dependency when prompting for values (for example, financial year variant and financial year) is not supported for SAP Crystal Reports for Enterprise, SAP BusinessObjects Web Intelligence, or SAP BusinessObjects Dashboards.

Defaults defined in the BEx query (not to be confused with default values for variables) are supported only by SAP BusinessObjects Dashboards and the Analysis products.

SAP BusinessObjects 4.x Connectivity for SAP Landscape: Metadata Support for BEx Queries							
BEx Query Element	Crystal Reports for Enterprise	Web Intelligence	Dashboards (formerly Xcelsius)	Analysis, edition for MS Office	Analysis, OLAP Edition	SAP Business-Objects Explorer	Universe (Relational)
Single Value Variable	✓	✓	✓	✓	✓	–	✗
Multiple Single Value Variables	✓	✓	✓	✓	✓	–	✗
Interval Variable	✓	✓	✗	✓	✓	–	✗
Selection Option Variable	✓ (!)	✓ (!)	✓ (!)	✓	✓	–	✗
Hierarchy Variable	✓	✓	✓ (!)	✓	✓	–	✗
Hierarchy Node Variable	✓	✓	✓ (!)	✓	✓	–	✗
Hierarchy Version Variable	✗	✗	✓	✓	✓	–	✗
Text Variable	✓	✓	✓	✓	✓	–	✗
EXIT Variable	✓	✓	✓	✓	✓	–	✗
Single Key Date Variable	✓	✓	✓ (!)	✓	✓	–	✗
Multiple Key Date Variable	✓	✗	✗	✓	✓	–	✗
Formula Variable	✓	✓	✓	✓	✓	–	✗
Default Values for Variables	✓	✓	✓	✓	✓	–	✗

Figure 3.5 Metadata Support Part 2

Figure 3.5 shows the support for the different types of variables you can create as part of your BEx query. As mentioned already, the relational universe on top of SAP NetWeaver BW is not able to support those variables. Some key items to be aware of:

▶ A selection option variable is fully supported only by the Analysis products. All other BI clients turn the selection option variable into an interval variable.

▶ Hierarchy version variables are not supported by SAP Crystal Reports for Enterprise or SAP BusinessObjects Web Intelligence.

▶ BEx queries with multiple key date variables are not supported using SAP BusinessObjects Web Intelligence or SAP BusinessObjects Dashboards.

▸ SAP BusinessObjects Dashboards combined with the BICS connectivity provided by SAP BusinessObjects Enterprise offers proper variable support only for single value and multi-single value variables. Hierarchy and hierarchy node variables are supported, but lack the cascading factor, which means the list of nodes is not updated after you select a hierarchy.

You will notice that in Figure 3.5 the column for SAP BusinessObjects Explorer does not state that the variables are supported; nor does it state that they are not supported. The reason behind this is simply that SAP BusinessObjects Explorer works on top of an indexed dataset and the user—at viewtime—cannot interact with those prompts. If you plan to leverage SAP BusinessObjects Explorer based on a relational universe on top of SAP NetWeaver BW, you can use the Universe (Relational) column to see the supported elements. Figure 3.6 outlines the support for the most common display settings from the BEx query:

▸ The defined scaling factor for a key figure is leveraged and the correct result set is shown. The scaling factor is shown as a separate field for each of the key figures configured with a scaling factor in SAP Crystal Reports for Enterprise, SAP BusinessObjects Web Intelligence, and SAP BusinessObjects Dashboards. For both of the Analysis products, the scaling factor is shown as part of the result set automatically.

▸ The option to configure a so-called local calculation (for example, a ranking) as part of the BEx query is supported only by SAP BusinessObjects Dashboards and the Analysis products. If you are using a BEx query configured with such a local calculation with Crystal Reports for Enterprise or Web Intelligence, the key figure with this configuration will not be available as part of the metadata; instead, it will simply be removed and not shown to the BI client.

▸ The option to leverage the display as a hierarchy setting from the BEx query is supported only by the Analysis products. For the other BI clients, such as Crystal Reports for Enterprise and Web Intelligence, there are options to design the report in a similar way.

SAP BusinessObjects 4.x Connectivity for SAP Landscape: Metadata Support for BEx Queries							
BEx Query Element	Crystal Reports for Enterprise	Web Intelligence	Dashboards (formerly Xcelsius)	Analysis, edition for MS Office	Analysis, OLAP Edition	SAP Business-Objects Explorer	Universe (Relational)
Scaling Factor	✓ (4.x)	✓ (4.x)	✓	✓	✓ (4.x)	✗	✗
Number of Decimals	✗	✗	✓	✓	✓	✗	✗
Display Result Rows (top/ bottom)	–	–	✓	✓	✓	✗	✗
Suppress Result Rows	–	–	✓	✓	✓	✗	✗
Calculate Result as... (local calculation)	✗	✗	✓	✓	✓	✗	✗
Display as hierarchy	✗	✗	✗	✓	✓ (4.x)	✗	✗
Sorting	✓	✓	✓	✓	✓	✗	✗
Hide/Unhide	✓	✓	✓	✓	✓	✗	✗
Reverse +/- signage	✓	✓	✓	✓	✓	✗	✗

Figure 3.6 Metadata Support Part 3

Figure 3.7 shows the support for more advanced concepts, such as conditions and exceptions, and the option to create reports based on master data:

► The support for conditions is limited to the Analysis products in the 4.x release. Support for conditions for the other BI client products is planned for a future version.

► Exceptions are supported only by the Analysis products. For products such as SAP Crystal Reports for Enterprise, SAP BusinessObjects Web Intelligence, and SAP BusinessObjects Dashboards, you can leverage the functionality provided by each of the tools to achieve the same goal. For example, you can leverage highlighting and conditional formatting in SAP Crystal Reports for Enterprise and alerts in SAP BusinessObjects Web Intelligence.

BEx Query Element	Crystal Reports for Enterprise	Web Intelligence	Dashboards (formerly Xcelsius)	Analysis, edition for MS Office	Analysis, OLAP Edition	SAP Business-Objects Explorer	Universe (Relational)
Conditions in rows	✗	✗	✗	✓	✓	✗	✗
Conditions in columns	✗	✗	✗	✓	✓	✗	✗
Conditions on selected characteristic	✗	✗	✗	✓	✓	✗	✗
Exceptions	✗	✗	✗	✓	✓	✗	✗
Empty/non empty	✓	✓	✓	✓	✓	✗	✗

Figure 3.7 Metadata Support Part 4

Based on the superior support for your existing SAP NetWeaver BW metadata and the option to share the same metadata across all the different BI client tools, we highly recommend leveraging direct connectivity to SAP NetWeaver BW using the BICS connectivity option. The connectivity option provided by the relational universe can be a compelling option for those scenarios where you need to combine your data stored in SAP NetWeaver BW with another data source. So, as a rule of thumb: Use the direct BICS connection to BEx queries unless you want to combine SAP NetWeaver BW with another data source.

3.4   Relational Access to SAP ECC

As shown in Figure 3.8, the SAP BusinessObjects 4.x release gives you several options for connecting directly to the information in your SAP ERP system.

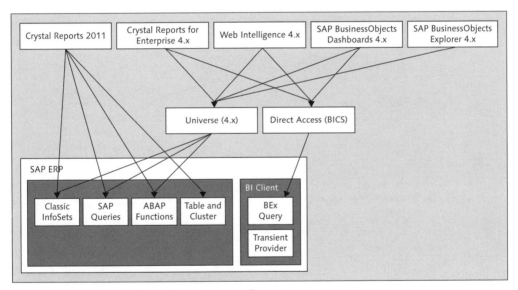

Figure 3.8 SAP BusinessObjects BI and SAP ERP

SAP Crystal Reports 2011 offers the same data connectivity options that are available with SAP Crystal Reports 2008, which means that SAP Crystal Reports 2011 is able to connect directly to classic InfoSets, SAP queries, ABAP functions, and tables in your SAP ERP system.

In addition to these options, release 4.x allows you to create a universe based on a classic InfoSet, SAP queries, and ABAP functions as well. These universes can then be leveraged by SAP Crystal Reports for Enterprise, SAP BusinessObjects Web Intelligence, SAP BusinessObjects Dashboards, and SAP BusinessObjects Explorer.

An alternative to the universe-based approach is the option to use the transient provider (which is available with SAP ERP 6.0, enhancement package 05) and the direct access method using the BI Consumer Services (BICS) layer, which then can be used by SAP Crystal Reports for Enterprise, SAP BusinessObjects Web Intelligence, and SAP BusinessObjects Dashboards.

As part of the SAP BusinessObjects 4.x release, the semantic layer is able to leverage a classic InfoSet, ABAP functions, and SAP queries as data sources. Figure 3.9 shows the list of available sources when you establish a data foundation on top of an SAP ERP system.

Figure 3.9 Data Foundation

Each export as part of an ABAP function is returned as a single table (see Figure 3.10) in the semantic layer, and input parameters from ABAP functions or InfoSets are returned as input columns for these tables (see Figure 3.11). In addition, each input for an ABAP function and each table from an ABAP function are also presented as input columns. If the input is configured as an actual table, each field of the table definition is presented as an input column.

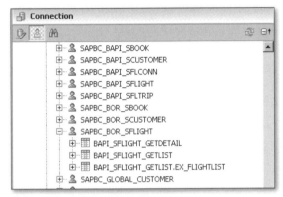

Figure 3.10 BAPI_SFLIGHT_GETDETAIL

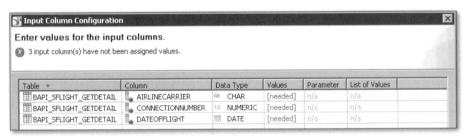

Figure 3.11 Input Columns

ABAP Function Tables

As described above, each table of an ABAP function is also presented as an input column. Because the interface is not able to recognize whether the table is really leveraged as an input, this can sometimes result in a situation where a result table is listed as an input column in the semantic layer data foundation. All tables leveraged as exports are shown correctly with the prefix "EX" as an export result set in the data foundation.

Figure 3.12 shows the resulting table of the BAPI_SFLIGHT_GETDETAIL function, where you can identify the result set returned as part of the FLIGHTDATA table and with the first set of columns marked as input columns.

Figure 3.12 Example BAPI_SFLIGHT_GETDETAIL

This new capability to create a semantic layer on top of your SAP ERP system allows you to go beyond SAP Crystal Reports 2008 for your operational reporting. You can leverage a single definition of the metadata for SAP Crystal Reports for Enterprise,

SAP BusinessObjects Web Intelligence, SAP BusinessObjects Dashboards, and SAP BusinessObjects Explorer.

We provide you with a step-by-step approach to creating a universe on top of SAP ERP as part of Section 4.3.

3.4.1 Recommendation for SAP ERP Access

We are often asked whether customers can report on top of their SAP ERP system without the need to create a complete data warehouse. The simple answer is "Yes." But you need to keep in mind that you are using your operational system in such a scenario for reporting and that you are putting an additional load—in addition to running your business—on the system. This is something you always should keep in mind when creating reports and analytics directly from the SAP ERP system.

There is, of course, a need to have real-time information, and there are even systems where there is no data warehouse at all as part of the overall landscape. From a technical viewpoint, it is possible to report on top of an SAP ERP system without a complete data warehouse. However, when considering this option, you have to remember that your SAP ERP system might not be sized for the additional load. In such scenarios, using SAP BusinessObjects Enterprise capabilities (such as scheduling a report and creating a publication, where you schedule a report for several users in a single step) will help to mitigate the risk that the reporting and analytics aspects impose on your day-to-day business operations.

3.5 Summary

In this chapter, you received an overview of the different connectivity options you can leverage as part of your SAP BusinessObjects BI platform. You learned some of the advantages and disadvantages of each connectivity option, and you should now have a better understanding of which connectivity is the best option for your requirements. In the next chapter we discuss SAP Crystal Reports for Enterprise, and provide step-by-step instructions about how you can connect SAP Crystal Reports for Enterprise to your SAP system.

In this chapter we look at how you can leverage Crystal Reports for Enterprise and Crystal Reports 2011 in combination with SAP NetWeaver BW and SAP ERP.

4 SAP Crystal Reports and SAP Landscapes

We look at which edition of SAP Crystal Reports is best suited for which requirements, and then we show you how to build your first report using SAP Crystal Reports with your SAP data.

4.1 SAP Crystal Reports 2011 or SAP Crystal Reports for Enterprise

With the release of SAP BusinessObjects 4.x, you will receive two editions of the SAP Crystal Reports designer environment: SAP Crystal Reports 2011, which is the successor to Crystal Reports 2008, and SAP Crystal Reports for Enterprise, which is a brand new design environment focused on a very tight integration with the SAP BusinessObjects BI platform.

The SAP Crystal Reports 2011 designer focuses on delivering incremental updates to the SAP Crystal Reports 2008 designer, whereas the SAP Crystal Reports for Enterprise environment focuses on delivering a completely new user experience, including a close integration with the SAP BusinessObjects platform. In addition, the SAP Crystal Reports for Enterprise edition is also the version that will be used for integration with SAP environments.

As shown in Figure 4.1 and Figure 4.2, you can see that SAP Crystal Reports for Enterprise and SAP Crystal Reports 2011 have very different options for connecting to your SAP system. SAP Crystal Reports 2011 offers the same data connectivity options as SAP Crystal Reports 2008. SAP Crystal Reports for Enterprise leverages the new data connectivity based on the BI Consumer Services (BICS), and is also able to leverage the universe-based approach.

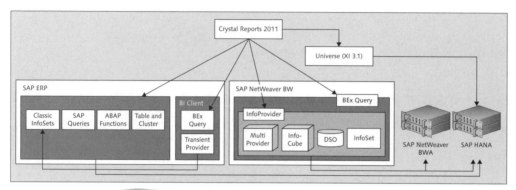

Figure 4.1 Crystal Reports 2011 Data Connectivity

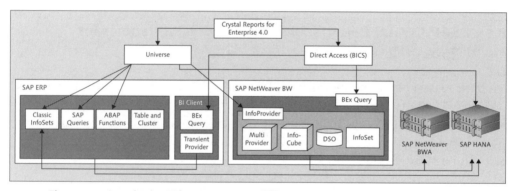

Figure 4.2 Crystal Reports for Enterprise Data Connectivity

In this chapter, the focus is on SAP Crystal Reports for Enterprise, as it is the long-term successor of SAP Crystal Reports 2008 and reflects the strategic direction for integration with SAP landscapes.

SAP Crystal Reports 2011 is only relevant for scenarios where you need access to your SAP ECC system and where you cannot leverage the transient provider from your SAP ECC system in combination with SAP Crystal Reports for Enterprise. As part of the 4.x release, SAP Crystal Reports for Enterprise is able to leverage the universe in combination with your SAP ECC system, except for the option to connect directly to the tables of the SAP ECC system.

4.2   Crystal Reports for Enterprise and SAP NetWeaver BW

In the following sections, we go into more detail using SAP Crystal Reports for Enterprise on top of SAP NetWeaver BW. The sections outline the connectivity between SAP Crystal Reports for Enterprise and your SAP system, and you'll learn how to build your first report using SAP Crystal Reports.

4.2.1   Data Connectivity Overview for SAP Crystal Reports for Enterprise

In Figure 4.2 you saw an overview of the SAP Crystal Reports for Enterprise capabilities to connect to your SAP NetWeaver BW system. SAP Crystal Reports for Enterprise offers two separate types of connectivity:

▶ SAP Crystal Reports for Enterprise is able to leverage the new direct access connectivity using the BI Consumer Services and connect directly to your BEx queries.

▶ SAP Crystal Reports for Enterprise is also able to leverage universe-based access connecting to the relational schema inside the SAP NetWeaver BW system.

As mentioned in Chapter 3, the direct access connectivity using BI Consumer Services is clearly the recommended approach, as it supports most of your existing metadata from SAP NetWeaver BW. In the next section, we review the level of metadata support for SAP Crystal Reports for Enterprise.

4.2.2   Supported and Unsupported SAP NetWeaver BW Elements for SAP Crystal Reports for Enterprise

Table 4.1 shows the supported and unsupported features of SAP Crystal Reports for Enterprise on top of SAP NetWeaver BW.

	Direct Access using BICS	Relational Universe Access
Direct access to InfoCube and MultiProvider	No	Yes
Access to BEx queries	Yes	Limited

Table 4.1   Metadata Support

	Direct Access using BICS	Relational Universe Access
Characteristic Values		
Key	Yes	Yes
Short description	Yes	Yes
Medium and long description	Yes	Yes
BEx Query Features		
Support for hierarchies	Yes	No
Support for free characteristics	Yes	Yes
Support for calculated and restricted key figures	Yes	No
Support for currencies and units	Yes	Yes
Support for custom structures	Yes	No
Support for formulas and selections	Yes	No
Support for filter	Yes	Yes
Support for display and navigational attributes	Yes	Yes
Support for conditions in rows	No	No
Support for conditions in columns	No	No
Support for conditions for fixed characteristics	No	No
Support for exceptions	No	No
Compounded characteristics	Limited	No
Constant selection	Yes	No
Default values in BEx query	No	No
Number scaling factor	Yes	No
Number of decimals	No	No
Calculate rows as (local calculation)	No	No

Table 4.1 Metadata Support (Cont.)

	Direct Access using BICS	Relational Universe Access
Sorting	Yes	No
Hide/unhide	Yes	No
Display as hierarchy	No	No
Reverse sign	Yes	No
Support for reading master data	Yes	No
Data Types		
Support for CHAR (characteristics)	Yes	Yes
Support for type NUMC (characteristics)	Yes as string value	Yes as string value
Support for DATS (characteristics)	Yes for Value description. Key is supported as string value	Yes for Value description. Key is supported as string value
Support for TIMS (characteristics)	Yes as string value	Yes as string value
Support for numeric key figures such as Amount and Quantity	Yes	Yes
Support for Date (key figures)	Yes	Yes
Support for Time (key figures)	Yes as string value	Yes as string value
SAP Variable—Processing Type		
User input	Yes	No
Authorization	Yes	No
Replacement path	Yes	No
SAP exit/custom exit	Yes	No
Precalculated value set	Yes	No

Table 4.1 Metadata Support (Cont.)

	Direct Access using BICS	Relational Universe Access
General Features for Variables		
Support for optional and mandatory variables	Yes	No
Support for key date dependencies	Yes	No
Support for default values	Yes	No
Support for personalized values	No	No
SAP Variables — Variable Type		
Single value	Yes	No
Multi-single value	Yes	No
Interval value	Yes	No
Selection option	Limited	No
Hierarchy variable	Yes	No
Hierarchy node variable	Yes	No
Hierarchy version variable	No	No
Text variable	Yes	No
EXIT variable	Yes	No
Single key date variable	Yes	No
Multiple key dates	Yes	No
Formula variable	Yes	No

Table 4.1 Metadata Support (Cont.)

Supported and Unsupported Features

As you can see, SAP Crystal Reports for Enterprise doesn't use the features of conditions and exceptions inside a BEx query. You can easily create exceptions in SAP Crystal Reports for Enterprise by using the highlighting capabilities, and you can create conditions in your report by using the Group Expert in combination with options such as a TopN or BottomN group. Keep in mind that a BEx query with a condition will transfer all of its records to Crystal Reports for Enterprise based on the missing support—not just the records that meet the condition in the BEx query.

For the limited support of compounded characteristics, you need to be aware that SAP Crystal Reports for Enterprise is not able to create a dependency between the compounded characteristics when used for prompting, which results in an independent list of values for each of the involved characteristics.

An often-asked question concerns the difference between accessing a BEx query and accessing an InfoCube directly. Table 4.2 shows the supported elements when accessing the BEx query or InfoCube level with the SAP BusinessObjects 4.x product suite.

SAP NetWeaver BW Metadata Element	Support Level
Characteristics (including time and unit)	InfoCube and BEx Query
Hierarchies	InfoCube and BEx Query
Key figures	InfoCube and BEx Query
Navigational attributes	BEx Query only
Display attributes	InfoCube and BEx Query
Calculated key figures / Formulas	BEx Query only
Restricted key figures	BEx Query only
Custom structures	BEx Query only
Variables	BEx Query only
Authorization variable	BEx Query only

Table 4.2   SAP NetWeaver BW Metadata Support

InfoCube Access

In addition to the differences shown in Table 4.2, you also should consider the fact that when accessing the InfoCube directly, you do not have the functionality to create authorization variables that will filter the data based on user authorizations. There are always options to address such a situation, but this is an important topic to consider in your deployment.

In Table 4.3 you can see how SAP Crystal Reports for Enterprise uses the elements from the BEx query when using the direct BICS data connectivity:

BEx Query Element	SAP Crystal Reports for Enterprise
Characteristic	For each characteristic you'll receive a field representing the key value and a field for the description, including short, medium, and long description.
Hierarchy	Each available hierarchy is shown as an external hierarchy in SAP Crystal Reports for Enterprise.
Key figure	Each key figure can have up to four elements: numeric value, unit, scaling factor, and formatted value. The formatted value is based on the user preferences configured in the SAP system.
Calculated/restricted key figure	Each calculated and restricted key figure is treated like a key figure. The user does not have access to the underlying definition in the SAP Crystal Reports for Enterprise designer.
Filter	Filters are applied to the underlying query but are not visible in the SAP Crystal Reports for Enterprise designer.
Display attribute	Display attributes become standard fields in the query panel and are grouped as subordinates of the linked characteristic.
Navigational attribute	Navigational attributes are treated the same way as characteristics.
Variables	Each variable with the property READY FOR INPUT results in a parameter field in SAP Crystal Reports for Enterprise.
Custom structure	A custom structure is available as an element in the query panel and each structure element can be selected or de-selected for the report.

Table 4.3 SAP NetWeaver BW Metadata Mapping for Crystal Reports for Enterprise

4.2.3 Creating Your First Report with SAP Crystal Report for Enterprise and SAP NetWeaver BW

You will now use the knowledge you've gained from the previous sections to create your first report with SAP Crystal Reports for Enterprise on top of the SAP NetWeaver BW system. When you create a new report with SAP Crystal Reports for Enterprise on top of SAP NetWeaver BW, you first need to establish the connection as part of your SAP BusinessObjects Enterprise system; then you can leverage the connection in SAP Crystal Reports for Enterprise.

In this example for creating a new SAP Crystal Reports for Enterprise report, we use a BEx query created on top of the SAP Demo cube (0D_SD_C03) with the following elements:

▶ Calendar Month/Year (0CALMONTH) and Sold-to Party (0D_SOLD_TO) in the rows

▶ Material (0D_MATERIAL) in the free characteristics

▶ Open Orders (0D_OORVALSC), Open Orders Quantity (0D_OORQTYBM), Costs (0D_COSTVALS), and Net Sales (0D_NETVAL_S) in the columns

▶ A optional interval variable for the Calendar Month/Year characteristics in the filter area

Allow External Access (Release for ODBO)

For BEx queries to be used in SAP Crystal Reports for Enterprise, you need to set the ALLOW EXTERNAL ACCESS property (in SAP NetWeaver BW 3.x, it's called RELEASED FOR ODBO). This property can be set in the BEx Query Designer.

Before you can start using SAP Crystal Reports for Enterprise in combination with the BEx query, you need to establish the data connectivity as part of the Central Management Console (CMC) of your SAP BusinessObjects Enterprise system.

1. To start the configuration of the data connection, log on to the Central Management Console (CMC). To reach the Central Management Console (CMC) open the URL *http://localhost:8080/BOE/CMC* in your browser.

2. Log on with an administrative account.

3. Navigate to the OLAP CONNECTIONS area (see Figure 4.3).

4. Use the NEW icon (⬚) to create a new OLAP connection.

5. Enter the details for your OLAP connection according to Table 4.4 with the values for your SAP system.

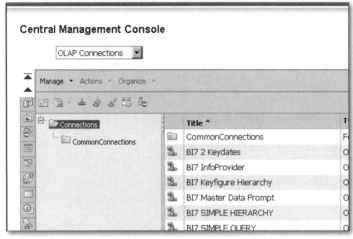

Figure 4.3 OLAP Connections

Field Name	Value Description
NAME	The name of the connection the user sees in SAP Crystal Reports for Enterprise.
DESCRIPTION (OPTIONAL)	Description for the connection. The value is optional.
PROVIDER	The type of connection. For our example connecting to SAP NetWeaver BW, select the SAP BUSINESS INFORMATION WAREHOUSE provider.
SERVER TYPE	Here you can select between an application server (SERVER) or a message server with a logon group (GROUP).
SYSTEM	The three-digit system ID of your SAP NetWeaver BW system. Example: IH1
SERVER	This is either the full qualified name of your application server or your message server, depending on the SERVER-TYPE you selected. Example: ihilgefort.dyndns.org
SYSTEM NUMBER	The two-digit system number of your SAP NetWeaver BW system. Example: 00

Table 4.4 OLAP Connection Parameters

Field Name	Value Description
CLIENT	The client number to which you would like to connect from your SAP NetWeaver BW system. Example: 800
LANGUAGE	The two-digit letter code for the language. Example: EN for English.
SAVE LANGUAGE	You can use this option to save the language, so that the setting in the user profile does not overwrite the setting in the connection.
AUTHENTICATION	Here you can select one of three options: PROMPT, SSO, or USER SPECIFIED.

Table 4.4 OLAP Connection Parameters (Cont.)

6. Click CONNECT (see Figure 4.4).

Figure 4.4 Log on to the Data Source

7. You are asked to enter your SAP credentials to log on to the SAP NetWeaver system. After doing so, you are presented with a list of InfoProviders and BEx queries (see Figure 4.5).

8. Choose the BEx query you created previously and click SELECT.

9. Set the AUTHENTICATION to the value SSO.

10. Click SAVE.

You have now created an OLAP connection as part of your SAP BusinessObjects Enterprise system, and you can now build your first report using SAP Crystal Reports for Enterprise.

Figure 4.5 Cube Browser

Based on this newly created OLAP connection, you can create your report using SAP Crystal Reports for Enterprise. You will build a report that shows the value of your open orders per month and provide the capability to perform a drill-down to the customer level.

1. Start SAP Crystal Reports for Enterprise by following the menu START • PROGRAMS • CRYSTAL REPORTS FOR ENTERPRISE 4 • CRYSTAL REPORTS FOR ENTERPRISE 4.

2. Select the menu FILE • NEW • FROM DATA SOURCE.

3. Select the BROWSE REPOSITORY menu option from SAP BUSINESSOBJECTS BUSINESS INTELLIGENCE PLATFORM.

4. As this is your first time using SAP Crystal Reports for Enterprise, you do not have any SAP BusinessObjects Enterprise server definitions (see Figure 4.6). SAP Crystal Reports for Enterprise relies on the semantic layer to provide the connection and therefore first needs to connect to the SAP BusinessObjects system to receive a list of connections.

5. Use the ⋯ icon to open the SAP BusinessObjects server definition dialog (see Figure 4.7).

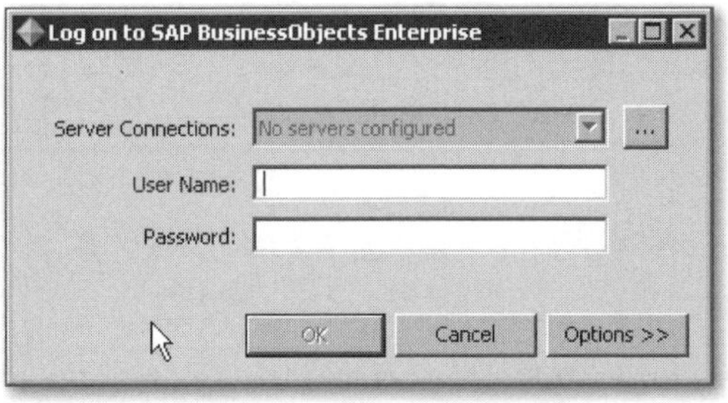

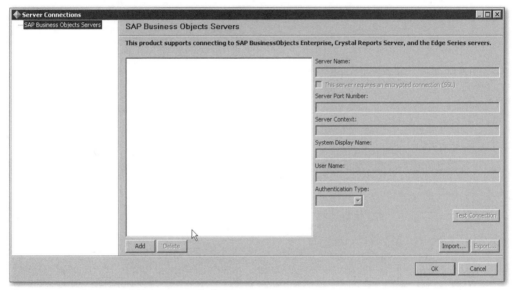

Figure 4.6 Log on to SAP BusinessObjects

Figure 4.7 SAP BusinessObjects Server Definition

6. Click ADD and enter the values according to Table 4.5.

In our example, we configured the OLAP connection to leverage SSO to the SAP NetWeaver BW system; therefore, make sure you use the SAP authentication when logging on to the SAP BusinessObjects Enterprise system.

7. Click OK.

8. Enter the necessary user and password. Remember to use your SAP credentials. The logon UI does not allow you to enter the system ID and client number; therefore, you need to enter your SAP credentials in the syntax: <System ID>~<Client Number>/<User Name>, for example IH1~800/INGO.

Field Name	Value
SERVER NAME	This is the name of your Java Application server. Example: BOEXI4
SERVER PORT NUMBER	This is the port of your Java Application server. Example: 8080
SERVER CONTEXT	This is the context for the deployment of the web services SDK. By default, this is `/dswsbobje/services`.
SYSTEM DISPLAY NAME	Enter a display name for the server definition.
USER NAME	Enter a user name that will be used as a default value.
AUTHENTICATION TYPE	Select the default authentication type. Example: SAP

Table 4.5 SAP BusinessObjects Server Definition

9. Click OK. You are presented with a list of available connections (see Figure 4.8).

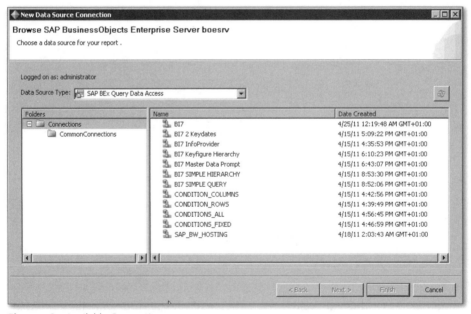

Figure 4.8 Available Connections

10. Select the previously created connection.

11. Click NEXT.

12. You are presented with the query panel, which allows you to select the elements from the BEx query for your report (see Figure 4.9).

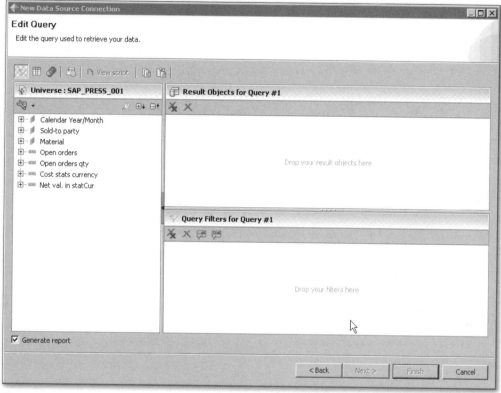

Figure 4.9 Query Panel

13. Add the following elements to the RESULT OBJECTS (see Figure 4.9):

    ▶ CALENDAR YEAR/MONTH

    ▶ SOLD-TO-PARTY

    ▶ MATERIAL

    ▶ OPEN ORDERS

14. Uncheck the GENERATE REPORT option.

15. Click FINISH. You are presented with the prompt dialog for the prompt resulting from the variables (see Figure 4.10). As the variable is optional, you can just click OK for now.

Figure 4.10 Prompting Screen

> **Optional Variables**
>
> If the underlying variable in the BEx query is configured to be an optional variable, SAP Crystal Reports for Enterprise will offer the option to leave the values empty, which removes the variable from the actual data retrieval to ensure that all records are considered.

16. Drag and drop the following fields from the DATA EXPLORER to the BODY area of your report:

    ▶ SOLD-TO-PARTY

    ▶ MATERIAL

    ▶ OPEN ORDERS

17. Open the GROUP menu on the INSERT tab.

18. Use CALENDAR YEAR/MONTH as the field to group (see Figure 4.11).

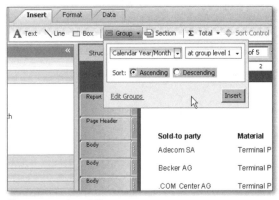

Figure 4.11 Insert Group

19. Click INSERT. Your report now contains a group based on the CALENDAR YEAR/ MONTH (see Figure 4.12).

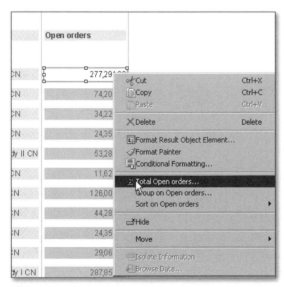

	Sold-to party	Material	Open orders
Report Header			
Page Header			
Group Header 1 Calendar Year/Month	01.2003		
Body	Adecom SA	Terminal P600 CN	277,291.00
Body	Becker AG	Terminal P600 CN	74,200.00
Body	.COM Center AG	Terminal P600 CN	34,228.00
Body	Netzwerk Berlin	Terminal P400 CN	24,354.00
Body	K.A.P.A. GmbH	Notebook Speedy II CN	53,280.00
Body	Omega Soft - Hardwar	Terminal P400 CN	11,622.00

Figure 4.12 Crystal Reports Grouping

20. Right-click on a value from OPEN ORDERS.

21. Select the TOTAL OPEN ORDERS menu (see Figure 4.13).

Figure 4.13 Inserting Summaries

22. Select the SUM OF option and FOR EACH GROUPING OF CALENDAR YEAR/MONTH (see Figure 4.14).

Figure 4.14 Summary Details

23. Right-click on the BODY section of your report.

24. Select the FORMAT BODY menu (see Figure 4.15).

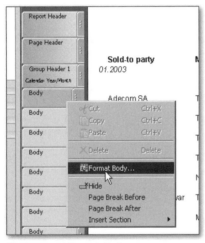

Figure 4.15 Format Body

25. Navigate to the GENERAL area.

26. Select the SHOW ON DRILL ONLY option (see Figure 4.16).

Page View or Structure View

Depending on your personal preference, you can design your report with the actual data shown in the PAGE view or you can use the STRUCTURE view, which shows you a more technical view of your report design.

Figure 4.16 Formatting Drill Options

27. Click CLOSE.

28. Move the subtotal field from the group footer to the group header with a simple drag and drop.

29. Right-click on the Group Footer 1 section.

30. Select the HIDE menu item.

31. Select the INSERT tab.

32. Open the menu CHART • BAR • SIDE-BY-SIDE BAR (see Figure 4.17).

Figure 4.17 Inserting Chart

33. Place the chart into the report header.

34. Click on the DATA tab in the chart (see Figure 4.18).

35. Drag and drop CALENDAR YEAR/MONTH from the Data Explorer to the CATEGORY (X).

36. Drag and drop OPEN ORDERS from the Data Explorer to the TOTAL (Y).

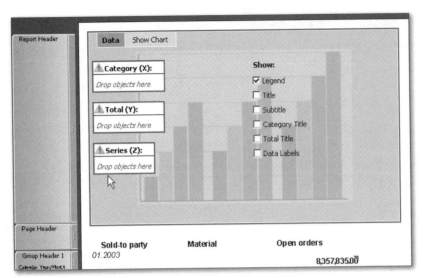

Figure 4.18 Chart Design

37. Click on SHOW CHART (see Figure 4.19).

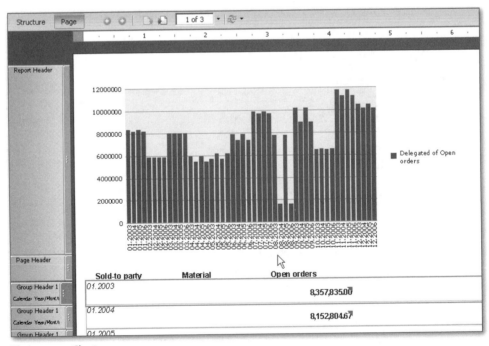

Figure 4.19 Chart

38. Navigate to the REFRESH symbol for your report (see Figure 4.20).

39. Select the PROMPT FOR PARAMETERS BEFORE REFRESH option.

40. Refresh your report.

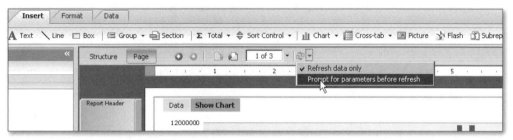

Figure 4.20 Refresh Report

41. Select parameter values for your prompt.

42. Click OK.

43. Select the menu FILE • SAVE AS (see Figure 4.21).

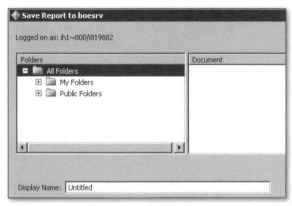

Figure 4.21 Save Report

44. Select a folder as part of your SAP BusinessObjects system.

45. Enter a name for your report.

46. Click SAVE.

You have now created a report with a group and a chart; both the group and the chart offer the opportunity to drill down into the details of your report.

In the next section, we use SAP Crystal Reports for Enterprise in combination with data from your SAP ERP system.

4.3 SAP Crystal Reports for Enterprise and SAP ERP

In addition to the capability to use the BEx query as a data source, SAP Crystal Reports for Enterprise is now—as part of the SAP BusinessObjects 4.x release—also able to establish a data connection directly to the data in the SAP ERP system by using the semantic layer on top.

As was shown in Figure 4.2, the semantic layer is able to connect towards classic InfoSets, ABAP functions, and InfoSet queries. These elements from your SAP ERP system can be used as metadata source for the universe. SAP Crystal Reports for Enterprise can then leverage the universe and retrieve the data directly from the SAP ERP system.

In the following steps you will set up a universe based on an ABAP function and then use SAP Crystal Reports for Enterprise to create your first report connecting to your SAP ERP system.

1. Start the Information Design tool by following the menu START • PROGRAMS • SAP BUSINESSOBJECTS BI PLATFORM 4 • SAP BUSINESSOBJECTS BI PLATFORM CLIENT TOOLS • INFORMATION DESIGN TOOL.

2. Select the menu FILE • NEW • PROJECT to create a new project for your universe (see Figure 4.22).

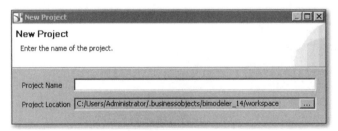

Figure 4.22 New Project

3. Enter a name for the new project and click FINISH.

4. Select the menu FILE • NEW • RELATIONAL CONNECTION to start the process to set up the data connection to your SAP ERP system.

5. Enter a name for the data connection and click NEXT (see Figure 4.23).

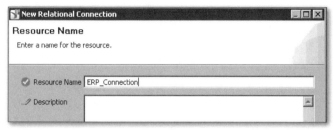

Figure 4.23 New Relational Connection

6. Select SAP ERP from the list of available options (see Figure 4.24).

Figure 4.24 Database Middleware

7. Click NEXT (see Figure 4.25).

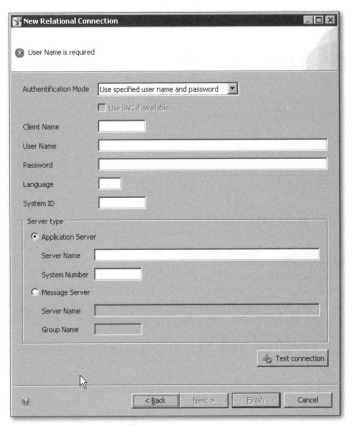

Figure 4.25 System Details

8. You now need to enter the necessary system details to establish the connection. Enter your SAP ERP system details and click NEXT (see Figure 4.26).

9. You can now limit the list of ABAP functions returned from the SAP system by entering criteria for either the function name or the function group.

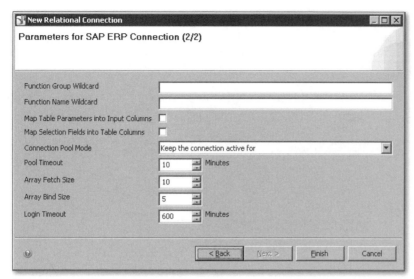

Figure 4.26 Connection Options

10. In addition, you can use the Map Table Parameters into Input Columns option to map the input parameters of an ABAP function into input columns for the table.

11. If you are using an InfoSet as a data source, you can now set the flag so that the configured selections from the InfoSet are turned into input columns for the table.

12. As the last step, you can configure several settings for the connection. For now, though, you can leave the default values.

13. Activate the Map Table Parameters into Input Columns option.

14. Click Finish.

Your data connection should now appear in your new project. The next step is to publish the connection to a repository. To do this, follow the steps below:

1. Right-click the connection and select Publish connection to a Repository (see Figure 4.27).

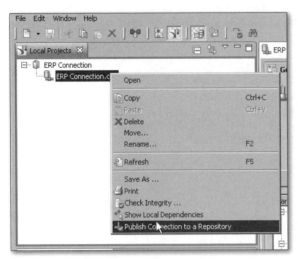

Figure 4.27 Publish Connection

2. You are asked to log on to your SAP BusinessObjects system. Log on with your credentials and click CONNECT (see Figure 4.28).

Figure 4.28 Repository Logon

3. Select a folder for your newly created connection and click FINISH.

4. You are asked whether you wish to create a shortcut for the connection. Click YES, as the shortcut is needed for the next steps (see Figure 4.29).

Figure 4.29 Creating Shortcut

5. Click CLOSE.

6. Select the menu FILE • NEW • DATA FOUNDATION.

7. Enter a name for the data foundation.

8. Click NEXT.

9. You are asked whether you would like to create a single-source or a multi-source foundation. For this example, select the SINGLE-SOURCE option (see Figure 4.30).

Figure 4.30 Data Foundation Type

10. Click NEXT.

11. Select the data connection shortcut you created in the previous step.

12. Click FINISH.

You can now open the connection as part of the data foundation and browse all available sources (see Figure 4.31).

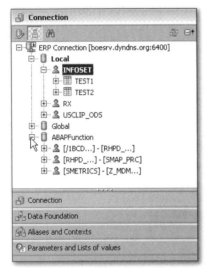

Figure 4.31 SAP ERP Sources

The data connection provides you access to the classic InfoSets, InfoSet queries, and ABAP functions. The listing shown in Figure 4.31 follows very specific logic:

▶ InfoSets are first grouped based on the InfoSet environment: local or global.

▶ Below the local or global environment the INFOSET entry contains a complete listing of the available InfoSets.

▶ The other entries below local or global represent the InfoSet query user groups, and below each user group the corresponding InfoSets are listed.

▶ The ABAP function entry contains a complete list of available ABAP functions organized on the first level by the name of the assigned function group.

For this example, use the `BAPI_FLIGHT_GETLIST` ABAP function from the `SAPBC_BAPI_SFLIGHT` function group.

1. Open the list of sources as part of your newly established connection (see Figure 4.32).

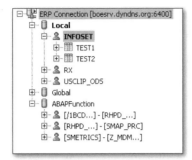

Figure 4.32 Data Connection

2. Navigate to the list of ABAP functions and navigate to the SAPBC_BAPI_SFLIGHT function group (see Figure 4.33).

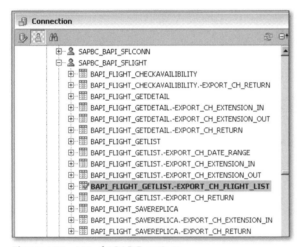

Figure 4.33 List of ABAP Functions

3. Navigate to the BAPI_FLIGHT_GETLIST BAPI function.

4. Notice that each export and table of the ABAP function is returned as a table as part of the data connection. For these reporting requirements, the most interesting table is the EXPORT_CH_FLIGHT_LIST.

5. Double-click the entry to select the table.

6. You are presented with the complete list of input columns. Click CANCEL for now.

Figure 4.34 Imported BAPI Function

7. As shown in Figure 4.34, the BAPI function is imported with several input columns, which are the result of the input parameters of the ABAP function itself.

8. Navigate to the PARAMETERS AND LIST OF VALUES area (see Figure 4.35).

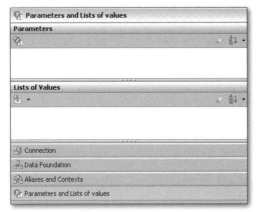

Figure 4.35 Parameters

9. Use the NEW PARAMETER ( ) icon in the PARAMETERS area to create a new parameter.

10. Define a parameter name and enter a prompt text (see Figure 4.36).

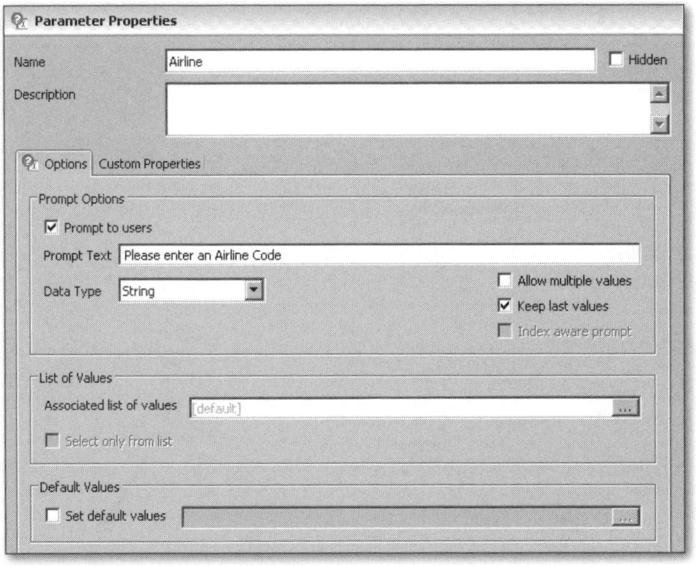

Figure 4.36 Parameter Properties

11. Ensure the ALLOW MULTIPLE VALUES option is unchecked.

Input Columns in SAP BusinessObjects 4.x

As part of the SAP BusinessObjects 4.x ability to create universes on top of your SAP ERP system, you face an important limitation: the input columns are limited to single values only. This has been acknowledged and is planned to be fixed as part of a service pack for the 4.x release.

12. Set the DATA TYPE to STRING.

13. Select the menu FILE • SAVE to save your changes.

14. Navigate back to the table in your DATA FOUNDATION.

15. Select the AIRLINE column and open the context menu (see Figure 4.37).

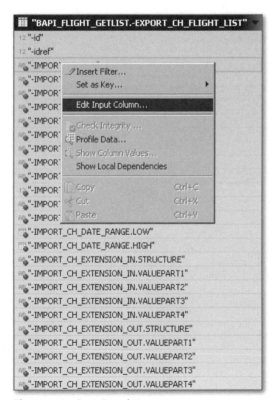

Figure 4.37 Data Foundation

16. Select the EDIT INPUT COLUMN menu item (see Figure 4.38).

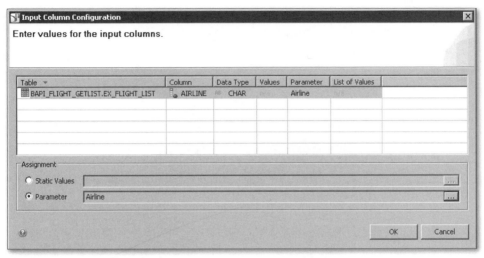

Figure 4.38 Input Column Configuration

17. Select the row for the AIRLINE column in the dialog.

18. Select the PARAMETER option.

19. Use the [...] button and select the newly created parameter.

20. Click OK.

21. Click OK.

22. Select the menu FILE • SAVE to save your changes.

23. Select the menu FILE • NEW • BUSINESS LAYER.

24. Select RELATIONAL DATA SOURCE.

25. Click NEXT.

26. Enter a name for the business layer.

27. Click NEXT.

28. Use the [...] icon and select your newly created DATA FOUNDATION.

29. Click OK.

30. Make sure the AUTOMATICALLY CREATE CLASSES AND OBJECTS option is checked (see Figure 4.39).

Figure 4.39 New Business Layer

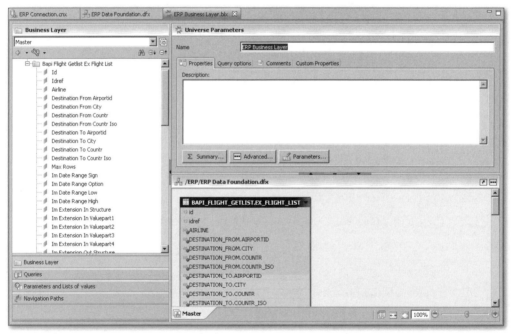

Figure 4.40 Business Layer Finished

> **Automatically Create Classes and Objects**
>
> In our example we use the option to automatically generate classes and objects to simply receive a complete list of objects in a quick fashion. You can use the standard mechanism to create classes and objects as well.

31. Click FINISH.

Finally, select the business layer in the local project (see Figure 4.41) and follow the steps below:

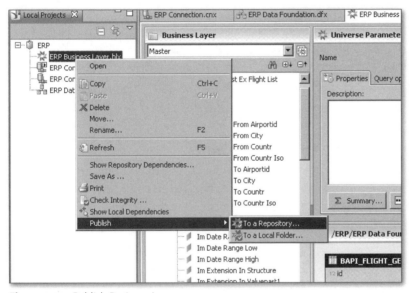

Figure 4.41   Publish Business Layer

1. Right-click and select PUBLISH • TO A REPOSITORY. You are presented with a set of checks that you can perform.

2. Click NEXT.

3. Select a folder for your universe.

4. Click FINISH.

5. Click CLOSE.

You now have a universe as part of your SAP BusinessObjects system, which is based on the `BAPI_FLIGHT_GETLIST` BAPI function. You can use this universe now with SAP Crystal Reports for Enterprise.

In this section you learned how you can use the semantic layer in combination with data sources from your SAP ERP system and SAP Crystal Reports for Enterprise. In the next section we look at SAP Crystal Reports 2011.

Known Limitation

As part of the SAP BusinessObjects 4.x release, the semantic layer provides you the option to establish a semantic layer on top of your SAP ECC system. The data sources that can be leveraged are ABAP functions, classic InfoSets, and SAP queries. These data sources are treated like a stored procedure in the semantic layer and therefore you cannot use the selected source itself as a source for a list of values for parameters. If you would like to provide your end users with a proper list of values, you will have to leverage one of the possible sources without pre-built parameters as a source for the list of values and link it to the actual source.

Recommendation for Semantic Layer and SAP ERP

As mentioned previously, the semantic layer provides you with the option to establish a universe on top of an ABAP function, classic InfoSet, or SAP query. Most of these sources do contain parameters/prompts and will therefore be treated like a stored procedure. You only have two options for creating a proper list of values for these sources:

▶ You can add several ABAP functions or InfoSets without parameters and link them to your source, which will require some effort and several additional sources (ABAP function, InfoSet) in addition to the actual source.

▶ You can set up a new InfoSet or ABAP function without any pre-built parameters/prompts.

Our recommendation is to set up new sources in the SAP ERP system without any pre-created parameters/prompts, as it is the simpler of the two options.

4.4 Crystal Reports 2011 and SAP ERP

When it comes to data connectivity to SAP NetWeaver BW, you should leverage SAP Crystal Reports for Enterprise. If your main requirements are for reporting on top of your SAP ERP system, SAP Crystal Reports 2011 can be an alternative.

4.4.1 Data Connectivity Overview

Figure 4.42 shows, at a high level, the options available for connecting SAP Crystal Reports to an SAP ERP system.

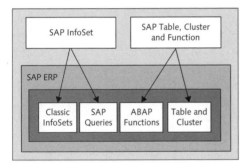

Figure 4.42 SAP Crystal Reports 2011 Data Connectivity for SAP ERP

Classic InfoSet and SAP Queries

The combined connectivity for classic InfoSets and SAP queries allows you to connect to InfoSets and SAP queries (sometimes referred to as ABAP queries) directly from SAP Crystal Reports 2011. When you create an SAP Crystal Reports 2011 object on top of an InfoSet or an SAP query, the newly created report will inherit all of the available metadata from the underlying SAP source. For an InfoSet and an SAP query, this includes items such as long text for key fields and the selections defined. Selections created in the InfoSet or SAP query result in parameter fields in SAP Crystal Reports 2011 that can be used to filter the actual result set.

The connectivity between InfoSets and SAP queries also honors the security on various levels:

▶ Each user viewing or designing a report based on an InfoSet or SAP query needs to authenticate against the SAP system. General access to the source is secured, but also the configured data-level security in the SAP system will be used.

▶ Crystal Reports 2011 differentiates between global and local InfoSets and SAP queries and honors the assignment to user groups (Transaction SQ02) as well.

Table and ABAP Functions

With the connectivity to tables and ABAP functions in your SAP ERP system, you can access ABAP functions, transparent tables, cluster tables, pool tables, and views with SAP Crystal Reports 2011. This connectivity provides you with dramatic flexibility for your SAP ERP reporting, because you can now use SAP Crystal Reports 2011 to directly access this information and leverage those sources. The connectivity references the ABAP Dictionary to retrieve all of the metadata for the tables, which includes items such as the language-dependent description of tables and fields.

When accessing ABAP functions in SAP Crystal Reports 2011, you can preprocess the data in ABAP before passing it to SAP Crystal Reports 2011. In addition, this connectivity allows you to use a large set of your existing ABAP reports in your SAP ERP system directly as a source for SAP Crystal Reports 2011. Therefore, you can use SAP Crystal Reports 2011 to create presentation-style reports based on your existing investment on the ABAP side.

ABAP functions that will be used in SAP Crystal Reports 2011 need to fulfill the following requirements:

▶ The ABAP function needs to have defined return types for each of the outputs.

▶ The ABAP function cannot use complete tables as input parameters.

▶ You cannot call entire programs. You can use only individual functions.

As an example, we use the BAPI_SFLIGHT_GETLIST ABAP function, shown in Listing 4.1.

```
FUNCTION BAPI_SFLIGHT_GETLIST
IMPORTING
    VALUE(FROMCOUNTRYKEY) LIKE  BAPISFDETA-COUNTRYFR
    VALUE(FROMCITY) LIKE  BAPISFDETA-CITYFROM
    VALUE(TOCOUNTRYKEY) LIKE  BAPISFDETA-COUNTRYTO
    VALUE(TOCITY) LIKE  BAPISFDETA-CITYTO
    VALUE(AIRLINECARRIER) LIKE  BAPISFDETA-CARRID DEFAULT SPACE
    VALUE(AFTERNOON) LIKE  BAPI_AUX-AFTERNOON DEFAULT SPACE
    VALUE(MAXREAD) LIKE  BAPI_AUX-MAXREAD DEFAULT 0
    EXPORTING
    VALUE(RETURN) LIKE  BAPIRET2 STRUCTURE  BAPIRET2
```

TABLES
   FLIGHTLIST STRUCTURE BAPISFLIST

Listing 4.1 ABAP Function BAPI_SFLIGHT_GETLIST

Given the above example, you'll receive a list of fields in SAP Crystal Reports (see Figure 4.43). All input parameters result in fields with a prefix "I_" in the technical name. The output fields are available in SAP Crystal Reports 2011, and the technical name depends on the type of output. In our case, the output is a table with the name FLIGHTLIST, so the fields are named with the prefix "T_" (for table) and the name of table (for example, T_FLIGHTLIST.CARRID). In SAP Crystal Reports 2011 you can either use the input parameters of an ABAP function in the record selection formula, or you can link fields from another table to these fields and use the values from the table as input for the ABAP function.

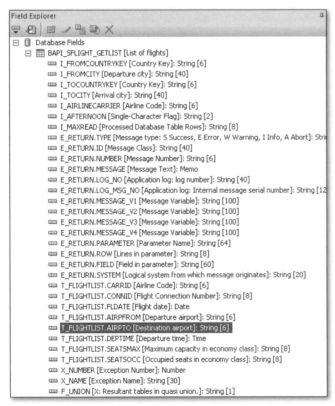

Figure 4.43 SAP Crystal Reports 2011 Field Explorer

Data Cluster

Data clusters are specific databases in the ABAP dictionary. The structure is divided into a standard section containing several fields and one large field for the actual data cluster. Usually, data clusters contain complex structures containing multiple pieces of information. The ABAP Dictionary might contain the table in which the data cluster is stored, but unfortunately the ABAP Dictionary does not contain the definition of the data cluster.

Therefore, the ABAP transports as part of the integration with your SAP system include a Cluster Definition Tool (Transaction ZCDD), which allows you to create a dictionary for the data cluster and to map the individual components to tables. The dictionary can then be used with the table, ABAP function, and data cluster connectivity in SAP Crystal Reports 2011.

Data Cluster Example

Because this book focuses on the installation and configuration of the SAP Business-Objects software in combination with your SAP landscape, explaining how you can configure your data cluster for the usage of SAP Crystal Reports 2011 goes beyond the scope of this book. The user's guide and administrator's guide for SAP BusinessObjects Enterprise contains a very good example of how you can map an existing data cluster to a structure that can be used in SAP Crystal Reports 2011. You can download the guide from *https://service.sap.com/bosap-instguides*.

4.4.2 Data-Level Security Editor

Because SAP Crystal Reports 2011 can access the tables directly, the ABAP transports for the integration with SAP systems also includes a tool that allows you to define the user security for tables and the data stored in those tables. Using this tool, not only can you define which users will have access to which tables, but you can configure row-level security.

In this section you'll learn how to configure global access (or global restriction) on all tables and how to configure data-level security on top of the tables in your SAP ERP system.

1. To configure global access or global restriction, start with the Security Definition Editor with Transaction /CRYSTAL/RLS (see Figure 4.44).

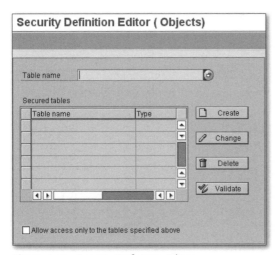

Figure 4.44 Security Definition Editor

2. If you want to restrict your users to a specific set of tables, you can select the
ALLOW ACCESS ONLY TO THE TABLES SPECIFIED ABOVE checkbox. By default, the
checkbox is not selected, and your users have access to all tables.

3. If you select the option to restrict your users to a specific set of tables, you first
need to create a new authorization object via Transaction SU21. In our example,
we name the authorization object ZTABCHECK. The authorization object needs
to contain one field; we call the field TABLE (see Figure 4.45).

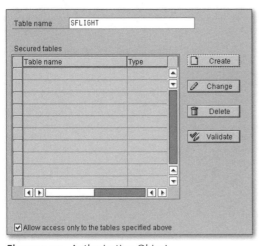

Figure 4.45 Authorization Object

4. After you create the authorization object, go back to the Security Definition Editor (Transaction /CRYSAL/RLS). Enter the name of the table you want to allow your users to access and click CREATE. We use the table SFLIGHT (see Figure 4.46). You can also use wildcards such as "*" to define the settings for multiple tables at once.

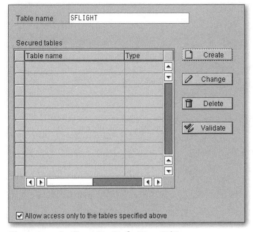

Figure 4.46 Security Definition Editor

5. In the next screen, click CREATE to set up a new authorization entry. You can select REFERENCE TO AN AUTHORIZATION OBJECT when asked for the entry type.

6. Enter your previously created authorization object (in our example ZTABCHECK) and click CREATE (see Figure 4.47).

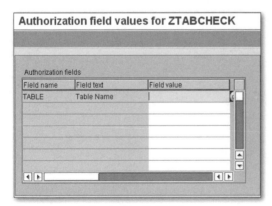

Figure 4.47 Authorization Field Values

7. Enter the table name (in our example SFLIGHT) as the FIELD VALUE and save your changes.

8. For the final step, you need to add the authorization object (in our example ZTABCHECK) to the role of your users and specify the table to which you want to grant access.

If you want to set up row-level security, the steps are very similar to those above.

1. Create a new authorization object with a single field in Transaction SU21. The field represents the table field that you use to define the row-level security. We use the field CARR_ID (carrier ID) to define the row-level security for the table SFLIGHT.

2. Start the Security Definition Editor (Transaction /CRYSTAL/RLS). Enter the name of the table where you want to define the row-level security (we use SFLIGHT) and click CREATE.

3. In the next screen, click CREATE to set up a new authorization entry. You can select REFERENCE TO AN AUTHORIZATION OBJECT when asked for the entry type.

4. Enter your previously created authorization object and click CREATE.

5. Enter the field name that you want to use to define the row-level security. In our example we use the field CARR_ID.

6. For the final step, you need to add the authorization object to the role of your users and specify as part of the role the actual value that you want the users to be able to use as row-level security for the field.

4.4.3 Creating Your First Report with SAP Crystal Reports 2011 and SAP ERP

You will now use the knowledge from the previous sections to create your first report with SAP Crystal Reports 2011 on top of an SAP ERP system.

1. Start SAP Crystal Reports 2011 using the menu START • ALL PROGRAMS • CRYSTAL REPORTS 2011 • CRYSTAL REPORTS 2011.

2. Follow the menu path FILE • NEW • STANDARD REPORT.

3. Double-click CREATE NEW CONNECTION. SAP Crystal Reports 2011 shows a list of available data sources configured on your machine. By scrolling down the list you can identify the SAP options as well (see Figure 4.48).

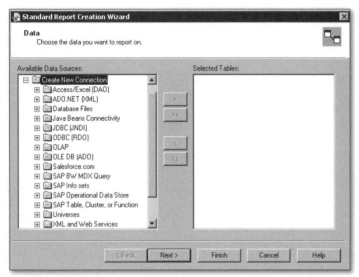

Figure 4.48 List of Data Sources

4. Double-click to select SAP TABLE, CLUSTER, or FUNCTION. You are asked to select the SAP system and to provide the necessary user credentials.

5. After a successful logon you are presented with three options: DATA DICTIONARY, ABAP FUNCTION MODULES, and DATA CLUSTER.

6. Select DATA DICTIONARY, right-click to open the context menu, and select OPTIONS.

7. To reduce the list of tables retrieved by SAP Crystal Reports 2011 you can configure a filter in the TABLE NAME LIKE field (see Figure 4.49). In our example we use the filter "s%". After changing the filter value, you need to refresh the connection by either pressing the [F5] button on your keyboard or right-clicking on your connection and selecting the REFRESH option.

8. Double-click DATA DICTIONARY. SAP Crystal Reports 2011 shows the tables from your SAP system. You can then add the SCARR, SPFLI, and SFLIGHT tables to the list of tables that will be used in SAP Crystal Reports 2011 (see Figure 4.50).

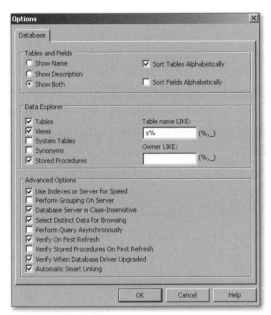

Figure 4.49 Options

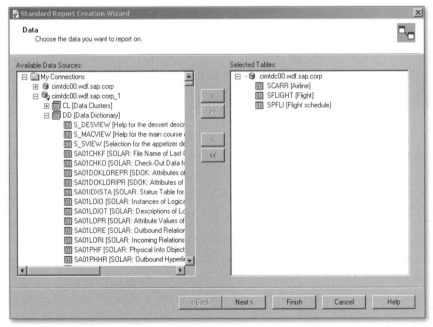

Figure 4.50 Selected Tables

9. In the next screen you can define the linking between the tables (see Figure 4.51). You have the option to define the linking yourself or to receive suggestions based on names or keys.

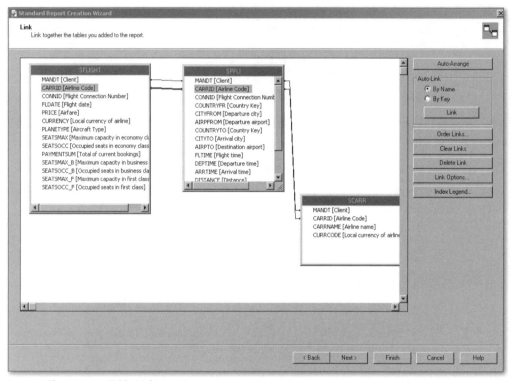

Figure 4.51 Table Linking

10. Click FINISH. You can now use all of the fields from all of the tables in SAP Crystal Reports 2011, and you can build your first SAP Crystal Reports 2011 objects on top of SAP ERP data—much like you created your first report on top of the BW query.

In this section we reviewed the capabilities of SAP Crystal Reports 2011 in combination with data from your SAP ERP system. If the new capabilities of the semantic layer in combination with SAP Crystal Reports for Enterprise do not provide enough functionality, SAP Crystal Reports 2011 can be an alternative.

In the next section, you will learn about some common migration scenarios for moving from SAP Crystal Reports 2008 to SAP Crystal Reports for Enterprise.

4.5 Migrating from SAP Crystal Reports 2008 to SAP Crystal Reports for Enterprise

In this section we focus on the steps necessary to migrate your existing content from SAP Crystal Reports 2008 to SAP Crystal Reports for Enterprise. We use an SAP Crystal Reports 2008 report based on SAP NetWeaver BW as an example, but you can use the steps below as a guideline for other sources as well.

Figure 4.52 shows the report that will be migrated. Our report is based on a BEx query and uses a hierarchy in combination with the hierarchical grouping in SAP Crystal Reports 2008. As a prerequisite to migrating this report to SAP Crystal Reports for Enterprise, you will need an OLAP connection configured in the Central Management Console (CMC) as outlined in Section 4.2.3.

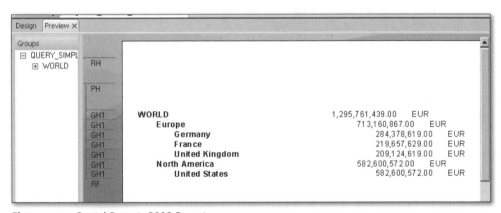

Figure 4.52 Crystal Reports 2008 Report

1. Start SAP Crystal Reports for Enterprise by following the menu START • ALL PROGRAMS • CRYSTAL REPORTS FOR ENTERPRISE 4 • CRYSTAL REPORTS FOR ENTERPRISE 4.

2. Select the menu FILE • OPEN and open your existing SAP Crystal Reports 2008 object. Remember that you need to be logged on to your SAP BusinessObjects system. You are presented with the migration dialog (see Figure 4.53).

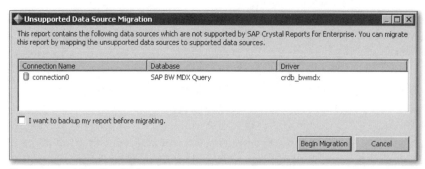

Figure 4.53 Migration Dialog

3. Click BEGIN MIGRATION.

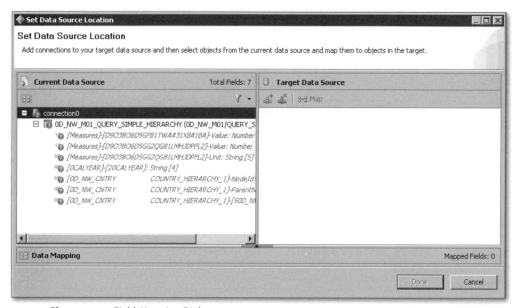

Figure 4.54 Field Mapping Dialog

4. In the field mapping dialog (see Figure 4.54) you are presented with the list of fields from your report on the left-hand side. On the right-hand side you add a data connection to your report, which will become the new data source.

Known Limitation in SAP BusinessObjects 4.x

As part of the 4.x release of SAP BusinessObjects, the mapping dialog for SAP Crystal Reports for Enterprise (at the point of writing this book) shows only the technical field names and not the field descriptions.

5. Use the ADD CONNECTION icon ( ) to add your new connection.

6. Select BROWSE REPOSITORY (see Figure 4.55).

Figure 4.55 Choose Data Source

7. Log on to your SAP BusinessObjects system.

8. Select the previously created connection from the SAP BEx QUERY DATA ACCESS category.

9. Click FINISH.

10. Select the BEx query from the list of available BEx queries.

11. Click OK.

You can now select the original field and the target field in your new connection. Then right-click to select the MAP option (see Figure 4.56). All mapped fields are shown below the data connections.

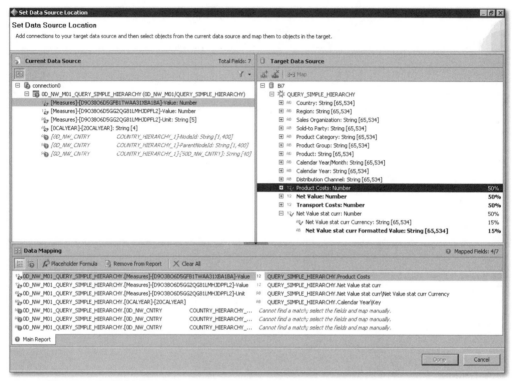

Figure 4.56 Field Mapping

For the hierarchy mapping you can map the HIERARCHY NODE ID from the SAP Crystal Reports 2008 report (not the PARENT NODE ID) to the hierarchy entry in the new connection (not to the level entries). To do so, follow the steps below.

1. For the PARENT NODE ID as part of the SAP Crystal Reports 2008 report, select the REMOVE FROM REPORT option in the mapping dialog.

2. Select the NODE ID entry from the SAP Crystal Reports 2008 report.

3. Now select the hierarchy entry in the list of available fields from the target connection. Remember not to select the level entries.

4. Right-click on the hierarchy entry and select the MAP menu item.

5. Click DONE.

6. As the hierarchical reporting in SAP Crystal Reports for Enterprise has changed, you need to do some fine-tuning. Navigate to the structure of your report (see Figure 4.57) and open the context menu of your group. Select the EDIT GROUP option.

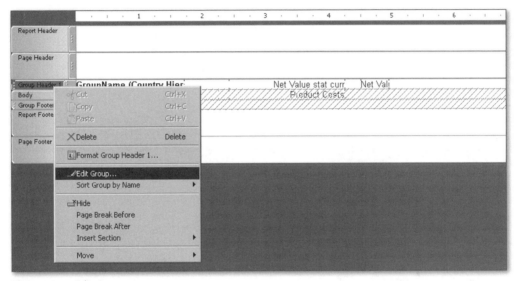

Figure 4.57 Edit Group

7. In the GROUPS dialog (see Figure 4.58), make sure you select the actual hierarchy for the display name and that you set the hierarchy type to EXTERNAL HIERARCHY.

8. Click OK.

Using the BW MDX Driver and the new direct BICS connection, you have now migrated a hierarchical report in SAP Crystal Reports 2008 to SAP Crystal Reports for Enterprise (see Figure 4.59).

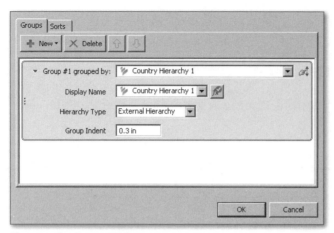

Figure 4.58 Groups Dialog

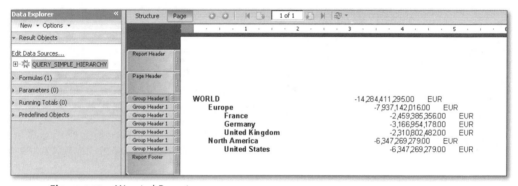

Figure 4.59 Migrated Report

4.6 Summary

In this chapter you received an overview of the data connectivity of SAP Crystal Reports for Enterprise and SAP Crystal Reports 2011 in combination with your SAP NetWeaver BW and SAP ERP system. In the next chapter you will learn more details about how you can use SAP BusinessObjects Web Intelligence as part of your overall SAP landscape.

SAP BusinessObjects Web Intelligence can be used on top of SAP NetWeaver BW and SAP ECC, offering end users an ad-hoc and self-service reporting solution.

5 SAP BusinessObjects Web Intelligence and SAP NetWeaver BW

In this chapter we go into detail about how you can use SAP BusinessObjects Web Intelligence 4.x to leverage data from your SAP NetWeaver BW and SAP ERP systems. We start by outlining the different connectivity options available to you, move on to the metadata mapping between SAP NetWeaver BW and your SAP BusinessObjects Web Intelligence query, and finally create our very first SAP BusinessObjects Web Intelligence report.

> **SAP BusinessObjects Menu Structure**
>
> The following chapters are based on SAP BusinessObjects release 4, enhancement package 01. In this release, the menu structure for launching SAP BusinessObjects Web Intelligence is START • PROGRAMS • SAP BUSINESSOBJECTS BI PLATFORM 4 • SAP BUSINESSOBJECTS BI PLATFORM • SAP BUSINESSOBJECTS BI PLATFORM JAVA BI LAUNCHPAD. You can start SAP BusinessObjects Web Intelligence in the BI launch pad using the menu APPLICATIONS • WEB INTELLIGENCE APPLICATION.
>
> If you are using the SAP BusinessObjects 4.0 products, the menu structure is START • PROGRAMS • SAP BUSINESSOBJECTS BI PLATFORM 4.0 • SAP BUSINESSOBJECTS BI PLATFORM • SAP BUSINESSOBJECTS PLATFORM JAVA BI LAUNCHPAD. You can start SAP BusinessObjects Web Intelligence in the BI launch pad using the menu APPLICATIONS • INTERACTIVE ANALYSIS.

5.1 SAP BusinessObjects Web Intelligence and SAP BW

In this section we review the integration of SAP BusinessObjects Web Intelligence with SAP NetWeaver BW. You will learn about the different data connectivity options and the support for the existing metadata, and will also create your very first SAP

BusinessObjects Web Intelligence report using data from your SAP NetWeaver BW system.

5.1.1   Data Connectivity Overview

Figure 5.1 shows an overview of the data connectivity for SAP BusinessObjects Web Intelligence with regard to the SAP NetWeaver BW and SAP ERP systems.

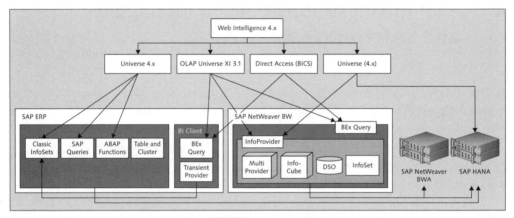

Figure 5.1   Data Connectivity for SAP BusinessObjects Web Intelligence and SAP NetWeaver BW

SAP BusinessObjects Web Intelligence 4.x is able to leverage BI Consumer Services (BICS) to utilize a direct access method connecting with the SAP NetWeaver BW system and the transient providers from your SAP ERP system. The transient provider requires SAP ECC 6.0, enhancement package 05. The direct access method does not require you to create an authored universe; instead, the direct access method allows you to connect directly against a BEx query. In addition, SAP BusinessObjects Web Intelligence 4.x is able to leverage the universe based on SAP NetWeaver BW. The authored universe relies on a relational data access method and provides access to the underlying relation schema of the InfoProviders.

In this section we review the different options for data connectivity of SAP Business-Objects Web Intelligence in combination with SAP NetWeaver BW. In the next section we review support for the metadata of your SAP NetWeaver BW system.

5.1.2   Supported and Unsupported SAP NetWeaver BW Elements

Table 5.1 shows the supported and unsupported features of the two connectivity options for SAP BusinessObjects Web Intelligence 4.x on top of SAP NetWeaver BW.

	Direct Access using BICS	Relational Universe Access
Direct access to InfoCube and MultiProvider	No	Yes
Access to BEx queries	Yes	Limited
Characteristic Values		
Key	Yes	Yes
Short description	Yes	Yes
Medium and long description	Yes	Yes
BEx Query Features		
Support for hierarchies	Yes	No
Support for free characteristics	Yes	Yes
Support for calculated and restricted key figures	Yes	No
Support for currencies and units	Yes	Yes
Support for custom structures	Yes	No
Support for formulas and selections	Yes	No
Support for filter	Yes	Yes
Support for display and navigational attributes	Yes	Yes
Support for conditions in rows	No	No
Support for conditions in columns	No	No
Support for conditions for fixed characteristics	No	No
Support for exceptions	No	No

Table 5.1   Supported and Unsupported BEx Query Features for SAP BusinessObjects Web Intelligence

	Direct Access using BICS	Relational Universe Access
Compounded characteristics	Limited	No
Constant selection	Yes	No
Default values in BEx query	No	No
Number scaling factor	Yes	No
Number of decimals	No	No
Calculate rows as (local calculation)	No	No
Sorting	Yes	No
Hide/unhide	Yes	No
Display as hierarchy	No	No
Reverse sign	Yes	No
Support for reading master data	Yes	No
Data Types		
Support for CHAR (characteristics)	Yes	Yes
Support for type NUMC (characteristics)	Yes as string value	Yes as string value
Support for DATS (characteristics)	Yes for Value description. Key is supported as string value	Yes for Value description. Key is supported as string value
Support for TIMS (characteristics)	Yes as string value	Yes as string value
Support for numeric key figures such as Amount and Quantity	Yes	Yes
Support for Date (key figures)	Yes	Yes
Support for Time (key figures)	Yes as string value	Yes as string value

Table 5.1 Supported and Unsupported BEx Query Features for SAP BusinessObjects Web Intelligence (Cont.)

	Direct Access using BICS	Relational Universe Access
SAP Variable—Processing Type		
User input	Yes	No
Authorization	Yes	No
Replacement path	Yes	No
SAP exit/custom exit	Yes	No
Precalculated value set	Yes	No
General Features for Variables		
Support for optional and mandatory variables	Yes	No
Support for key date dependencies	Yes	No
Support for default values	Yes	No
Support for personalized values	No	No
SAP Variables—Variable Type		
Single value	Yes	No
Multi-single value	Yes	No
Interval value	Yes	No
Selection option	Limited	No
Hierarchy variable	Yes	No
Hierarchy node variable	Yes	No
Hierarchy version variable	No	No
Text variable	Yes	No
EXIT variable	Yes	No
Single key date variable	Yes	No
Multiple key dates	No	No
Formula variable	Yes	No

Table 5.1 Supported and Unsupported BEx Query Features for SAP BusinessObjects Web Intelligence (Cont.)

Supported and Unsupported Features

As you can see, SAP BusinessObjects Web Intelligence doesn't support conditions and exceptions inside a BEx query. You can easily create exceptions in SAP BusinessObjects Web Intelligence by using the alerts functionality, and you can create conditions in your report by using the ranking functionality. Setting up the condition in SAP BusinessObjects Web Intelligence results in all data being transferred to the report itself; the ranking is done as part of the report and not as part of the backend.

In regard to the scaling factor, you should be aware that the number returned to SAP BusinessObjects Web Intelligence will reflect the correct scaling factor, and each key figure with a configured scaling factor will have a separate field with the scaling factor available.

For the limited support of compounded characteristics, you need to be aware that, when used for prompting, SAP BusinessObjects Web Intelligence is not able to create a dependency between the compounded characteristics. This results in an independent list of values for each of the involved characteristics.

In Table 5.2 you can see how the direct access method using the BICS option uses the elements from the BEx query, and how the objects are mapped to the query panel for SAP BusinessObjects Web Intelligence.

BEx Query Element	SAP BusinessObjects Web Intelligence
Characteristic	For each characteristic you'll receive a field representing the key value and a field for the description, including short, medium, and long description.
Hierarchy	Each available hierarchy is shown as an external hierarchy in SAP BusinessObjects Web Intelligence.
Key figure	Each key figure can have up to four elements: numeric value, unit, scaling factor, and formatted value. The formatted value is based on the user preferences configured in the SAP system.
Calculated/restricted key figure	Each calculated and restricted key figure is treated like a key figure. The user does not have access to the underlying definition in SAP BusinessObjects Web Intelligence.
Filter	Filters are applied to the underlying query but are not visible in SAP BusinessObjects Web Intelligence.

Table 5.2 SAP NetWeaver BW Metadata Mapping for SAP BusinessObjects Web Intelligence

BEx Query Element	SAP BusinessObjects Web Intelligence
Display attribute	Display attributes become standard fields in the query panel and are grouped as subordinates of the linked characteristic.
Navigational attribute	Navigational attributes are treated the same way as characteristics.
Variables	Each variable with the property "ready for input" results in a parameter field in SAP BusinessObjects Web Intelligence.
Custom structures	A custom structure is available as an element in the query panel and each structure element can be selected or de-selected for the report.

Table 5.2 SAP NetWeaver BW Metadata Mapping for SAP BusinessObjects Web Intelligence (Cont.)

In addition to the option to leverage the direct connection towards the BI Consumer Services (BICS) on top of the BEx query, you can also use the option to establish a universe on top of the InfoProvider in your SAP NetWeaver BW system. The level of support for the metadata from the InfoProvider is described in Section 3.3.2 of Chapter 3. In Section 5.4 you can follow the steps to establish a relational universe on top of your InfoProvider, and also learn how to create a SAP BusinessObjects Web Intelligence report.

In this section we reviewed the level of support for the existing metadata of your SAP NetWeaver BW system, considering both the direct access method and creating a relational universe on top of the SAP NetWeaver BW InfoProvider. In the next section we review the option to connect SAP BusinessObjects Web Intelligence to your data in SAP ECC.

5.2   SAP BusinessObjects Web Intelligence and SAP ERP

As part of the 4.x release of SAP BusinessObjects, you can now also establish a connection with the semantic layer on top of your SAP ERP system. You can see the known limitations outlined in Section 3.4 of Chapter 3. In Section 4.3 of Chapter 4, you can follow the steps to establish a universe on top of the SAP ERP system in combination with SAP Crystal Reports for Enterprise, but remember that the steps to create the semantic layer are identical because the semantic layer is shared across multiple tools. As shown in Figure 5.1, SAP BusinessObjects Web Intelligence is able to leverage the semantic layer from the 4.x release and connect to classic InfoSets, ABAP functions, and SAP queries. In addition, SAP BusinessObjects Web Intelligence is able to leverage the local BI client of the SAP ERP system and to leverage a BEx query on top of a transient provider, which is a capability available starting with enhancement package 05 of SAP ERP 6.0.

In the next section you will learn how to create a report with SAP BusinessObjects Web Intelligence using a direct BICS connection to SAP NetWeaver BW.

5.3   Creating Your First Report for SAP NetWeaver BW (BICS)

In this section you will create your first SAP BusinessObjects Web Intelligence report based on SAP NetWeaver BW, using the same query used for the first SAP Crystal Reports for Enterprise example. Because SAP BusinessObjects Web Intelligence and SAP Crystal Reports for Enterprise share the connections, you can leverage the connection you created previously in the Central Management Console (CMC) for SAP Crystal Reports for Enterprise. You can find the details of the query in Section 4.2.3.

Optional Variables

If the underlying variable in the BEx query is configured to be an optional variable, SAP BusinessObjects Web Intelligence shows the word *optional* behind the prompting text, and you can run the query without entering any values. If you don't enter any values for the variable, SAP BusinessObjects Web Intelligence will remove the variable from the actual data retrieval to ensure that all records are considered.

---

1. Log on to the BI launch pad via the menu START • PROGRAMS • SAP BUSINESS-OBJECTS BI PLATFORM 4 • SAP BUSINESSOBJECTS BI PLATFORM • SAP BUSINESS-OBJECTS BI PLATFORM JAVA BI LAUNCH PAD.

2. Log on to the system using your SAP credentials and the AUTHENTICATION option SAP.

3. Select the menu APPLICATIONS (see Figure 5.2).

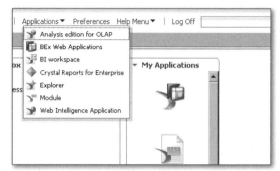

Figure 5.2 Menu Applications

4. Select the WEB INTELLIGENCE APPLICATION entry.

5. In the toolbar use the NEW (⬜) icon to create a new report (see Figure 5.3).

Figure 5.3 SAP BusinessObjects Web Intelligence Toolbar

6. Select the BEx option (see Figure 5.4).

Figure 5.4 Create a New Document

7. Click OK. The list of available connections is shown (see Figure 5.5).

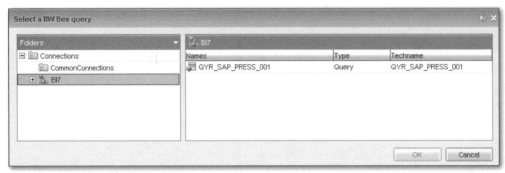

Figure 5.5 List of Connections

8. Select the previously created connection, select the BEx query, and click OK.

9. You are now presented with the query panel—similar to SAP Crystal Reports for Enterprise. Add the following elements to the RESULT OBJECTS:

   ▶ SOLD-TO-PARTY

   ▶ MATERIAL

   ▶ CALENDAR YEAR/MONTH

   ▶ NET VALUE

   ▶ OPEN ORDERS

Figure 5.6 SAP BusinessObjects Web Intelligence Query Panel

10. Click RUN QUERY. As your BEx query contains a variable for the CALENDAR MONTH/YEAR, you are presented with the prompt for the CALENDAR MONTH/ YEAR (see Figure 5.7).

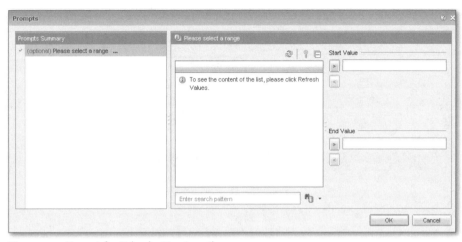

Figure 5.7 Prompt for Calendar Year/month

11. You can use the REFRESH icon ( ) to refresh the list of values.

12. As the variable is optional you can leave the selection empty for now.

13. Click OK without selecting values for the prompt.

You are presented with a standard table and you can now design your first SAP BusinessObjects Web Intelligence report (see Figure 5.8). To do so, follow the steps below:

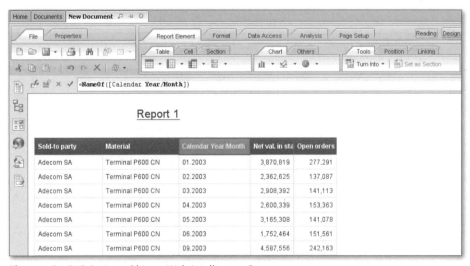

Figure 5.8 SAP BusinessObjects Web Intelligence Report

1. Select an entry from the CALENDAR YEAR/MONTH column.

2. Right-click to open the context menu.

3. Select the SET AS SECTION menu (see Figure 5.9).

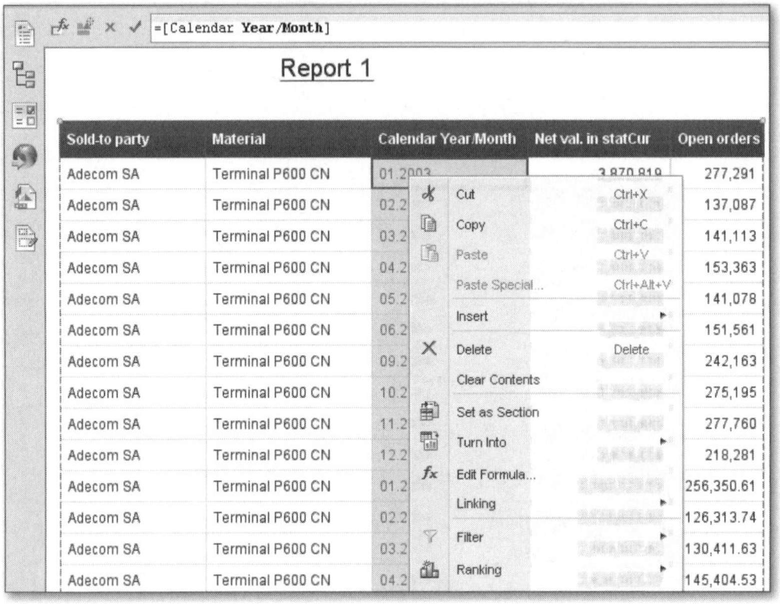

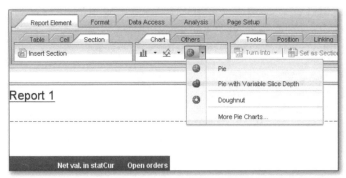

Figure 5.9 Menu Set as Section

4. Navigate to the REPORT ELEMENT tab.

5. Navigate to the CHART tab (see Figure 5.10).

Figure 5.10 Chart Menu

6. Select the PIE option.

7. Place the chart next to your table. As the chart is not defined yet, the chart will be shown as a gray chart. You can now drag and drop the elements from the list of available objects to the chart.

> **Charting in SAP BusinessObjects Web Intelligence**
>
> When you start creating charts in SAP BusinessObjects Web Intelligence, you have the option to simply drag and drop objects from the list of available objects into the chart. Alternatively, you can use the menu TURN INTO • MORE TRANSFORMATIONS in the TOOLS tab of the REPORT ELEMENT tab. The MORE TRANSFORMATIONS option provides a more fine-grained control over the chart definition.

8. Drag and drop the MATERIAL dimension to the chart.

9. Drag and drop the NET VALUE measure to the chart. After you add those two objects to your chart, notice that the chart will not show the data. Instead, it shows a warning.

> **Database Delegated Key Figures**
>
> Based on the direct access method using BI Consumer Services, all available key figures are treated as "database delegated" key figures, which means that the BI client tool will try to get the aggregated numbers from the underlying source.
>
> In the above example, the chart references a different level of aggregation than the main report; therefore, you will have to refresh the report.

10. Use the REFRESH icon (☙) in the toolbar to refresh the report.

11. Confirm the values for the prompt. The chart should now be displayed.

12. Select an entry from the MATERIAL column.

13. With a simple drag and drop, move the MATERIAL in front of the SOLD-TO-PARTY column.

14. Now select an entry from the MATERIAL column.

15. Navigate to the REPORT ELEMENT tab.

16. Navigate to the TABLE LAYOUT tab (see Figure 5.11).

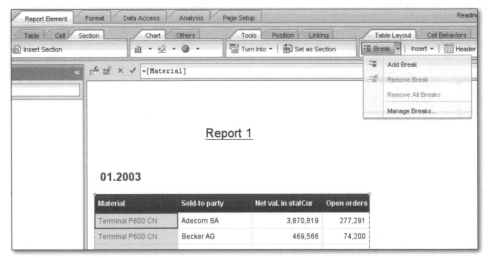

Figure 5.11 Table Layout

17. Select the ADD BREAK menu.

18. Select an entry from the NET VALUE column.

19. Navigate to the ANALYSIS tab.

20. Navigate to the FUNCTIONS tab (see Figure 5.12).

Figure 5.12 Functions

21. Select the SUM option.

22. Repeat the steps for the OPEN ORDERS column.

23. Navigate to the FILE tab.

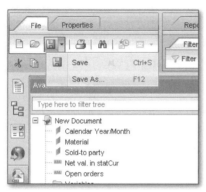

Figure 5.13 Menu File

24. Use the SAVE icon to save the report to your SAP BusinessObjects system.

In this section you created your first SAP BusinessObjects Web Intelligence report using the direct access method leveraging BI Consumer Services connecting to a BEx query. In the next section you will learn how to migrate your existing SAP BusinessObjects Web Intelligence XI 3.1 reports using OLAP universes to the direct access method using the BI Consumer Services.

5.4   Creating Your First Report for SAP NetWeaver BW (Relational Universe)

In addition to the option to leverage a direct connection towards the BEx query using the BI Consumer Services (BICS), you can also establish a relational universe on top of your InfoProviders in the SAP NetWeaver BW system. The list of unsupported metadata is shown in Section 3.3.2. In the following steps, we show you how to create a universe using a relational connection on top of an InfoProvider from the SAP Demo content. Then we show you how to create a SAP BusinessObjects Web Intelligence report on top of the newly created universe.

1. Start the Information Design tool by following the menu START • PROGRAMS • SAP BUSINESSOBJECTS BI PLATFORM 4 • SAP BUSINESSOBJECTS BI PLATFORM CLIENT TOOLS • INFORMATION DESIGN TOOL.

2. Select the menu FILE • NEW • PROJECT to create a new project for your universe.

3. Enter a name for the new project and click FINISH.

4. Select the WINDOW menu and make sure the REPOSITORY RESOURCES window is shown.

5. In the REPOSITORY RESOURCES window select the INSERT SESSION menu to establish a session in your SAP BusinessObjects system (see Figure 5.14).

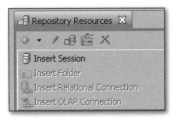

Figure 5.14 Repository Resources

6. Log on with your credentials.

7. Click OK.

8. Open the context menu of your established server connection in the CONNECTIONS area (see Figure 5.15).

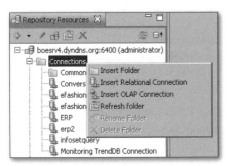

Figure 5.15 Connections

9. Select the INSERT RELATIONAL CONNECTION menu item.

SAP NetWeaver BW Connection

To establish a relational connection with SAP NetWeaver BW, you need to first establish a session in the SAP BusinessObjects system, and then create a connection starting with the repository of your SAP BusinessObjects system. This is slightly different than the usual workflow.

10. Enter a name for the connection.

11. Click NEXT.

12. Select the SAP NETWEAVER BW connection type (see Figure 5.16).

Figure 5.16 Relational Connection

13. Click NEXT.

14. Enter the necessary details of your SAP NetWeaver BW system (see Figure 5.17):

    ▶ Client number

    ▶ User and password

    ▶ Language

    ▶ System ID

    ▶ Application server and system number, or message server and logon group

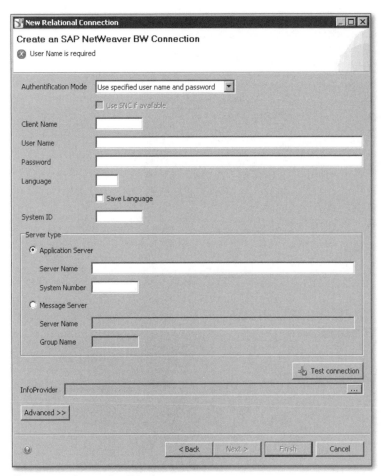

Figure 5.17 Connection Details

Authentication Mode

You can set the AUTHENTICATION MODE to USE SINGLE-SIGN ON, but this requires your SAP BusinessObjects system to be configured with SAP authentication.

15. You can use the SAVE LANGUAGE option to save your settings as configured in the relational connection. If you leave the checkbox open, the user can influence the language by setting the user preferences in the BI launch pad.

16. Use the ... button next to INFOPROVIDER to receive a list of possible InfoProviders (see Figure 5.18).

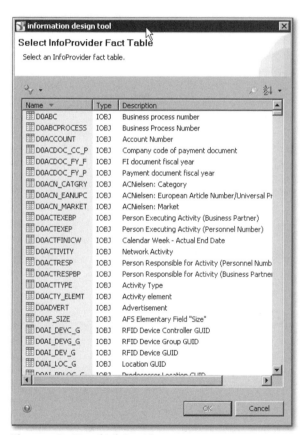

Figure 5.18 List of InfoProviders

17. You can use the filter as part of the screen to limit the list of InfoProviders based on the type of InfoProvider (see Figure 5.19).

   ▶ IOBJ: InfoObject

   ▶ CUBE: InfoCube

   ▶ ODSO: Operational Data Store

   ▶ MRPO: MultiProvider

   ▶ VIRT: Virtual InfoProvider

Figure 5.19 List of Filters

18. In our example we use the MultiProvider 0D_NW_M01 from the NetWeaver Demo Model.

19. Click OK.

20. Click FINISH.

21. You are asked whether you would like to create a shortcut for your connection. Click YES.

22. Click CLOSE.

SAP NetWeaver BW Star Schema

The following is only basic information about the tables shown in the list of available tables. We recommended that you consider the documentation on SAP NetWeaver BW for further details:

▶ The fact table of the InfoProvider is shown with the prefix "I".

▶ Master data tables are shown with the prefix "D".

▶ Text tables are shown with the prefix "T".

---

23. Select your local project.

24. Select the menu FILE • NEW • DATA FOUNDATION.

25. Enter a name for the data foundation.

26. Click NEXT.

27. Select the MULTI-SOURCE ENABLED option. The connection towards SAP NetWeaver BW is not available when using the single source option.

28. Click NEXT. You are asked to log on to your SAP BusinessObjects system.

29. Enter your credentials.

30. Click NEXT.

31. Select the shortcut that was created for the connection established previously.

32. Click NEXT (see Figure 5.20).

Figure 5.20 Define Connection Properties

33. Click ADVANCED.

34. Ensure that the AUTOMATICALLY CREATE TABLES AND JOINS option is activated.

35. Click FINISH.

You are presented with a default generated star schema for the selected InfoProvider. You can find out more about the known limitations in Section 3.3.2.

36. Select your local project.

37. Select the menu FILE • NEW • BUSINESS LAYER.

38. Select the RELATIONAL DATA SOURCE entry.

39. Click NEXT.

40. Enter a name for the business layer.

41. Click NEXT.

42. Click the 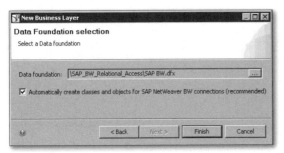 button and select the newly created data foundation.

Figure 5.21 New Business Layer

43. Ensure that AUTOMATICALLY CREATE CLASSES AND OBJECTS FOR SAP NETWEAVER BW CONNECTIONS (RECOMMENDED) is activated.

44. Click FINISH (see Figure 5.22).

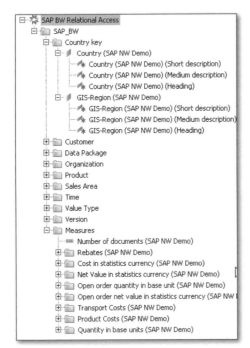

Figure 5.22 Created Business Layer

You are presented with a list of classes, dimensions, and measures that have been generated based on the information retrieved from SAP NetWeaver BW.

45. Right-click the newly generated business layer entry as part of your local project (see Figure 5.23).

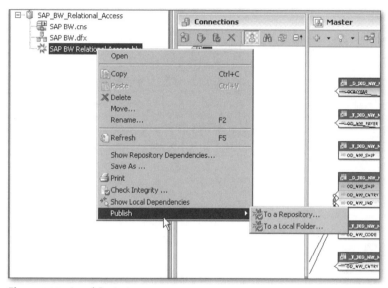

Figure 5.23 Local Project

46. Select the menu PUBLISH • TO A REPOSITORY.

47. Select the integrity checks you would like to perform.

48. Click NEXT.

49. Select a folder for the universe.

50. Click FINISH.

51. Click CLOSE.

You have created a universe based on a relational connection on top of a Multi-Provider in SAP NetWeaver BW. You can use SAP Crystal Reports for Enterprise, SAP BusinessObjects Web Intelligence, SAP BusinessObjects Dashboards, and SAP BusinessObjects Explorer on top of this universe.

In this section you created your first universe based on a relational connection with SAP NetWeaver BW. In the next section you will learn how you can migrate a

SAP BusinessObjects Web Intelligence report using a XI 3.1 OLAP universe to SAP BusinessObjects Web Intelligence 4.x using the new direct connectivity.

5.5 Migration from SAP BusinessObjects Web Intelligence XI 3.1 to 4.x

In this section you will learn about the steps required to migrate a SAP Business-Objects Web Intelligence report from release XI 3.1 (based on an OLAP universe) to release 4.x (based upon the direct link towards SAP NetWeaver BW) using the BI Consumer Service connectivity.

Figure 5.24 shows the SAP BusinessObjects Web Intelligence report with a chart, a table, and a section. The report is based on an OLAP universe from the XI 3.1 release.

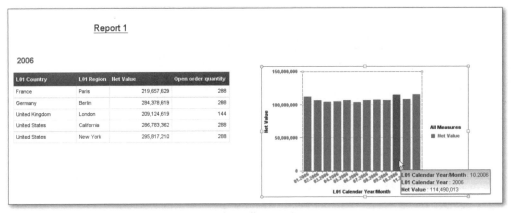

Figure 5.24 SAP BusinessObjects Web Intelligence Report

Migrating SAP BusinessObjects Web Intelligence Reports using SAP NetWeaver BW Data

If you would like to migrate your XI 3.1 SAP BusinessObjects Web Intelligence reports to the new platform using the new BICS connectivity, you need to set up the connection towards SAP NetWeaver BW in the Central Management Console before starting the migration process.

1. Log on to the BI launch pad via the menu START • PROGRAMS • SAP BUSINESS-OBJECTS BI PLATFORM 4 • SAP BUSINESSOBJECTS BI PLATFORM • SAP BUSINESS-OBJECTS PLATFORM JAVA BI LAUNCH PAD.

2. Log on to the system using your SAP credentials and the SAP authentication option.

3. Select the DOCUMENTS tab.

4. Select the FOLDERS item.

5. Navigate to the folder where you saved the SAP BusinessObjects Web Intelligence XI 3.1 report.

6. Select the report.

7. Right-click on the report and open the context menu.

8. Select the MODIFY menu item.

9. Navigate to the DATA ACCESS tab.

10. Navigate to the TOOLS tab (see Figure 5.25).

Figure 5.25 Data Access

11. Select the CHANGE SOURCE menu item .

12. Select the underlying query (see Figure 5.26).

13. Select the SPECIFY A NEW DATA SOURCE option.

14. Select the BEx option.

15. Select the connection to the SAP NetWeaver BW system based on the direct BICS connection.

16. Select your connection.

17. Select the BEx query.

18. Click OK (see Figure 5.27).

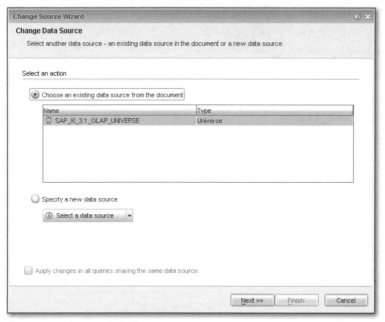

Figure 5.26 Change Data Source

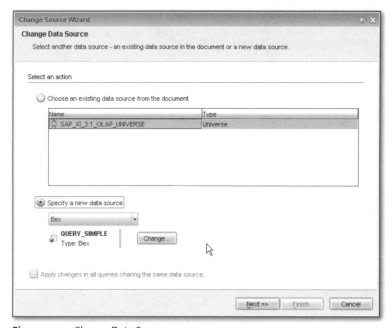

Figure 5.27 Change Data Source

19. Click Next (see Figure 5.28).

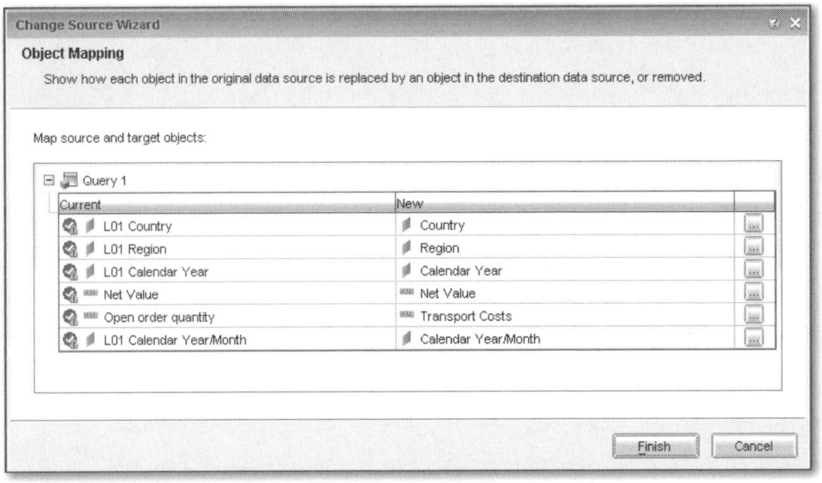

Figure 5.28 Object Mapping

20. You are presented with a mapping dialog of the objects that are used in the existing SAP BusinessObjects Web Intelligence report and those that are available in the new data connection. You can use the ▪▪▪ button to change the mapping.

21. Click Finish.

Your report should now point to the new data connection. You should be able to save your changes and refresh the report.

5.6 Summary

In this chapter you learned about the different data connectivity options for SAP BusinessObjects Web Intelligence 4.x as part of your overall SAP landscape. In addition, you learned how the metadata from your SAP NetWeaver BW system is mapped to the SAP BusinessObjects Web Intelligence query panel, and how you can create your first report on top of data coming from your SAP NetWeaver BW system. Finally, you learned how you can migrate your existing SAP BusinessObjects Web Intelligence XI 3.1 reports (based on OLAP universes) to SAP BusinessObjects Web Intelligence 4.x. In the next chapter you will learn how to leverage SAP BusinessObjects Analysis, edition for Microsoft Office, in combination with SAP NetWeaver BW.

In this chapter you will learn how you can leverage SAP BusinessObjects Analysis, edition for Microsoft Office in combination with SAP NetWeaver BW and use the product as a premium successor for your BEx Analyzer workbooks.

6 SAP BusinessObjects Analysis, Edition for Microsoft Office and SAP NetWeaver BW

In this chapter you will learn about the data connectivity options and the level of support for the metadata in SAP NetWeaver BW, and you will create your very first workbook using SAP BusinessObjects Analysis, edition for Microsoft Office.

6.1 Data Connectivity Overview

Figure 6.1 shows the data connectivity between SAP BusinessObjects Analysis, edition for Microsoft Office and your SAP NetWeaver BW, SAP ERP, and SAP HANA system.

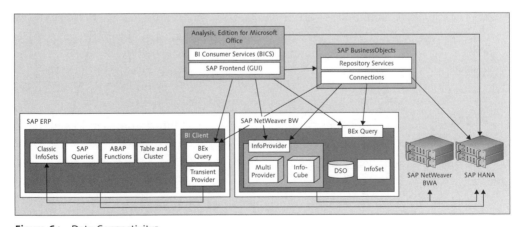

Figure 6.1 Data Connectivity

SAP BusinessObjects Analysis, edition for Microsoft Office can be leveraged in combination with the SAP BusinessObjects BI platform or in a so-called "lean deployment," where SAP BusinessObjects Analysis, edition for Microsoft Office is deployed without the use of the SAP BusinessObjects BI platform. In regard to data connectivity, SAP BusinessObjects Analysis, edition for Microsoft Office is able:

- To leverage a direct access method using BI Consumer Services (BICS) to the InfoProvider and BEx queries from your SAP NetWeaver BW system.

- To leverage a direct access method using BICS with BEx queries based on transient providers in the SAP ERP system. The transient provider requires SAP ECC 6.0, enhancement package 05.

- To leverage the shared connections from the SAP BusinessObjects BI platform using the direct access method based on BICS.

- To establish a direct link to SAP HANA.

As you can see in Figure 6.1, you can leverage SAP BusinessObjects Analysis, edition for Microsoft Office with or without the deployment of the SAP BusinessObjects BI platform. Below we list some of the disadvantages of deploying SAP Business-Objects Analysis, edition for Microsoft Office without the SAP BusinessObjects BI platform and some of the advantages that the SAP BusinessObjects BI platform can add to your overall BI landscape.

The disadvantages of deployment without the SAP BusinessObjects BI platform are:

- All connections toward any SAP NetWeaver BW system have to be created on each client computer as part of the SAP frontend.

- Microsoft Excel and PowerPoint documents can be shared only on some form of the central shared folder, as there is no central repository.

- The SAP frontend has to be deployed on each client computer that will leverage SAP BusinessObjects Analysis, edition for Microsoft Office.

- Such a deployment does not offer any form of administration services in terms of access to Microsoft Excel and PowerPoint documents.

- Such a deployment does not leverage any form of a central lifecycle mechanism, which means that there is no automated way of populating shared documents from development to a QA or production environment.

The advantages of integrated deployment with the SAP BusinessObjects BI platform are:

▶ Users can centrally save, open, and share documents created with SAP BusinessObjects Analysis, edition for Microsoft Office by storing them via the SAP BusinessObjects BI platform system.

▶ Administrators can create connections to the SAP NetWeaver BW system centrally and control access to those connections in the SAP BusinessObjects BI platform system.

▶ Administrators can assign authorizations to centrally stored documents created with SAP BusinessObjects Analysis, edition for Microsoft Office and control access to these documents on a user and group level.

▶ Administrators can leverage the SAP BusinessObjects lifecycle management console to follow documents and connections from development, to QA, to a production environment.

▶ When SAP BusinessObjects Analysis, edition for Microsoft Office is deployed combined with the SAP BusinessObjects BI platform there is no need to have the SAP frontend deployed on the client, because users can share connections via the SAP BusinessObjects BI platform system.

In this section we reviewed the different data connectivity options available with SAP BusinessObjects Analysis, edition for Microsoft Office. In the next section you will learn about the level of support of your existing metadata from SAP NetWeaver BW in combination with SAP BusinessObjects Analysis, edition for Microsoft Office.

6.2 Supported and Unsupported SAP NetWeaver BW Elements

In this section we review the level of support for your existing metadata inside the SAP NetWeaver BW system for SAP BusinessObjects Analysis, edition for Microsoft Office. Table 6.1 shows which of the objects are supported when using SAP BusinessObjects Analysis, edition for Microsoft Office as the BI client tool.

	Direct Access using BICS
Direct access to InfoCube and MultiProvider	Yes
Access to BEx queries	Yes
Characteristic Values	
Key	Yes
Short description	Yes
Medium and long description	Yes
BEx Query Features	
Support for hierarchies	Yes
Support for free characteristics	Yes
Support for calculated and restricted key figures	Yes
Support for currencies and units	Yes
Support for custom structures	Yes
Support for formulas and selections	Yes
Support for filter	Yes
Support for display and navigational attributes	Yes
Support for conditions in rows	Yes
Support for conditions in columns	Yes
Support for conditions for fixed characteristics	Yes
Support for exceptions	Yes
Compounded characteristics	Yes
Constant selection	Yes
Default values in BEx query	Yes
Number scaling factor	Yes
Number of decimals	Yes
Calculate rows as (local calculation)	Yes

Table 6.1 Supported and Unsupported BEx Query Features for SAP BusinessObjects Analysis, Edition for Microsoft Office

	Direct Access using BICS
Sorting	Yes
Hide/unhide	Yes
Display as hierarchy	Yes
Reverse sign	Yes
Support for reading master data	Yes
Data Types	
Support for CHAR (characteristics)	Yes
Support for NUMC (characteristics)	Yes
Support for DATS (characteristics)	Yes
Support for TIMS (characteristics)	Yes
Support for numeric key figures such as Amount and Quantity	Yes
Support for Date (key figures)	Yes
Support for Time (key figures)	Yes
SAP Variables—Processing Type	
User input	Yes
Authorization	Yes
Replacement path	Yes
SAP exit / custom exit	Yes
Precalculated value set	Yes
General Features for Variables	
Support for optional and mandatory variables	Yes
Support for key date dependencies	Yes
Support for default values	Yes
Support for personalized values	No

Table 6.1 Supported and Unsupported BEx Query Features for SAP BusinessObjects Analysis, Edition for Microsoft Office (Cont.)

	Direct Access using BICS
SAP Variables — Variable Type	
Single value	Yes
Multi-single value	Yes
Interval value	Yes
Selection option	Yes
Hierarchy variable	Yes
Hierarchy node variable	Yes
Hierarchy version variable	Yes
Text variable	Yes
EXIT variable	Yes
Single key date variable	Yes
Multiple key dates	Yes
Formula variable	Yes

Table 6.1 Supported and Unsupported BEx Query Features for SAP BusinessObjects Analysis, Edition for Microsoft Office (Cont.)

In Table 6.2 you can see how the direct access method using the BICS option uses elements from the BEx query and how the objects are mapped to the navigation panel for SAP BusinessObjects Analysis, edition for Microsoft Office.

BEx Query Element	SAP BusinessObjects Analysis, Edition for Microsoft Office
Characteristic	For each characteristic you'll receive a field, and with the menu members you can decide which part of the characteristic is shown as part of the overall result.
Hierarchy	Each available hierarchy is shown as an external hierarchy and can be leveraged as part of the crosstab. In addition, you can leverage hierarchy levels as part of your crosstab; for example, you can show all members of Level 2 of the hierarchy.

Table 6.2 SAP NetWeaver BW Metadata Mapping for SAP BusinessObjects Analysis, Edition for Microsoft Office

BEx Query Element	SAP BusinessObjects Analysis, Edition for Microsoft Office
Key figure	Each key figure is shown with the unit and scaling factor information.
Calculated/restricted key figure	Each calculated and restricted key figure is treated like a key figure. The user does not have access to the underlying definition in SAP BusinessObjects Analysis, edition for Microsoft Office.
Filter	Filters are applied to the underlying query and are visible in the navigation panel as part of the FILTER area in the INFORMATION tab.
Display attribute	Display attributes become standard fields in the navigation panel and are grouped as subordinates of the linked characteristic.
Navigational attribute	Navigational attributes are treated the same way as characteristics.
Variable	Each variable with the property READY FOR INPUT results in a prompt. You can leverage the PROMPTS menu to provide the necessary input values.
Custom Structure	A custom structure is available as an element in the navigation panel and each structure element can be selected or de-selected for the report.

Table 6.2 SAP NetWeaver BW Metadata Mapping for SAP BusinessObjects Analysis, Edition for Microsoft Office (Cont.)

In addition to the details on how SAP BusinessObjects Analysis, edition for Microsoft Office supports your existing metadata from SAP NetWeaver BW, we would like to highlight the fact that the terms that are used in SAP BusinessObjects Analysis, edition for Microsoft Office are different from those that you might be used to in BEx Analyzer. Table 6.3 maps those terms.

As you can see in Table 6.1 and Table 6.2, SAP BusinessObjects Analysis, edition for Microsoft Office strongly supports existing metadata from SAP NetWeaver BW and provides you with a feature-rich successor to your BEx Analyzer. In the next section, you will learn the first steps of working with SAP BusinessObjects Analysis, edition for Microsoft Office.

BEx Query	SAP BusinessObjects Analysis, Edition for Microsoft Office
Key figure	Measure
Characteristic	Dimension
Variable	Prompt
Characteristic value	Member
Condition	Filter by measure
Exception	Conditional formatting

Table 6.3 Terms in SAP BusinessObjects Analysis, Edition for Microsoft Office

6.3 Creating Your First Workbook in SAP BusinessObjects Analysis, Edition for Microsoft Office

In the following steps you will learn how to use some of the basic functionality of SAP BusinessObjects Analysis, edition for Microsoft Office. You will leverage the connection created previously in the Central Management Console (CMC) of your SAP BusinessObjects BI platform system.

1. Start SAP BusinessObjects Analysis for Microsoft Excel by following the menu START • ALL PROGRAMS • SAP BUSINESSOBJECTS • ANALYSIS FOR MICROSOFT EXCEL.

2. Navigate to the ANALYSIS tab.

3. Select the menu INSERT • SELECT DATA SOURCE (see Figure 6.2).

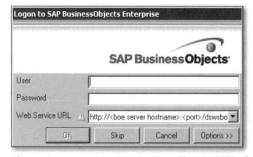

Figure 6.2 Log on to SAP BusinessObjects BI Platform

4. You are asked to log on to your SAP BusinessObjects BI platform system or you can use the Skip option and leverage the connection with your local SAP GUI. In our example we use the shared connection from our SAP BusinessObjects BI platform system.

5. In the field for the Web Service URL replace the placeholders with the values for your SAP BusinessObjects system.

    ▶ BOE Server Hostname: Here you need to enter the name of your Java application server that is used as part of your SAP BusinessObjects BI platform system.

    ▶ Port: Here you need to enter the port of your Java application server that is used as part of your SAP BusinessObjects BI platform system.

6. Click on Options (see Figure 6.3).

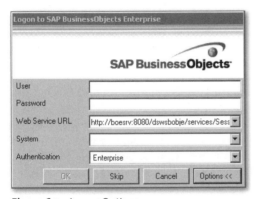

Figure 6.3 Logon Options

7. Enter the name of your system into the System field. Here you should enter the name of your Central Management Server (CMS).

8. Select SAP as the Authentication.

9. Enter your SAP credentials. Because you cannot enter the SAP system ID and the client number in separate fields, you need to enter your SAP user in the following syntax `<SAP System ID>~<SAP Client Number>/<SAP User>`.

10. Enter your password.

11. Click OK. The list of available connections from the SAP BusinessObjects BI platform system is shown (see Figure 6.4).

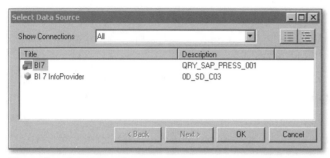

Figure 6.4 Select Data Source

12. Select the previously established connection.

13. Click OK. You are asked to log on to the SAP system again.

14. Enter the SAP credentials.

15. Click OK.

You are presented with the data according to the layout defined by the BEx query (see Figure 6.5).

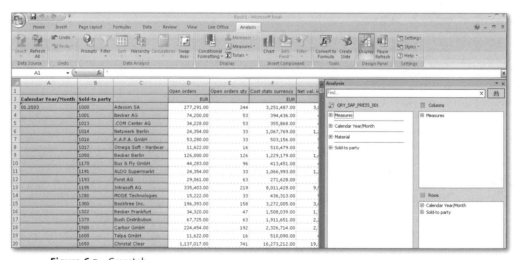

Figure 6.5 Crosstab

16. Select the SOLD-TO PARTY entry in the ROWS area of the navigation panel and drag and drop it to an empty area of the navigation panel so that it is removed from the result set (see Figure 6.6).

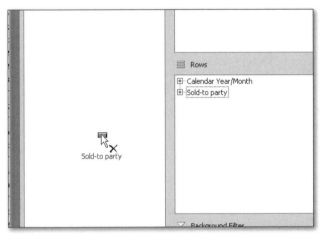

Figure 6.6   Remove Sold-to Party

17. Now right-click on the MEASURES in the COLUMNS.

18. Click the FILTER BY MEMBER menu (see Figure 6.7).

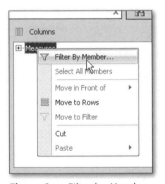

Figure 6.7   Filter by Member

19. You are presented with the list of available members (see Figure 6.8). Select the COSTS and NET VALUE entry.

Figure 6.8 Member Selector

20. Now navigate to the ANALYSIS ribbon and click PAUSE REFRESH (see Figure 6.9).

Figure 6.9 Pause Refresh

21. Drag and drop the MATERIAL item from the navigation panel on top of the CALENDAR MONTH/YEAR item so that it replaces CALENDAR MONTH/YEAR.

22. Now click again on the PAUSE REFRESH item in the ANALYSIS ribbon (see Figure 6.10).

	A	B	C
1		Cost stats currency	Net val. in statCur
2	**Material**	EUR	EUR
3	CN Service Plus	167,751,876.64	241,362,315.92
4	Monitor flat 17 CN	771,615,521.90	1,021,134,957.52
5	Monitor flat 21 CN	629,486,674.68	670,408,981.36
6	Notebook Speedy I CN	1,172,649,613.64	1,360,239,999.12
7	Notebook Speedy II CN	494,824,926.70	614,790,723.56
8	Terminal P400 CN	849,590,785.34	881,370,895.92
9	Terminal P600 CN	961,186,787.86	1,061,558,927.88
10	**Overall Result**	**5,047,006,186.76**	**5,850,866,801.28**
11			

Figure 6.10 Updated Crosstab

23. The PAUSE REFRESH function allows you to defer the update of your workbook until you enable it. In this way, you can perform several navigation steps and then perform a single update to reflect all changes.

24. Select a member of MATERIAL as part of your crosstab (see Figure 6.11).

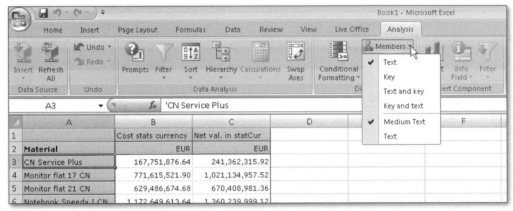

Figure 6.11 Members Formatting

25. Select the MEMBERS option from the ANALYSIS ribbon.

26. Select the TEXT entry and choose TEXT in the lower part as well.

27. Select an entry from MEASURES.

28. Select the MEASURES menu from the ANALYSIS ribbon (see Figure 6.12).

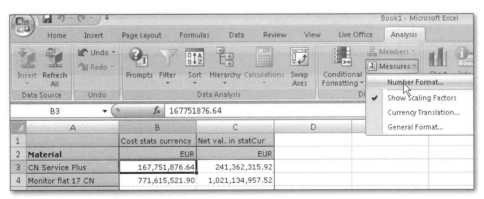

Figure 6.12 Measure Formatting

29. Format your measure with a scaling factor of 1000 and 0 decimal places (see Figure 6.13).

Figure 6.13 Number Formatting

30. Click OK.

31. Select the column header for the NET VALUE measure.

32. Select the menu FILTER • FILTER BY MEASURE • MOST DETAILED DIMENSION IN ROWS • EDIT (see Figure 6.14).

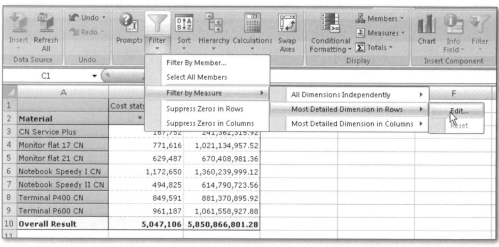

Figure 6.14 Filter by Measure

33. Select the TOP N option.

34. Enter the value "5".

35. Click ADD (see Figure 6.15). You are presented with the top five materials (see Figure 6.16).

Figure 6.15 Top N Filter by Measure

	A	B	C
1		Cost stats currency	Net val. in statCur
2	**Material**	* 1,000 EUR	EUR
3	Monitor flat 17 CN	771,616	1,021,134,957.52
4	Monitor flat 21 CN	629,487	670,408,981.36
5	Notebook Speedy I CN	1,172,650	1,360,239,999.12
6	Terminal P400 CN	849,591	881,370,895.92
7	Terminal P600 CN	961,187	1,061,558,927.88
8	**Overall Result**	**5,047,106**	**5,850,866,801.28**
9			

Figure 6.16 Top 5 Material

36. Now drag and drop the SOLD-TO PARTY dimension on top of the MATERIAL dimension in the navigation panel so that it replaces the MATERIAL dimension. You are presented with the top five SOLD-TO PARTY members (see Figure 6.17).

	A	B	C	D
1			Cost stats currency	Net val. in statCur
2	**Sold-to party**		* 1,000 EUR	EUR
3	1650	Christal Clear	265,414	479,368,757.60
4	2210	DelBont Industries	224,503	266,880,688.80
5	3300	Minerva Industries	335,995	399,962,309.90
6	3510	Star Supermarkets	264,927	315,388,974.00
7	4151	Toro Motor Company	522,903	507,622,850.10
8	**Overall Result**		**5,047,106**	**5,850,866,801.28**

Figure 6.17 Top 5 Sold-to-Party

37. Remember that your underlying BEx query contains a variable for the Calendar Month/Year. Use the PROMPTS menu in the ANALYSIS ribbon to open the prompts dialog (see Figure 6.18).

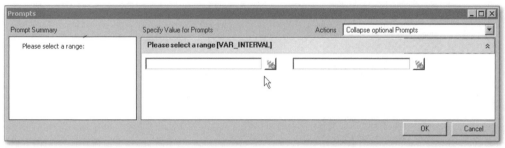

Figure 6.18   Prompt Dialog

38. You can use the MEMBER SELECTOR icon ( ) to open the member selector.

39. Enter an interval for the twelve months of the current year.

40. Click OK.

41. Now select an entry in your crosstab.

42. Select the CREATE SLIDE menu from the ANALYSIS ribbon (see Figure 6.19).

Figure 6.19   Create Slide

43. When prompted, log on to the SAP system.

44. Depending on your default settings and the data volume, you are asked to configure how the data is shown in the slides in Microsoft PowerPoint (see Figure 6.20).

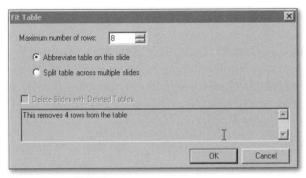

Figure 6.20 Fit Table

45. Set MAXIMUM NUMBER OF ROWS to 8.

46. Select the ABBREVIATE TABLE ON THIS SLIDE option.

47. Click OK (see Figure 6.21).

		Cost stats currency	Net val. in statCur
Sold-to party		*** 1,000 EUR**	**EUR**
1650	Christal Clear	265,414	479,368,757.60
2210	DelBont Industries	224,503	266,880,688.80
3300	Minerva Industries	335,995	399,962,309.90
3510	Star Supermarkets	264,927	315,388,974.00
4151	Toro Motor Company	522,903	507,622,850.10
Overall Result		5,047,106	5,850,866,801.28

Figure 6.21 SAP BusinessObjects Analysis for Microsoft PowerPoint

The crosstab is turned into a Microsoft PowerPoint presentation using SAP Business-Objects Analysis for Microsoft PowerPoint, and you can now use the Analysis ribbon in Microsoft PowerPoint to format your slides further.

In this section your learned some of the basic steps of SAP BusinessObjects Analysis, edition for Microsoft Office. In the next chapter we look into more details of SAP BusinessObjects Analysis, edition for OLAP.

6.4   Summary

In this chapter you learned how you can leverage SAP BusinessObjects Analysis, edition for Microsoft Office in combination with data from your SAP NetWeaver BW system. You also learned how the product supports the existing metadata from your SAP NetWeaver BW system. In the next chapter you will learn more about SAP BusinessObjects Analysis, edition for OLAP.

In this chapter you will learn how you can leverage SAP BusinessObjects Analysis, edition for OLAP in combination with SAP NetWeaver BW and use the product as a premium successor for you BEx Web Analyzer reporting.

7   SAP BusinessObjects Analysis, Edition for OLAP and SAP NetWeaver BW

To begin our discussion, we'll look at the data connectivity options, learn about the metadata support for SAP NetWeaver BW, and then explore the product itself by learning some basic first steps.

7.1   Data Connectivity Overview

Figure 7.1 shows the data connectivity between SAP BusinessObjects Analysis, edition for OLAP and your SAP NetWeaver BW and SAP ERP system.

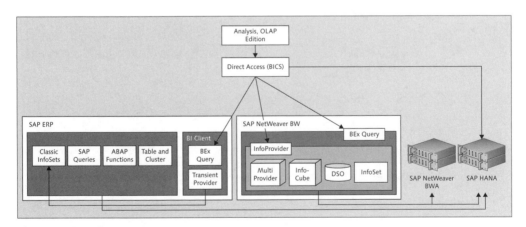

Figure 7.1   Data Connectivity

SAP BusinessObjects Analysis, edition for OLAP shares the connection established as part of the SAP BusinessObjects BI platform with the other BI client products.

SAP BusinessObjects Analysis, edition for OLAP is able to leverage the direct BICS connection towards your SAP NetWeaver BW system, connecting to the BEx query and InfoProvider level. In addition, SAP BusinessObjects Analysis, edition for OLAP is also able to leverage the connection towards the BEx query, using the transient provider as part of your SAP ERP system; the transient provider requires SAP ECC 6.0, enhancement package 05. SAP BusinessObjects Analysis, edition for OLAP is also able to establish a direct link to SAP HANA using the BICS connectivity.

7.2 Supported and Unsupported SAP NetWeaver BW Elements

In this section we review the level of support for your existing metadata inside the SAP NetWeaver BW system for SAP BusinessObjects Analysis, edition for OLAP. Table 7.1 shows which of the objects are supported when using SAP BusinessObjects Analysis, edition for OLAP as a BI client tool.

	Direct Access using BICS
Direct access to InfoCube and MultiProvider	Yes
Access to BEx queries	Yes
Characteristic Values	
Key	Yes
Short description	Yes
Medium and long description	Yes
BEx Query Features	
Support for hierarchies	Yes
Support for free characteristics	Yes
Support for calculated and restricted key figures	Yes
Support for currencies and units	Yes
Support for custom structures	Yes
Support for formulas and selections	Yes

Table 7.1 Supported and Unsupported BEx Query Features for SAP BusinessObjects Analysis, Edition for OLAP

	Direct Access using BICS
Support for filter	Yes
Support for display and navigational attributes	Yes
Support for conditions in rows	Yes
Support for conditions in columns	Yes
Support for conditions for fixed characteristics	Yes
Support for exceptions	Yes
Compounded characteristics	Yes
Constant selection	Yes
Default values in BEx query	Yes
Number scaling factor	Yes
Number of decimals	Yes
Calculate rows as (local calculation)	Yes
Sorting	Yes
Hide/unhide	Yes
Display as hierarchy	Yes
Reverse sign	Yes
Support for reading master data	Yes
Data Types	
Support for CHAR (characteristics)	Yes
Support for NUMC (characteristics)	Yes
Support for DATS (characteristics)	Yes
Support for TIMS (characteristics)	Yes
Support for numeric key figures such as Amount and Quantity	Yes
Support for Date (key figures)	Yes
Support for Time (key figures)	Yes

Table 7.1 Supported and Unsupported BEx Query Features for SAP BusinessObjects Analysis, Edition for OLAP (Cont.)

	Direct Access using BICS
SAP Variable—Processing Type	
User input	Yes
Authorization	Yes
Replacement path	Yes
SAP exit/custom exit	Yes
Precalculated value set	Yes
General Features for Variables	
Support for optional and mandatory variables	Yes
Support for key date dependencies	Yes
Support for default values	Yes
Support for personalized values	No
SAP Variables—Variable Type	
Single value	Yes
Multi-single value	Yes
Interval value	Yes
Selection option	Yes
Hierarchy variable	Yes
Hierarchy node variable	Yes
Hierarchy variable	Yes
Text variable	Yes
EXIT variable	Yes
Single key date variable	Yes
Multiple key dates	Yes
Formula variable	Yes

Table 7.1 Supported and Unsupported BEx Query Features for SAP BusinessObjects Analysis, Edition for OLAP (Cont.)

In Table 7.2, you can see how the direct access method using the BICS option uses the elements from the BEx query and how the objects are mapped to the navigation panel for SAP BusinessObjects Analysis, edition for OLAP.

BEx Query Element	SAP BusinessObjects Analysis, Edition for OLAP
Characteristic	For each characteristic you'll receive a field, and with the context menu in the layout panel you can decide which part of the characteristic is shown as part of the overall result.
Hierarchy	Each available hierarchy is shown as an external hierarchy and can be leveraged as part of the crosstab. In addition, you can leverage hierarchy levels as part of your crosstab; for example, you can show all members of Level 2 of the hierarchy.
Key figure	Each key figure is shown with the unit and scaling factor information.
Calculated/restricted key figure	Each calculated and restricted key figure is treated like a key figure. The user does not have access to the underlying definition in SAP BusinessObjects Analysis, edition for OLAP.
Filter	Filters are applied to the underlying query but end users cannot see that the list of available members was limited by a filter in the underlying BEx query.
Display attribute	Display attributes become standard fields in the navigation panel and are grouped as subordinates of the linked characteristic.
Navigational attribute	Navigational attributes are treated the same way as characteristics.
Variable	Each variable with the property READY FOR INPUT results in a prompt. You can leverage the REFRESH menu in the data panel to provide the necessary input values.
Custom structure	A custom structure is available as an element in the navigation panel and each structure element can be selected or de-selected for the report.

Table 7.2 SAP NetWeaver Business Warehouse Metadata Mapping for SAP BusinessObjects Analysis, Edition for OLAP

In addition to the details on how SAP BusinessObjects Analysis, edition for OLAP supports your existing metadata from SAP NetWeaver BW, we would like to highlight the fact that SAP BusinessObjects Analysis, edition for OLAP uses the same terms as SAP BusinessObjects Analysis, edition for Microsoft Office—and that they are different from the BEx Analyzer and BEx Web Analyzer terms. To see the details, refer back to Table 6.3 in Chapter 6.

SAP BusinessObjects Analysis, edition for OLAP is a premium successor to Voyager from SAP BusinessObjects and for BEx Web Analyzer on the SAP NetWeaver BW side. As you can see, the rich support of your existing metadata from your SAP NetWeaver BW system and the option to leverage your existing BEx queries make SAP BusinessObjects Analysis, edition for OLAP a compelling option for those use cases where you would like to provide analytical reporting to your end users in a web environment. In the next section we will discuss some of the basic steps for using SAP BusinessObjects Analysis, edition for OLAP.

7.3 Creating Your First Workbook in SAP BusinessObjects Analysis, Edition for OLAP

In this section you will learn the basic steps of SAP BusinessObjects Analysis, edition for OLAP. You will leverage the connection that we established previously with SAP Crystal Reports for Enterprise.

1. Open the BI launch pad via START • PROGRAMS • SAP BUSINESSOBJECTS BI PLATFORM 4 • SAP BUSINESSOBJECTS BI PLATFORM • SAP BUSINESSOBJECTS BI PLATFORM JAVA BI LAUNCH PAD.

2. Log on to the SAP BusinessObjects BI platform system using your SAP credentials and the SAP authentication.

3. Select the menu APPLICATIONS • ANALYSIS EDITION FOR OLAP (see Figure 7.2).

4. Select the connection created previously.

SAP BusinessObjects Analysis, OLAP Edition and OLAP Connections

If you created a connection pointing directly to the InfoProvider, you can use the NEXT button shown in Figure 7.2 to retrieve a list of BEx queries from the selected InfoProvider. If your connection is pointing to a BEx query already—as in our example—you can simply click OK.

Figure 7.2 Open Data Source

5. Click OK (see Figure 7.3).

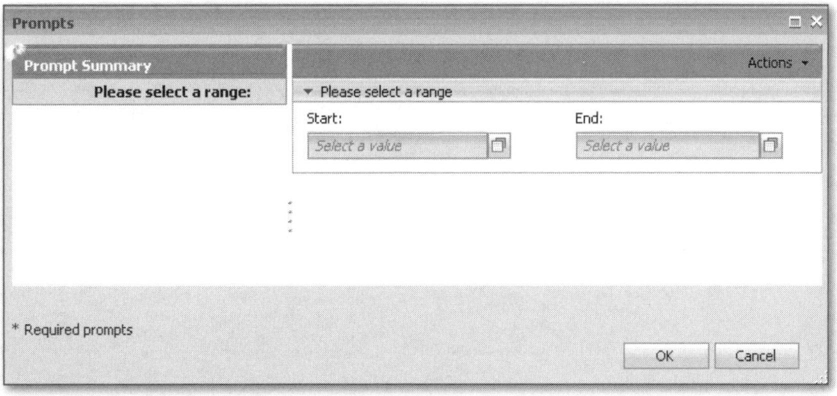

Figure 7.3 Prompting Dialog

6. You are presented with the prompting dialog, as your underlying BEx query contains a variable. You can use the Member Selector icon (📋) to open the list of available members (see Figure 7.4).

7. Select a range for the CALENDAR MONTH/YEAR to show the data for the current year.

8. Click OK.

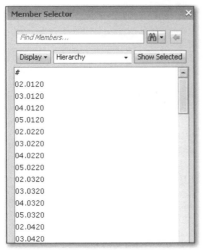

Figure 7.4 Member Selector

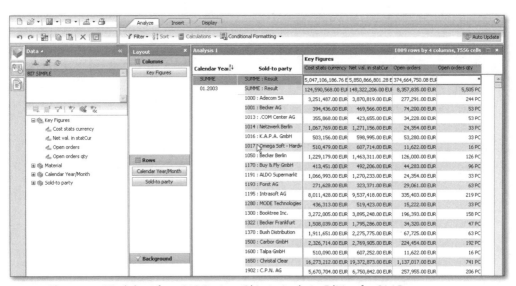

Figure 7.5 Worksheet from SAP BusinessObjects Analysis, Edition for OLAP

You are presented with the default layout defined by the underlying BEx query. In addition, you are shown all the available panels of SAP BusinessObjects Analysis, edition for OLAP:

► The DATA panel provides you with access to the connections and the available elements of your worksheet.

> ▸ The LAYOUT panel allows you to define the layout of your crosstab by using simple drag and drop navigation, as well as using the context menus.

> ▸ The ANALYSIS area in your worksheet presents the actual result set in the form of a crosstab or a chart to the end user.

9. Select the CALENDAR MONTH/YEAR entry in the ROWS and move it to an empty area in the DATA panel to remove it from the result set (see Figure 7.6).

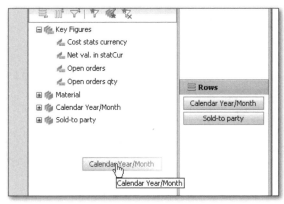

Figure 7.6 Navigation Step

10. Right-click on the KEY FIGURES entry in COLUMNS.

11. Select the menu FILTER • BY MEMBER (see Figure 7.7).

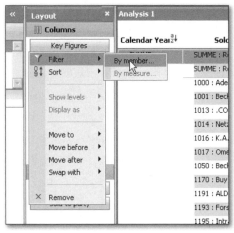

Figure 7.7 Filter By Member

12. Select the key figures NET VALUE and OPEN ORDERS.

13. Click OK.

14. Click the AUTO UPDATE button (top right corner).

15. Drag and drop the MATERIAL dimension from the DATA panel to the LAYOUT panel on top of the SOLD-TO PARTY dimension so that it replaces SOLD-TO PARTY (see Figure 7.8).

Figure 7.8 Exchanging Dimensions

16. Now click the AUTO UPDATE button again. Your worksheet is now getting updated. The AUTO UPDATE option allows you to defer the update and perform several navigation steps and trigger the update after you finish with the navigation steps.

17. Select a member of the MATERIAL dimension in the crosstab.

18. Open the context menu with a right click. Select the menu REORDER MEMBERS • MOVE.

19. Now navigate to the first member of the Material dimension in your crosstab.

20. Right-click on the member and select the men REORDER MEMBERS • INSERT BEFORE (see Figure 7.9).

21. You can use the REORDER MEMBERS menu to create your own custom order. You can also use a simple drag and drop to select a member and move it to a new place in the list of members.

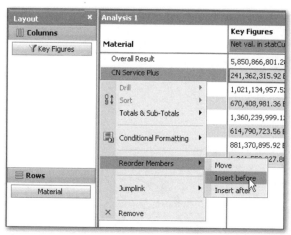

Figure 7.9 Reorder Members

22. Now right-click on the MATERIAL dimension in the LAYOUT panel (see Figure 7.10).

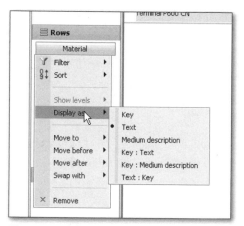

Figure 7.10 Display Members

23. Select the menu DISPLAY AS • KEY: TEXT.

24. Select the column header for the NET VALUE key figure.

25. Navigate to the DISPLAY tab (see Figure 7.11).

Figure 7.11 Display Menu

26. Select the MEASURE FORMAT menu (see Figure 7.12).

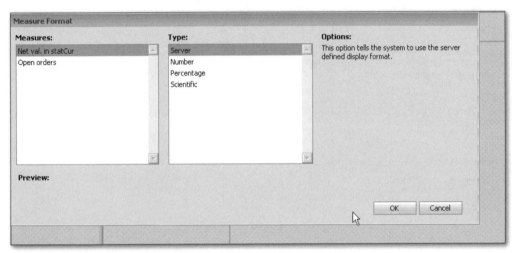

Figure 7.12 Measure Format

27. You can now configure how the key figure will be displayed. The SERVER setting will format the key figure as configured in the BEx query. Select the NUMBER option.

28. Click OK.

29. Right-click on the MATERIAL dimension in the LAYOUT panel (see Figure 7.13).

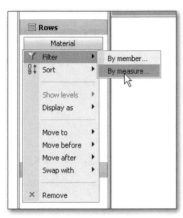

Figure 7.13 Context Menu

30. Select the menu FILTER • BY MEASURE (see Figure 7.14).

Figure 7.14 Filter By Measure

31. Use the NET VALUE as the BASED ON option.

32. Set the TOP N option for INCLUDE MEMBERS.

33. Enter the value "5".

34. Click ADD.

35. Click OK.

36. Navigate to the INSERT tab.

37. Select the CLUSTERED COLUMN option (see Figure 7.15). You are presented with a chart as part of your worksheet (see Figure 7.16).

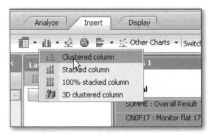

Figure 7.15   Insert Chart

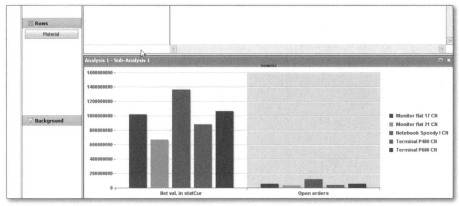

Figure 7.16   Chart

38. Navigate to the EXPORT menu (see Figure 7.17).

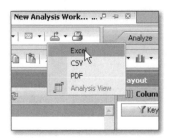

Figure 7.17   Export Menu

39. Select the Excel option.

40. Select both elements from your worksheet to be exported (see Figure 7.18).

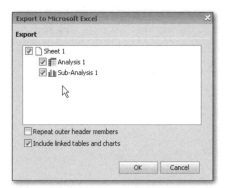

Figure 7.18   Export to Microsoft Excel

41. Click OK. You are presented with a Microsoft Excel spreadsheet.

42. Navigate back to your report.

43. Click Save (see Figure 7.19).

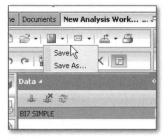

Figure 7.19   Save Menu

44. Save your worksheet to your SAP BusinessObjects server.

In this section you learned some of the basic navigation steps in SAP Business-Objects Analysis, edition for OLAP. In the next chapter we review the details of SAP BusinessObjects Dashboards in combination with your SAP landscape.

7.4   Summary

In this chapter you learned about the support of your existing metadata from SAP NetWeaver BW in combination with SAP BusinessObjects Analysis, edition for OLAP. You learned about the different data connectivity options and you got started with the first basic steps in the product itself. In the next chapter you will learn more details about SAP BusinessObjects Dashboards.

In this chapter you will learn how you can leverage SAP BusinessObjects Dashboards in combination with SAP NetWeaver BW and create compelling dashboards for your executives.

8 SAP BusinessObjects Dashboards and SAP Landscapes

This chapter will review the different data connectivity options for SAP Business-Objects Dashboards and SAP NetWeaver BW, and explain the level of metadata support. You will create your very first SAP BusinessObjects Dashboards objects visualizing data from your SAP system.

8.1 SAP BusinessObjects Dashboards and SAP NetWeaver BW

In this section you will learn about different options to connect SAP Business-Objects Dashboards to your SAP NetWeaver BW system. We review the different options for data connectivity and the level of support for your existing metadata in the SAP NetWeaver BW system.

8.1.1 Data Connectivity Overview

In Figure 8.1 you can see the various options for how you can connect from SAP BusinessObjects Dashboards to your SAP landscape.

SAP BusinessObjects Dashboards 4.x has several options for connecting to the data available in your SAP landscape. SAP BusinessObjects Dashboards can:

► Establish direct connectivity against a BEx query in the SAP NetWeaver BW system using BICS available in the SAP NetWeaver BW system itself.

► Establish direct connectivity against a BEx query in the SAP NetWeaver BW system using the direct access method via BICS provided by the SAP Business-Objects system.

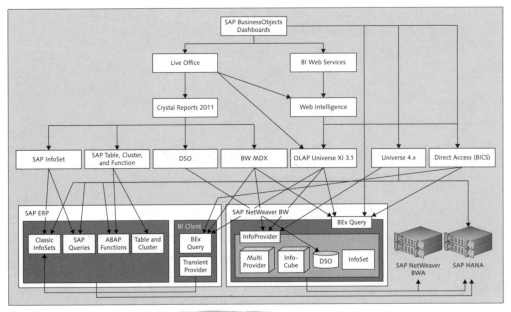

Figure 8.1 SAP BusinessObjects Dashboards Data Connectivity

- ▶ Leverage the universe as part of the SAP BusinessObjects 4.x platform and leverage the relational access towards the SAP NetWeaver BW system.

- ▶ Leverage the universe as part of the SAP BusinessObjects 4.x platform and leverage the relational access towards the SAP ERP system.

- ▶ Leverage Live Office as a source and in that way enable SAP BusinessObjects Dashboards to use SAP BusinessObjects Web Intelligence and SAP Crystal Reports 2011 as data sources for the dashboards.

- ▶ Leverage BI Web Services from the SAP BusinessObjects stack and use SAP BusinessObjectsWeb Intelligence reports via the BI Web Services as a data source for the dashboards.

As you can see from Figure 8.1, SAP BusinessObjects Dashboards offers three options for connecting directly to the SAP NetWeaver BW system. We already mentioned the main differences between the relational access using the universe and the direct access method using BICS in Chapter 3. Our recommendation to use the direct access method also holds true for SAP BusinessObjects Dashboards.

You have two data connectivity methods available for SAP BusinessObjects Dashboards using the BICS layer. First, you can connect SAP BusinessObjects Dashboards directly against the BEx query in the SAP NetWeaver BW system without the usage of SAP BusinessObjects; this uses the BICS layer from the SAP NetWeaver BW system and therefore does require the BI Java part of your SAP NetWeaver BW system. An SAP BusinessObjects Dashboards object using this connection must be hosted by the SAP NetWeaver system and cannot be hosted by the SAP BusinessObjects system. Second, SAP BusinessObjects Dashboards is now, with release 4.x, also able to use the shared connection using the BICS layer from the SAP BusinessObjects system. Such dashboards can be hosted with all your other content types as part of the SAP BusinessObjects system.

In this section you have received a brief overview of the different data connectivity options for SAP BusinessObjects Dashboards and how you can visualize your corporate data using SAP BusinessObjects Dashboards. In the next section we review in more detail the level of metadata support when using SAP NetWeaver BW as a source.

8.1.2   Supported and Unsupported SAP NetWeaver BW Elements

Table 8.1 shows the level of support for your existing SAP NetWeaver BW metadata for the two data connectivity options that leverage the BICS layer.

	Direct Access using BICS as Part of SAP BusinessObjects	Direct Access using BICS as Part of SAP NetWeaver BW
Direct access to InfoCube and MultiProvider	No	No
Access to BEx queries	Yes	Yes
Characteristic Values		
Key	Yes	Yes
Short description	Yes	Yes
Medium and long description	Yes	Yes
BEx Query Features		
Support for hierarchies	Yes	Limited

Table 8.1 Supported and Unsupported BEx Query Features for SAP BusinessObjects Dashboards

	Direct Access using BICS as Part of SAP BusinessObjects	Direct Access using BICS as Part of SAP NetWeaver BW
Support for free characteristics	Yes	Yes
Support for calculated and restricted key figures	Yes	Yes
Support for currencies and units	Yes	Yes
Support for custom structures	Yes	Yes
Support for formulas and selections	Yes	Yes
Support for filter	Yes	Yes
Support for display and navigational attributes	Yes	Navigational attributes only
Support for conditions in rows	No	Yes
Support for conditions in columns	No	Yes
Support for conditions for fixed characteristics	No	Yes
Support for exceptions	No	No
Compounded characteristics	Limited	Yes
Constant selection	Yes	Yes
Default values in BEx query	No	Yes
Number scaling factor	Yes	Yes
Number of decimals	No	Yes

Table 8.1 Supported and Unsupported BEx Query Features for SAP BusinessObjects Dashboards (Cont.)

	Direct Access using BICS as Part of SAP BusinessObjects	Direct Access using BICS as Part of SAP NetWeaver BW
Calculate rows as (local calculation)	No	Yes
Sorting	Yes	Yes
Hide/unhide	Yes	Yes
Display as hierarchy	No	No
Reverse sign	Yes	Yes
Support for reading master data	Yes	Yes
Data Types		
Support for CHAR (characteristics)	Yes	Yes
Support for NUMC (characteristics)	Yes as string value	Yes as string value
Support for DATS (characteristics)	Yes as string value	Yes as string value
Support for TIMS (characteristics)	Yes as string value	Yes as string value
Support for numeric key figures such as Amount and Quantity	Yes	Yes
Support for Date (key figures)	Yes as string value	Yes as string value
Support for Time (key figures)	Yes as string value	Yes as string value
SAP Variable—Processing Type		
User input	Yes	Yes
Authorization	Yes	Yes

Table 8.1 Supported and Unsupported BEx Query Features for SAP BusinessObjects Dashboards (Cont.)

	Direct Access using BICS as Part of SAP BusinessObjects	Direct Access using BICS as Part of SAP NetWeaver BW
Replacement path	Yes	Yes
SAP exit/custom exit	Yes	Yes
Precalculated value set	Yes	Yes
General Features for Variables		
Support for optional and mandatory variables	Yes	Yes
Support for key date dependencies	Yes	Yes
Support for default values	Limited	Limited
Support for personalized values	No	No
SAP Variables—Variable Type		
Single value	Yes	Yes
Multi-single value	Yes	Yes
Interval value	No	Yes
Selection option	No	Yes
Hierarchy variable	Limited	Yes
Hierarchy node variable	Limited	Yes
Hierarchy version variable	Limited	Yes
Text variable	Yes	Yes
EXIT variable	Yes	Yes
Single key date variable	Yes	Yes
Multiple key dates	Yes	Yes
Formula variable	Yes	Yes

Table 8.1 Supported and Unsupported BEx Query Features for SAP BusinessObjects Dashboards (Cont.)

In Table 8.2 you can see the details on how SAP BusinessObjects Dashboards is leveraging the available BEx query elements when you would use the direct access BICS method without using SAP BusinessObjects, which means you are using BICS as part of SAP NetWeaver BW.

BEx Query Element	SAP BusinessObjects Dashboards (BICS as part of SAP NetWeaver BW)
Characteristic	Each characteristic is supported with the elements configured in the underlying BEx query. For example, if the characteristic is configured to be displayed with the medium text only, SAP BusinessObjects Dashboards will show the medium text only, even though the characteristic also has a key value.
Hierarchy	Hierarchies are transformed into levels and SAP BusinessObjects Dashboards puts all levels into a single column; therefore, it is very difficult to create a hierarchical report.
Key figure	Each key figure is shown with the unit and scaling factor information. In addition you have the option to switch between a raw and a formatted display of the key figures, where the formatted option is incorporating the unit, thousand separator, and decimals into the display.
Calculated/restricted key figure	Each calculated and restricted key figure is treated like a key figure. The user does not have access to the underlying definition in SAP BusinessObjects Dashboards.
Filter	Filters are applied to the underlying query and SAP BusinessObjects Dashboards provides the information about the predefined filters as part of the data connection.
Display attribute	Display attributes are not supported as part of this data connectivity.
Navigational attribute	Navigational attributes are treated the same way as characteristics.
Variable	Each variable with the property READY FOR INPUT results in an input variable as part of the data connection details. In addition, SAP BusinessObjects Dashboards is also able to leverage the run time from BEx web reporting to prompt the users.

Table 8.2 SAP NetWeaver BW Metadata Mapping for SAP BusinessObjects Dashboards

BEx Query Element	SAP BusinessObjects Dashboards (BICS as part of SAP NetWeaver BW)
Custom structure	A custom structure is available as a single element in the data structure and users cannot select single structure elements.

Table 8.2 SAP NetWeaver BW Metadata Mapping for SAP BusinessObjects Dashboards (Cont.)

Table 8.3 shows the details of how SAP BusinessObjects Dashboards can leverage the shared connection from your SAP BusinessObjects system using the direct access method involving BICS.

BEx Query Element	SAP BusinessObjects Dashboards (BICS as Part of SAP BusinessObjects)
Characteristic	For each characteristic you receive a field representing the key value and a field for the description, including short, medium, and long description.
Hierarchy	Each available hierarchy is shown as an external hierarchy in SAP BusinessObjects Dashboards.
Key figure	Each key figure can have up to four elements: numeric value, unit, scaling factor, and formatted value. The formatted value is based on the user preferences configured in the SAP system.
Calculated/restricted key figure	Each calculated and restricted key figure is treated like a key figure. The user does not have access to the underlying definition in SAP BusinessObjects Dashboards.
Filter	Filters are applied to the underlying query but are not visible in SAP BusinessObjects Dashboards.
Display attribute	Display attributes become standard fields in the query panel and are grouped as subordinates of the linked characteristic.
Navigational attribute	Navigational attributes are treated the same way as characteristics.
Variable	Each variable with the READY FOR INPUT property results in a prompt available in SAP BusinessObjects Dashboards.

Table 8.3 SAP NetWeaver BW Metadata Mapping for SAP BusinessObjects Dashboards with SAP BusinessObjects

BEx Query Element	SAP BusinessObjects Dashboards (BICS as Part of SAP BusinessObjects)
Custom structure	A custom structure is available as an element in the query panel and each structure element can be selected or de-selected for the report.

Table 8.3 SAP NetWeaver BW Metadata Mapping for SAP BusinessObjects Dashboards with SAP BusinessObjects (Cont.)

In this section we reviewed the level of support for SAP BusinessObjects Dashboards in combination with your existing metadata in your SAP NetWeaver BW system. In the next section we review the options for connecting SAP BusinessObjects Dashboards to the data in your SAP ERP system.

8.2 SAP BusinessObjects Dashboards and SAP ERP

SAP BusinessObjects Dashboards, as part of the 4.x release, is able to leverage the close integration with the semantic layer and in that way establish a connection using the universe on top of the SAP ERP system. The known limitations are outlined in Section 3.4 of Chapter 3.

In Section 4.3 of Chapter 4 you can follow the steps for how to establish a universe on top of the SAP ERP system in combination with SAP Crystal Reports for Enterprise. Remember that the steps for creating the semantic layer are identical because the semantic layer is shared across multiple tools.

As shown in Figure 8.1, SAP BusinessObjects Dashboards is able to do the following:

▶ Leverage the semantic layer from the 4.x release to establish data connectivity towards SAP ERP.

▶ Leverage Live Office in combination with reports based on SAP Crystal Reports 2011 to leverage data from the SAP ERP system.

▶ Leverage the direct BICS connectivity on top of a BEx query in the local BI client of the SAP ERP system based upon a transient provider. The transient provider requires SAP ERP 6.0, enhancement package 05 or higher.

In the next section you will learn the steps for creating a report with SAP Business-Objects Dashboards and data coming from SAP NetWeaver BW using the direct BICS connection.

SAP BusinessObjects Dashboards and SAP ERP Activity

You will notice that in the next section both activities are based on a BEx query from SAP NetWeaver BW. The steps on how to leverage data from your SAP ERP data with SAP BusinessObjects Dashboards follows the same logic as those shown in Section 8.3.2, with the only difference being that you would use a universe based on top of your SAP ERP system.

8.3 Creating Your First Dashboard with SAP Business-Objects Dashboards

In this section you will create two simple dashboards using SAP BusinessObjects Dashboards. The first example is with the direct access method using the BICS layer provided directly by SAP NetWeaver BW, without the use of SAP BusinessObjects Enterprise. The second example uses the new capabilities of SAP BusinessObjects Dashboards 4.x with the BICS connectivity provided by your SAP BusinessObjects system.

8.3.1 SAP BusinessObjects Dashboards and Direct Access via SAP NetWeaver BW

In this section we review the integration between SAP BusinessObjects Dashboards and SAP NetWeaver BW using the direct access via BICS provided by SAP NetWeaver BW. Remember that this integration requires the BI Java portion of the SAP NetWeaver BW system, and the SAP BusinessObjects Dashboards object will have to be hosted inside the SAP NetWeaver BW system, not inside the SAP BusinessObjects system.

For our example we use a BEx query based on the SAP NetWeaver Actuals and Plan MultiProvider demo cubes (0D_NW_M01) (see Figure 8.2).

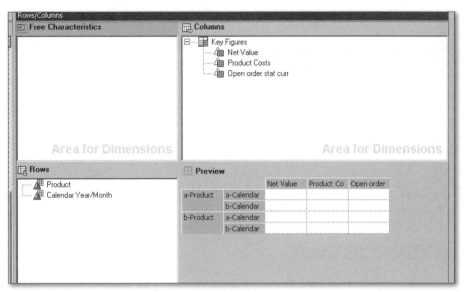

Figure 8.2 BEx Query

The BEx query contains the Product and Calendar Year/Month characteristics as well as the Net Value, Product Costs, and Open Orders key figures. In addition, the BEx query contains a variable for Calendar Year (see Figure 8.3).

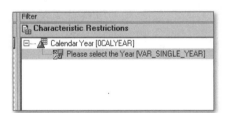

Figure 8.3 Variable

You can start building your first dashboard now.

1. Start the SAP BusinessObjects Dashboards Designer via the menu START • PROGRAMS • DASHBOARDS • DASHBOARDS.

2. Select the menu FILE • NEW • NEW to create a blank canvas.

3. Select the menu DATA • CONNECTIONS.

4. Click ADD.

5. Select the SAP NETWEAVER BW CONNECTION entry (see Figure 8.4).

Figure 8.4   Data Manager

6. Click BROWSE and log on to your SAP system.

7. Select the BEx query.

8. In the DEFINITION tab, enter a unique name for your new connection.

Figure 8.5   Input Values

► The INPUT VALUES area (see Figure 8.5) of your new connection provides you with the fields for setting up filters and for providing input to any variables from the underlying BEx query.

► The OUTPUT VALUES area (see Figure 8.6) provides you access to the characteristics, variables, static filters, information, and messages. But, most importantly, OUTPUT VALUES contains the CROSS-TAB DATA entry, which gives you access to the actual data being returned from your SAP NetWeaver BW system.

Figure 8.6   Output Values

► The CHARACTERISTICS area allows you to access the key and text for each characteristic that you can use for a list of values (see Figure 8.7).

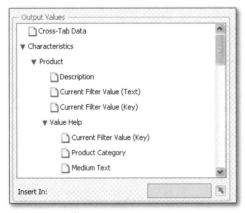

Figure 8.7   Characteristics

▶ The VARIABLES area (see Figure 8.8) provides you access to the information needed for a list of values for the variables from the underlying BEx query. This information is not only for the characteristics available, but also for related items of the characteristics, such as display attributes.

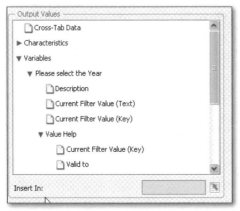

Figure 8.8 Variables

▶ The STATIC FILTER area provides you with the information about any predefined filters as part of the BEx query.

▶ The INFORMATION area (see Figure 8.9) allows you to incorporate the usual BEx text elements as part of your dashboard and provide details, such as the latest change to the underlying BEx query.

Figure 8.9 Information

▶ The MESSAGES area (see Figure 8.10) gives you access to any error messages.

Figure 8.10 Messages

9. Navigate to the DATA PREVIEW tab (see Figure 8.11).

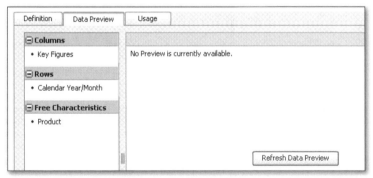

Figure 8.11 Data Preview

Result Set

The result set returned from SAP NetWeaver BW contains additional information for the data being returned. As you can see in Figure 8.12, the first two rows contain information like labels, currencies, and units.

Key Figures	Billed Quantity	Net Sales
Product	ST	* 1.000 USD
PDS01	106282	132657.301
PDS02	126389	115240.45
PDS03	99792	124532.786
PDS12	33237	170818.32
Overall Result	365700	543248.857

Figure 8.12 Sample Data Set

10. Make sure the Calendar Year/Month characteristic is the only entry in the Rows area.

11. Click REFRESH DATA PREVIEW. You are shown a preview of the data that will be returned. The structure shown here is important because you will have to select a range in the spreadsheet when defining the CROSS-TAB DATA entry from OUTPUT VALUES.

12. Navigate to the USAGE tab (see Figure 8.13).

Figure 8.13 Usage

13. Ensure that the REFRESH BEFORE COMPONENTS ARE LOADED item is selected.

14. Navigate back to the DEFINITION tab.

15. Select the CROSS-TAB DATA entry from the OUTPUT VALUES.

16. Click the icon () next to the INSERT IN option.

17. Select a range from A1 to D20 in the spreadsheet.

18. Click OK.

19. Open the list of entries in the VARIABLES area of the OUTPUT VALUES.

20. Select the KEY entry from the VALUE HELP for the variable (see Figure 8.14).

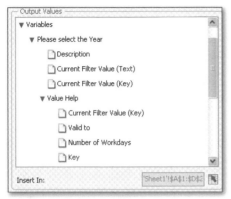

Figure 8.14 Output Values

21. Click the icon () next to the INSERT IN option.

22. Select a range from F1 to F20 in the spreadsheet.

23. Click OK.

24. Select the entry for the variable in the INPUT VALUES (see Figure 8.15).

Figure 8.15 Variables Input

25. Click the icon () next to the INSERT IN option.

26. Select cell H1 from the spreadsheet.

27. Click OK.

28. Navigate to the USAGE tab.

29. Click the icon (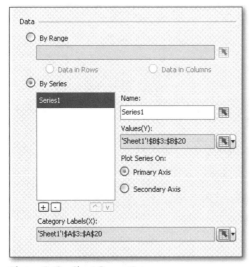) next to the TRIGGER CELL option.

30. Select cell H1 from the spreadsheet.

31. Click OK.

32. Select the WHEN VALUE CHANGES option.

33. Click CLOSE to close the Data Manager.

34. Select the menu VIEW • COMPONENTS to make sure that you can see the components.

35. Drag and drop a COLUMN CHART from the CHARTS area to your canvas.

36. Right-click on the chart and select the PROPERTIES menu.

37. Enter NET VALUE BY MONTH as TITLE.

38. Remove the SUBTITLE.

39. Activate the BY SERIES option for the DATA.

40. Use the "+" sign to add a new data series.

41. Click the icon () next to the VALUES (Y) option.

42. Select a range from B3 to B20 in the spreadsheet.

43. Click the icon () next to the CATEGORY LABELS (X) option.

44. Select a range from A3 to A20 in the spreadsheet (see Figure 8.16).

Figure 8.16 Chart Properties

45. Navigate to the BEHAVIOR tab.

46. Activate the IGNORE AT END-OF-RANGE ONLY IN SERIES and IN VALUES options.

47. Drag and drop a LIST BOX from the SELECTORS next to the chart.

48. Right-click on the listbox and select the PROPERTIES menu.

49. Click the icon (🔲) next to the LABELS option.

50. Select a range from F1 to F20 in the spreadsheet.

51. Set the INSERTION TYPE to VALUE.

52. Click the icon (🔲) next to the SOURCE DATA option.

53. Select a range from F1 to F20 in the spreadsheet.

54. Click OK.

55. Click the icon (🔲) next to the DESTINATION option.

56. Select a range from H1 in the spreadsheet.

57. Click OK (see Figure 8.17).

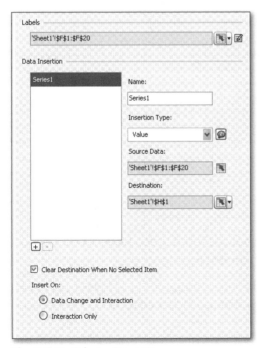

Figure 8.17 Selector Properties

58. Select the menu SAP • PUBLISH to save your dashboard to the SAP NetWeaver BW system.

59. Select the menu SAP • LAUNCH to view the dashboard (see Figure 8.18).

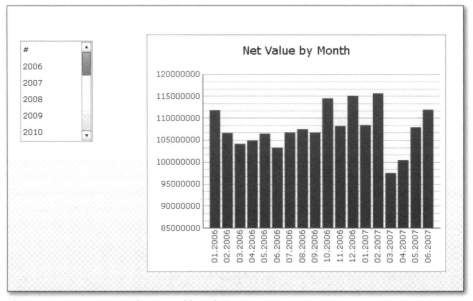

Figure 8.18 SAP BusinessObjects Dashboards Preview

You have created a SAP BusinessObjects Dashboards object based on a BEx query from SAP NetWeaver BW allowing you to select a year. Each time the selection changes, the chart will be updated live against the data from the SAP NetWeaver BW system. In the next section you will create a similar dashboard using the same BEx query, but this time you will leverage the shared connection from the SAP BusinessObjects system.

8.3.2 SAP BusinessObjects Dashboards and Direct Access to SAP NetWeaver BW via SAP BusinessObjects

In this section you will use the shared connection from the SAP BusinessObjects system. In the following example we use a BEx query based on the SAP NetWeaver demo model as shown in Figure 8.19.

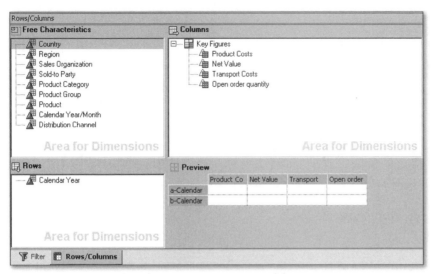

Figure 8.19 BEx Query based on NetWeaver Demo Model

The BEx query also contains a variable as shown in Figure 8.20. This variable is an optional variable for the dimension (characteristic) PRODUCT and allows the user to select multiple single values.

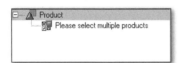

Figure 8.20 BEx Query Variable

SAP BusinessObjects Dashboards uses the same OLAP connection from your SAP BusinessObjects system, which you have used before with SAP Crystal Reports for Enterprise and SAP BusinessObjects Web Intelligence. For the following steps we assume that you have already established an OLAP connection in the Central Management Console. If you are unsure about how to set up the OLAP connection, review the steps in Section 4.2.3.

1. Start SAP BusinessObjects Dashboards by following the menu START • PROGRAMS • DASHBOARDS • DASHBOARDS.

2. Select the menu FILE • NEW • NEW.

3. Select the menu VIEW • QUERY BROWSER to ensure that the QUERY BROWSER is shown (see Figure 8.21).

Figure 8.21 Query Browser

4. Click the ADD QUERY button.

5. Log on to your SAP BusinessObjects BI platform system.

6. You are presented with the list of possible data sources. Select the option BEx (see Figure 8.22).

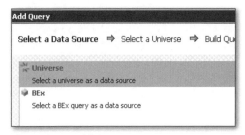

Figure 8.22 Add Query

7. Click NEXT.

8. Select the connection towards the BEx query (see Figure 8.23).

Figure 8.23 BEx Connections

9. Click Next.

10. You are presented with the shared query panel and you can now select the dimensions (characteristics) and measures (key figures) (see Figure 8.24). In our example we use a simple query, returning the net value by country.

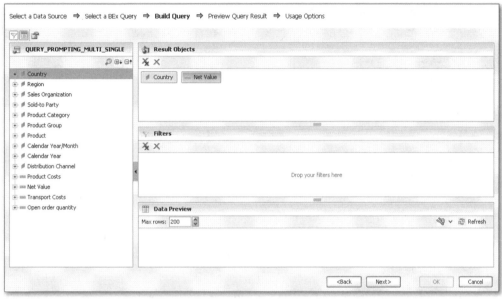

Figure 8.24 Query Panel

11. Click Next.

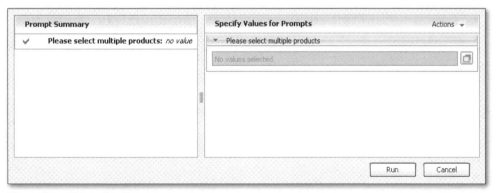

Figure 8.25 Prompting Screen

12. Because your underlying BEx query also includes a variable, you are presented with a prompting screen. You can leave the list of selected values empty for now, as the variable is optional (see Figure 8.25).

13. Click RUN. You are presented with a data preview (see Figure 8.26).

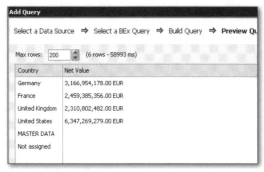

Figure 8.26   Data Preview

14. Click NEXT.

15. In the next step you are presented with connection options. Ensure that the REFRESH BEFORE COMPONENTS ARE LOADED option is checked (see Figure 8.27).

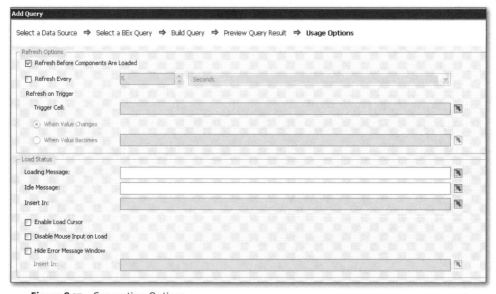

Figure 8.27   Connection Options

16. Click OK. You can see the details of your configured query in the QUERY BROWSER (see Figure 8.28).

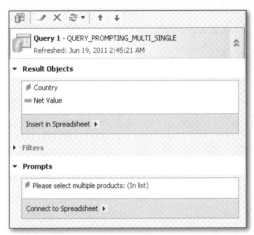

Figure 8.28 Query Browser

17. The QUERY BROWSER contains the RESULT OBJECTS and the PROMPTS, which are based on the variable from the underlying BEx query.

18. Select the VIEW • COMPONENTS menu to ensure that you see the available components.

19. Drag and drop a pie chart from the CHARTS area to your empty canvas.

20. Right-click on the pie chart and use the PROPERTIES menu item (see Figure 8.29).

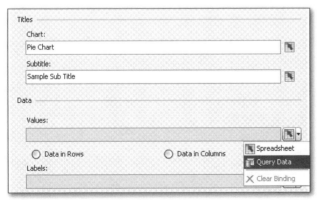

Figure 8.29 Chart Properties

21. Select the QUERY DATA option for the VALUES item (see Figure 8.29).

22. Select the NET VALUE entry (see Figure 8.30).

Figure 8.30 Direct Data Binding

23. Click OK.

24. Select the QUERY DATA option for the LABELS item.

25. Select the COUNTRY entry.

26. Click OK.

27. Select the VIEW • QUERY BROWSER menu to ensure the QUERY BROWSER is shown.

28. Select the prompt based on the variable from the BEx query in the PROMPTS area (see Figure 8.31).

Figure 8.31 Prompts

29. Select the prompt and drag it onto the empty canvas (see Figure 8.32). A default prompting dialog is generated based on the definition of the prompt.

30. Select the FILE • PREVIEW menu. You should now see a preview of your dashboard and you should be able to select values from the prompt and select the corresponding data (see Figure 8.33).

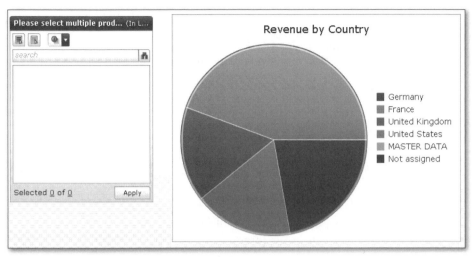

Figure 8.32 SAP BusinessObjects Dashboards Canvas

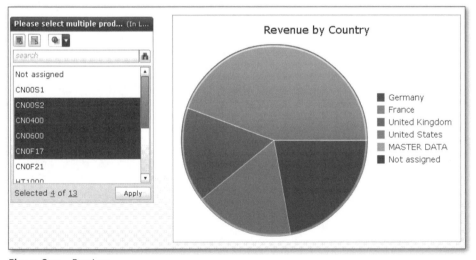

Figure 8.33 Preview

31. Select the menu FILE • SAVE TO PLATFORM.

32. Select the folder and enter a name for the SAP BusinessObjects Dashboards objects.

33. Click SAVE.

You can now log on to the BI launch pad and view your dashboard leveraging data from SAP NetWeaver BW.

In this section you learned how to leverage the direct connection to SAP NetWeaver BW and how to use the direct binding option in SAP BusinessObjects Dashbards 4.x.

8.4   Summary

In this chapter you learned how you can leverage SAP BusinessObjects Dashboards in combination with information stored in your SAP NetWeaver BW and SAP ERP system. You reviewed the level of support for your existing metadata and created your first dashboard using SAP BusinessObjects Dashboards. In the next chapter we review SAP BusinessObjects Explorer in combination with your corporate data.

In this chapter you will learn how you can leverage SAP BusinessObjects Explorer in combination with data from your SAP ERP and your SAP NetWeaver BW systems.

9   SAP BusinessObjects Explorer and SAP Landscapes

SAP BusinessObjects Explorer allows you to leverage universes, Microsoft Excel spreadsheets, SAP BW Accelerator (BWA), and SAP HANA as data sources. This chapter focuses on leveraging universes.

9.1   SAP BusinessObjects Explorer and SAP NetWeaver BW

In this section we focus on the integration of SAP BusinessObjects Explorer with your data stored in SAP NetWeaver BW. You will learn about the data connectivity options, the level of support for your existing metadata, and how to create your first information space on top of data coming from your SAP NetWeaver BW system.

9.1.1   Data Connectivity Overview

Before we look into the details of how SAP BusinessObjects Explorer is able to leverage all the elements from your SAP NetWeaver BW system, we look at the different options for connecting to the system.

Figure 9.1 shows the different data connectivity options for SAP BusinessObjects Explorer:

▶ SAP BusinessObjects Explorer is able to leverage the relational access approach using the universe on top of an SAP NetWeaver BW InfoProvider and can create a disk-based index for the data.

▶ SAP BusinessObjects Explorer is able to establish a direct link to SAP NetWeaver BW Accelerator (BWA) or SAP HANA and leverage the pre-created indexes from those systems. It does not have to create another disk-based index for the data.

▶ SAP BusinessObjects Explorer is also able to use the universe connectivity to SAP HANA and leverage the information being returned to create a disk-based index. Here it is important to recognize that, when using the universe-based approach for SAP BusinessObjects Explorer on top of SAP HANA, that SAP BusinessObjects Explorer is not leveraging the pre-built indexes from SAP HANA.

▶ In addition—not shown in Figure 9.1—SAP BusinessObjects Explorer is also able to create a disk-based index on Microsoft Excel spreadsheets. The spreadsheets can be uploaded on-demand or they can be stored as part of the SAP BusinessObjects system.

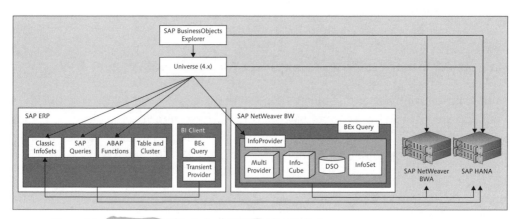

Figure 9.1 SAP BusinessObjects Explorer Data Connectivity

You will notice that SAP BusinessObjects Explorer as part of the SAP BusinessObjects 4.x release is not able to leverage the direct access method using the BICS layer towards SAP NetWeaver BW. Therefore, you have the choice of only the relational universe approach or SAP NetWeaver BWA/SAP HANA in combination with SAP NetWeaver BW.

In situations where you do not have SAP NetWeaver BWA or SAP HANA as part of your SAP landscape, SAP BusinessObjects Explorer can still be a key pillar of your overall BI strategy, but you will have to create disk-based indexes and the data volume that you can leverage will be limited. As a rule of thumb, you should be able to leverage around 2.5 to 3 million rows of data.

In the next section we review the level of support for the existing metadata in more detail.

9.1.2 Supported and Unsupported SAP NetWeaver BW Elements

As shown in Table 9.1, a large set of your existing metadata from SAP NetWeaver BW is not available when using the relational universe access method. In cases where the metadata is not supported directly, it does not automatically mean that the information is not available at all. As outlined in Section 3.3.2, you can re-create some of the missing information as part of the universe.

	Relational Universe Access
Direct access to InfoCube and MultiProvider	Yes
Access to BEx queries	Limited
Characteristic Values	
Key	Yes
Short description	Yes
Medium and long description	Yes
BEx query features	
Support for hierarchies	No
Support for free characteristics	Yes
Support for calculated and restricted key figures	No
Support for currencies and units	Yes
Support for custom structures	No
Support for formulas and selections	No
Support for filter	Yes
Support for display and navigational attributes	Yes
Support for conditions in rows	No

Table 9.1 Supported and Unsupported BEx Query Features for SAP BusinessObjects Explorer

	Relational Universe Access
Support for conditions in columns	No
Support for conditions for fixed characteristics	No
Support for exceptions	No
Compounded characteristics	No
Constant selection	No
Default values	No
Number scaling factor	No
Number of decimals	No
Calculate rows as (local calculation)	No
Sorting	No
Hide/unhide	No
Display as hierarchy	No
Reverse sign	No
Support for reading master data	No
Data Types	
Support for CHAR (characteristics)	Yes
Support for NUMC (characteristics)	Yes as string value
Support for DATS (characteristics)	Yes as string value
Support for TIMS (characteristics)	Yes as string value
Support for Date (key figures)	Yes
Support for Time (key figures)	Yes as string value
SAP Variable — Processing Type	
User input	No
Authorization	No
Replacement path	No

Table 9.1 Supported and Unsupported BEx Query Features for SAP BusinessObjects Explorer (Cont.)

	Relational Universe Access
SAP exit/custom exit	No
Precalculated value set	No
General Features for Variables	
Support for optional and mandatory variables	No
Support for key date dependencies	No
Support for default values	No
Support for personalized values	No
SAP Variables — Variable Type	
Single value	No
Multi-single value	No
Interval value	No
Selection option	No
Hierarchy variable	No
Hierarchy node variable	No
Hierarchy version variable	No
Text variable	No
EXIT variable	No
Single key date variable	No
Multiple key dates	No
Formula variable	No

Table 9.1 Supported and Unsupported BEx Query Features for SAP BusinessObjects Explorer (Cont.)

Based on the level of support for your existing metadata in SAP NetWeaver BW and the missing option to leverage the BICS layer for more of the pre-existing metadata (such as hierarchies and calculated key figures), we recommend that you evaluate the option to add SAP NetWeaver BWA or SAP HANA to your overall SAP landscape. This enables you to leverage larger volumes of data and achieve a higher degree of metadata support.

In this section we reviewed the options to use SAP BusinessObjects Explorer in combination with data from your SAP NetWeaver BW system and the level of support for your existing metadata. In the next section we review the connection options on top of your SAP ERP system.

9.2 SAP BusinessObjects Explorer and SAP ERP

In the previous section we discussed the options for connecting SAP BusinessObjects Explorer with the data in your SAP NetWeaver BW system. You can also leverage the semantic layer and in that way use SAP BusinessObjects Explorer directly with your SAP ERP system.

As shown in Figure 9.2, SAP BusinessObjects Explorer is able to leverage the universe on top of your SAP ERP system and use classic InfoSets, SAP queries, and ABAP functions as a source for a disk-based index. If you are looking for an option to leverage large volumes of data in combination with SAP BusinessObjects Explorer, we recommend that you consider the option to add SAP HANA to your landscape, push the information from your SAP ERP system into SAP HANA, and then use the direct link from SAP BusinessObjects Explorer to SAP HANA.

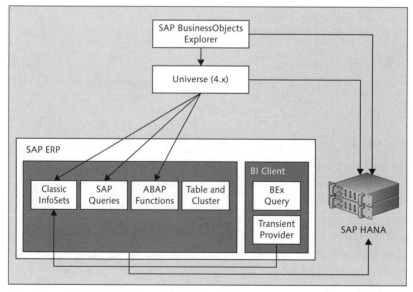

Figure 9.2 SAP BusinessObjects Explorer and SAP ERP

Since the 4.x release of SAP BusinessObjects, you can also establish a connection with the semantic layer on top of your SAP ERP system; Section 3.4 of Chapter 3 outlines the known limitations. In Section 4.3 of Chapter 4, you can follow the steps for establishing a universe on top of the SAP ERP system in combination with SAP Crystal Reports for Enterprise. Remember that the steps to create the semantic layer are identical because the semantic layer is shared across multiple tools.

It is important to recognize that, when you use SAP BusinessObjects Explorer in combination with a universe on top of the data source, you are creating a disk-based index, and the volume of data that can be leveraged is limited. The limit is around 2.5 to 3 million rows of information, but it also depends on the type of information—numeric or textual. If you would like to leverage more data in combination with SAP BusinessObjects Explorer, you should consider the option of using SAP HANA or SAP BW Accelerator.

In this section we reviewed the options for leveraging SAP BusinessObjects Explorer in combination with SAP ERP. In the next section you will learn to create a relational universe on top of SAP NetWeaver BW and then to create your own information space with SAP BusinessObjects Explorer.

9.3   Creating Your First SAP BusinessObjects Explorer Information Space

In the previous sections you learned about the options available for leveraging your corporate data as part of SAP BusinessObjects Explorer. In this section you will leverage a universe on top of SAP NetWeaver BW and create your own information space.

> **SAP BusinessObjects Explorer and SAP NetWeaver BW Accelerator**
>
> The complete details of integrating SAP BusinessObjects Explorer in combination with SAP NetWeaver BW Accelerator can be found in the SAP PRESS book *Inside SAP BusinessObjects Explorer*.

9.3.1 SAP BusinessObjects Explorer and Relational Access to SAP NetWeaver BW

You will now create a relational universe on top of a SAP NetWeaver BW InfoProvider, and then use the universe to establish an information space and create a disk-based index with SAP BusinessObjects Explorer.

1. Start the Information Design tool by following the menu START • PROGRAMS • SAP BUSINESSOBJECTS BI PLATFORM 4 • SAP BUSINESSOBJECTS BI PLATFORM CLIENT TOOLS • INFORMATION DESIGN TOOL.

2. Select the FILE • NEW • PROJECT menu to create a new project for your universe.

3. Enter a name for the new project and click FINISH.

4. Select the WINDOW menu and make sure that the REPOSITORY RESOURCES window is shown.

5. Select the INSERT SESSION menu to establish a session to your SAP BusinessObjects system (see Figure 9.3).

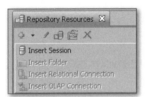

Figure 9.3 Repository Resources

6. Log on with your credentials.

7. Click OK.

8. Open the context menu of your established server connection in the CONNECTIONS area (see Figure 9.4).

9. Select the INSERT RELATIONAL CONNECTION menu item.

SAP NetWeaver BW Connection

To establish a relational connection to SAP NetWeaver BW, you need to first establish a session in the SAP BusinessObjects system, and then create a connection starting with the repository of your SAP BusinessObjects system. This is slightly different from the usual workflow.

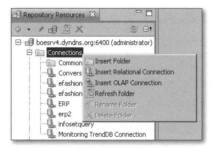

Figure 9.4 Connections

10. Enter a name for the connection.

11. Click NEXT.

12. Select the SAP NETWEAVER BW connection type (see Figure 9.5).

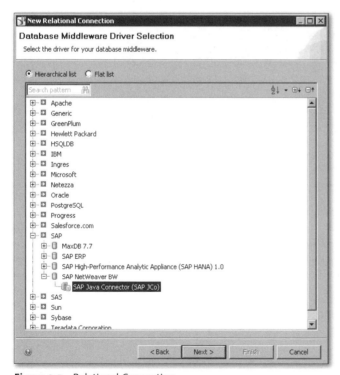

Figure 9.5 Relational Connection

13. Click NEXT.

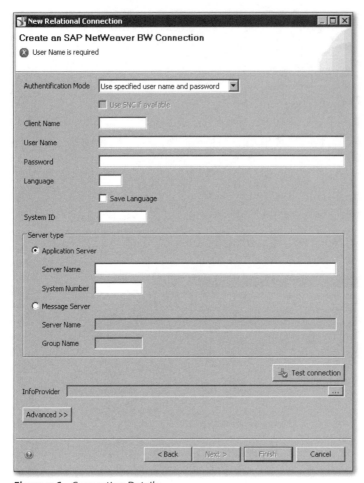

Figure 9.6 Connection Details

14. Enter the necessary details of your SAP NetWeaver BW system (see Figure 9.6):

   ▶ CLIENT NUMBER

   ▶ USER AND PASSWORD

   ▶ LANGUAGE

   ▶ SYSTEM ID

   ▶ APPLICATION SERVER and SYSTEM NUMBER or MESSAGE SERVER and LOGON
      GROUP

Authentication Mode

You can set the AUTHENTICATION MODE to USE SINGLE-SIGN ON, but this requires your SAP BusinessObjects system to be configured with SAP authentication.

15. You can use the SAVE LANGUAGE option to save your settings as configured in the relational connection. If you leave the checkbox open, the user can influence the language by setting the user preferences in the BI launch pad.

16. Use the ⋯ button next to INFOPROVIDER to receive a list of possible InfoProviders (see Figure 9.7).

Figure 9.7 List of InfoProviders

17. You can use the filter as part of the screen to limit the list of InfoProviders based on the type of InfoProvider:

    ▶ IOBJ = InfoObject

    ▶ CUBE = InfoCube

    ▶ ODSO = Operational Data Store

    ▶ MRPO = MultiProvider

    ▶ VIRT = Virtual InfoProvider

18. In our example we use the MultiProvider 0D_NW_M01 from the NetWeaver demo model.

19. Click OK.

20. Click FINISH.

21. You are asked whether you would like to create a shortcut for your connection. Click Yes.

22. Click CLOSE.

23. Select your local project.

24. Select the FILE • NEW • DATA FOUNDATION menu.

25. Enter a name for the data foundation.

26. Click NEXT.

27. Select the MULTI-SOURCE ENABLED option. The connection to SAP NetWeaver BW is not available when using the single source option.

28. Click NEXT. You are asked to log on to your SAP BusinessObjects system.

29. Enter your credentials.

30. Click NEXT.

31. Select the shortcut that was created for the connection you established previously.

32. Click NEXT (see Figure 9.8).

33. Click ADVANCED.

34. Ensure that the AUTOMATICALLY CREATES TABLES AND JOINS option is activated.

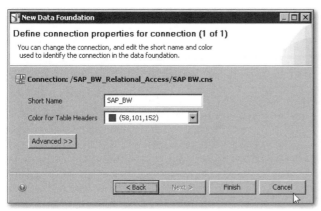

Figure 9.8 Define Connection Properties

35. Click FINISH. You are presented with a default generated star schema for the selected InfoProvider. You can find out more about the known limitations associated with this in Section 3.3.2.

36. Select your local project.

37. Select the FILE • NEW • BUSINESS LAYER menu.

38. Select the RELATIONAL DATA SOURCE entry.

39. Click NEXT.

40. Enter a name for the business layer.

41. Click NEXT.

42. Use the [...] button and select the newly created data foundation (see Figure 9.9).

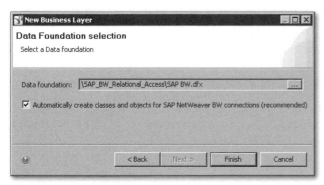

Figure 9.9 New Business Layer

43. Ensure that the AUTOMATICALLY CREATE CLASSES AND OBJECTS FOR SAP NETWEAVER BW CONNECTIONS (RECOMMENDED) option is activated.

44. Click FINISH. You are presented with a list of classes, dimensions, and measures that have been generated based on the information retrieved from SAP NetWeaver BW.

45. Right-click the newly generated business layer entry as part of your local project.

46. Select the PUBLISH • TO A REPOSITORY menu.

47. Select the integrity checks you would like to perform.

48. Click NEXT.

49. Select a folder for the universe.

50. Click FINISH.

51. Click CLOSE.

You have created a universe on top of SAP NetWeaver BW, which you can use in the next steps to create a new information space.

1. Log on to the BI launch pad via the menu START • PROGRAMS • SAP BUSINESS-OBJECTS BI PLATFORM 4 • SAP BUSINESSOBJECTS BI PLATFORM • SAP BUSINESS-OBJECTS BI PLATFORM JAVA BI LAUNCH PAD.

2. Select SAP AS AUTHENTICATION mode.

3. User your SAP credentials to log on.

4. Navigate to the APPLICATIONS menu.

5. Select EXPLORER.

6. Select the MANAGE SPACES menu (see Figure 9.10).

7. Select the previously generated universe.

8. Click NEW.

9. Enter a name for the new information space (see Figure 9.11).

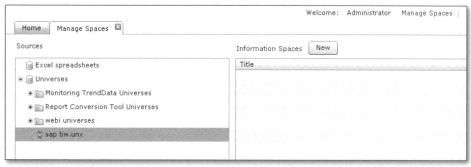

Figure 9.10 Manage Spaces

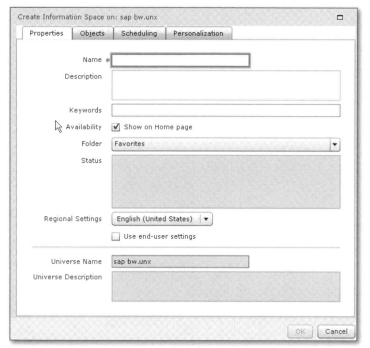

Figure 9.11 Create Information Space

10. Navigate to the OBJECTS tab (see Figure 9.12).

11. You can now add the dimensions and key figures you would like index to the list of facets, measures, and filters. Simply select the objects from the universe and add them to the list of objects on the right-hand side.

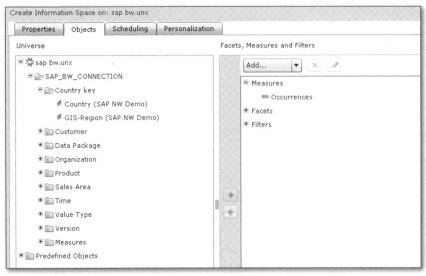

Figure 9.12 Information Space Objects

12. In our example we use the dimensions and measures as shown in Figure 9.13.

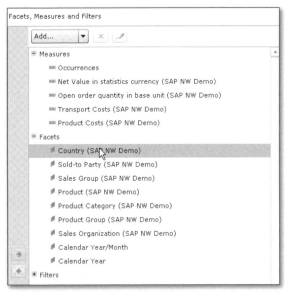

Figure 9.13 Configured Facets

13. Select one of the dimension objects from the FACETS area (see Figure 9.14).

Figure 9.14 Details

14. For each object you can use the DETAILS area on the right-hand side and specify the type of dimension object.

    The SCHEDULING tab allows you to set up a regular scheduling process for the indexing of the data retrieved by the universe.

    The PERSONALIZATION tab allows you to leverage data retrieved from another information space to apply additional data-level security to your newly created information space.

15. Click OK. The new information space is listed now for the data source (see Figure 9.15).

Figure 9.15 Information Space

16. Use the INDEX NOW icon () to create a disk-based index of the data.

    Depending on the data volume, you will receive a positive status update (see Figure 9.16) in a short period of time.

Figure 9.16 Status Successful

17. Navigate to the HOME tab.

18. Click REFRESH.

19. Select your new information space (see Figure 9.17).

Figure 9.17 Information Space

You can now change the visualization type in the lower part, select members of the data set in the upper part, or simply use common words and search for the information with the FIND option in the tools.

In this section you learned how you can leverage a relational universe on top of SAP NetWeaver BW and create your very own information space.

9.4 Summary

In this chapter you received an overview of how you can leverage SAP Business-Objects Explorer in combination with data from your SAP ERP and your SAP NetWeaver BW system. You learned how you can leverage the pre-existing metadata and how you can set up your own information space. In the next chapter we review Live Office and the BI Web Services.

SAP BusinessObjects Live Office and BI Web Services in combination with SAP BusinessObjects Dashboardscan be used for data retrieval.

10 SAP BusinessObjects Live Office and BI Web Services

In this section you will learn how you can use SAP BusinessObjects Live Office and the BI Web Services in combination with SAP BusinessObjects for data retrieval. The focus of the section is not to explain the usage of SAP BusinessObjects Live Office as a plug-in into the Microsoft Office environment, as this would go beyond the scope of this book; the focus here is really to show how you can use SAP BusinessObjects Live Office and BI Web Services to bring data into SAP BusinessObjects Dashboards.

10.1 Using Live Office and BI Web Services

In Chapter 8, you learned about the different data connectivity options for SAP BusinessObjects Dashboards. You learned that you can connect directly from SAP BusinessObjects Dashboards to the BEx query in the SAP NetWeaver BW system. You also learned that you can use the integration with the semantic layer. Both of these options are what we would call "on-demand" options—or "real-time" options—which means that the data shown in the SAP BusinessObjects Dashboard object is retrieved live from the underlying source.

SAP BusinessObjects BI Web Services allows you to retrieve the data from SAP BusinessObjects Web Intelligence 4.x reports or use parts of your reports; for example, you might have a table in an SAP BusinessObjects Web Intelligence report that contains a calculation, and you would like to include the calculation in the dashboard. In addition, BI Web Services allows you to leverage data from an instance; in this way, you can offload the processing of the data to the SAP Business-Objects system, and your dashboard simply leverages the pre-scheduled report.

> ### Using Publications as Part of the Server Environment
>
> A publication is the counterpart to the Information Broadcasting functionality from SAP NetWeaver, and allows you to schedule a report for several users and user groups while still keeping the data-level security intact (because a publication is able to run a single or multi-pass bursting process). There is a functionality gap in BI Web Services when it comes to leveraging publications as part of the SAP BusinessObjects BI platform server environment. BI Web Services is able to leverage a publication (as of release 4.x) only when the outcome of the publication is posted to each user's inbox, which becomes a problem from an administrative point of view because you also have to manage all the instances.
>
> For more on publications, please see Chapter 11.

SAP BusinessObjects Live Office allows you to leverage content from SAP Crystal Reports 2011, SAP BusinessObjects Web Intelligence, and universes inside the Microsoft Office environment. In combination with SAP BusinessObjects Dashboards, you can leverage SAP BusinessObjects Live Office to retrieve data "on-demand" from an SAP Crystal Report 2011 report or an SAP BusinessObjects Web Intelligence report. You can also leverage the data from scheduled instances and from a publication. SAP BusinessObjects Live Office is especially interesting for customers with an investment in SAP Crystal Reports 2011 objects, where they would like to leverage data as part of dashboards. This is because BI Web Services focuses on SAP BusinessObjects Web Intelligence reports only.

In short, both products allow you to leverage "on-demand" data and, to a certain degree, both products allow you to use scheduled reports. In addition, SAP BusinessObjects Live Office allows you to leverage publications, which becomes an important option when preparing dashboards for hundreds of recipients. SAP BusinessObjects Live Office is also able to use SAP Crystal Reports 2011 and SAP BusinessObjects Web Intelligence as sources.

10.2 SAP BusinessObjects Dashboards and SAP Business-Objects Live Office

In this section we use SAP BusinessObjects Live Office in combination with SAP BusinessObjects Dashboards, and treat SAP BusinessObjects Live Office as the data source for our dashboard.

In our example we start with an SAP Crystal Reports 2011 report, which shows the net value per country and product with a grouping done by calendar year (see Figure 10.1).

2006	Country (SAP NW Demo)	Product (SAP NW Demo)	Net Value Value
	Germany	Notebook Standard 15	62,041,979.00
	Germany	Notebook Standard 17	59,551,005.00
	Germany	PDA Standard	34,017,305.00
	Germany	PDA Professional	32,001,759.00
	Germany	Compact Screen 17	46,849,109.00
	Germany	Large Screen 21	49,917,462.00
	France	Notebook Standard 15	54,262,111.00
	France	Notebook Standard 17	49,641,831.00
	France	PDA Standard	24,862,588.00
	France	PDA Professional	27,518,292.00
	France	Compact Screen 17	31,676,233.00
	France	Large Screen 21	31,696,574.00
	United Kingdom	Notebook Basic 15	46,227,927.00
	United Kingdom	Notebook Basic 17	45,361,501.00
	United Kingdom	Easy Hand III	24,543,421.00
	United Kingdom	Easy Hand V	23,194,019.00
	United Kingdom	Ergo Screen	35,769,086.00

Figure 10.1 Sample Report

In the next set of steps we use this report and share the data with SAP Business-Objects Dashboards:

1. Assuming you have SAP BusinessObjects Live Office installed, start Microsoft Excel.

2. Navigate to the LIVE OFFICE ribbon (see Figure 10.2).

Figure 10.2 Live Office Ribbon

3. Select the APPLICATION OPTIONS menu item.

4. Navigate to the ENTERPRISE tab (see Figure 10.3).

Figure 10.3 Options

5. Activate the USE SPECIFIED LOGON CRITERIA option.

6. Enter the web service URL for your SAP BusinessObjects BI platform system. The default URL is *http://< application server>:<port>/dswsbobje/services/session* where the <application server> is replaced with the full qualified name of your Java application server and <port> is replaced with the port number for the application server.

7. Set the AUTHENTICATION to SAP.

8. Click OK.

9. Select the CRYSTAL REPORTS menu option from the LIVE OFFICE ribbon (see Figure 10.4).

10. Log on to your SAP BusinessObjects system with your SAP credentials. If you left the user empty as part of the Application options, you will receive an error message, as SAP BusinessObjects Live Office tries to authenticate the user

entered in the options. The SAP BusinessObjects Live Office dialog does not provide you with separate input options for the SAP system ID and SAP client number; therefore, you need to enter your SAP credentials in the following syntax: <SAP System ID>~<SAP Client number>/<SAP User Name>.

Figure 10.4 Insert Crystal Reports

11. You are presented with the folders from your SAP BusinessObjects system and you can select the report (see Figure 10.5).

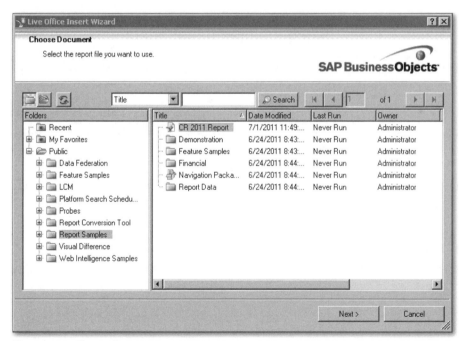

Figure 10.5 Choose Document

12. Select the report from the folder and click NEXT (see Figure 10.6).

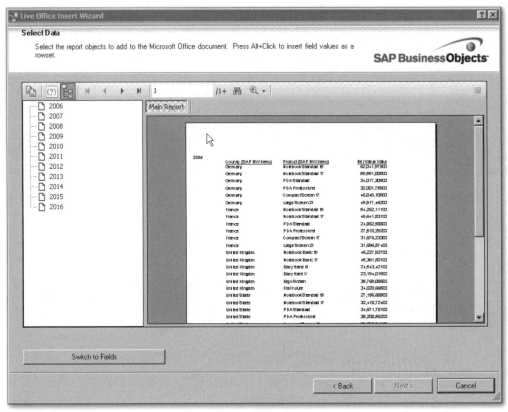

Figure 10.6 Crystal Reports Object

13. The report is shown and you can now select parts of the report. In our case, the raw data is most relevant; therefore, we are most interested in the list of fields. Click SWITCH TO FIELDS (see Figure 10.7).

14. You can now add the fields required for the dashboard to the list of selected fields. For our example, we use the Country dimension and the Net Value key figure.

15. Click NEXT.

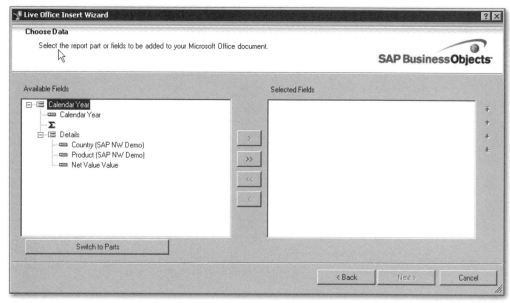

Figure 10.7　List of Fields

16. In this step you can add an additional filter for the result set (see Figure 10.8).

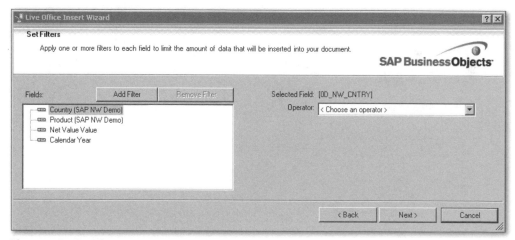

Figure 10.8　Set Filters

17. Click NEXT.
18. Click FINISH (see Figure 10.9).

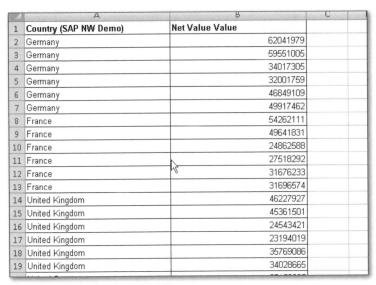

Figure 10.9 Result Set in Live Office

19. Select the REFRESH OPTIONS menu item from the LIVE OFFICE ribbon (see Figure 10.10).

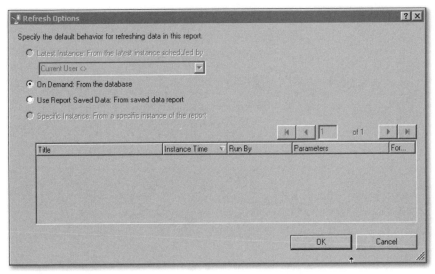

Figure 10.10 Refresh Options

20. Here you can configure whether the report should receive the data on-demand, from an instance, from saved data, or from a specific instance.

21. Use the SAVE TO REPOSITORY menu item from the LIVE OFFICE ribbon (see Figure 10.11).

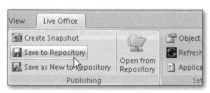

Figure 10.11 Live Office Ribbon

22. Enter a name for the SAP BusinessObjects Live Office object.

23. Click SAVE.

24. Close Microsoft Excel.

25. Select the menu START • PROGRAMS • DASHBOARDS • DASHBOARDS.

26. Create a blank SAP BusinessObjects Dashboards model using the FILE • NEW menu.

27. Select the DATA • IMPORT FROM PLATFORM menu.

28. You receive a warning that any existing data might now be overwritten. Click YES.

29. Log on to your SAP BusinessObjects system.

30. Select the SAP BusinessObjects Live Office document from the previous steps.

31. Click OPEN.

32. Select the DATA • CONNECTIONS menu.

33. Click ADD.

34. Select the LIVE OFFICE CONNECTIONS entry.

35. Select the newly created connection entry (see Figure 10.12).

36. Replace the <webserver> placeholder in the SESSION URL field with the name of your application server for the SAP BusinessObjects system.

37. Navigate to the USAGE tab.

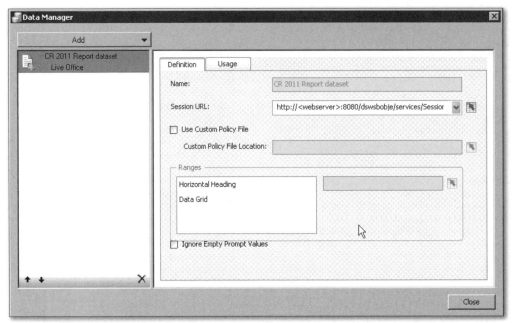

Figure 10.12 Data Manager

38. Activate the REFRESH BEFORE COMPONENTS ARE LOADED option.

39. Click CLOSE.

You now have the data retrieved via SAP BusinessObjects Live Office available in SAP BusinessObjects Dashboards, and you can use all available components to create a dashboard with the retrieved information (see Figure 10.13).

SAP BusinessObjects Live Office inside SAP BusinessObjects Dashboards
In the previous steps, you used SAP BusinessObjects Live Office outside of SAP Business-Objects Dashboards and imported the Live Office document into the SAP BusinessObjects Dashboards environment. You can also activate Live Office inside the SAP BusinessObjects Dashboards environment. In the menu FILE • PREFERENCES, select the EXCEL OPTION category. This allows you to activate the LIVE OFFICE COMPATIBILITY, which enables you to use SAP BusinessObjects Live Office inside of SAP BusinessObjects Dashboards.

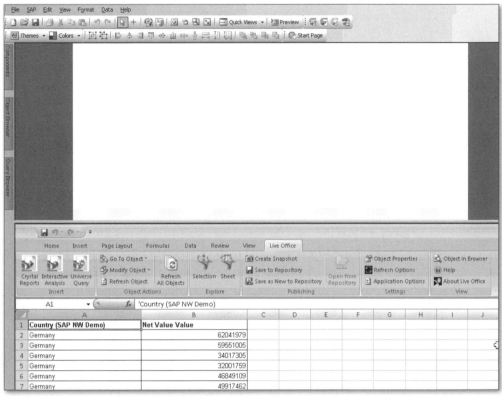

Figure 10.13 SAP BusinessObjects Dashboards

In this section we reviewed the workflow for how you can use SAP BusinessObjects Live Office in combination with SAP BusinessObjects Dashboards, and in that way leverage data from an SAP Crystal Reports 2011 object. In the next section we use BI Web Services and leverage the data from an SAP BusinessObjects Web Intelligence document.

Prompts and Publications

If you would like to leverage prompts of the underlying report as part of the SAP BusinessObjects Live Office and SAP BusinessObjects Dashboards workflow, you can use the OBJECT PROPERTIES menu of the LIVE OFFICE ribbon. As part of the OBJECT PROPERTIES, you will see a PROMPTS tab and you can bind the parameter to the Microsoft Excel spreadsheet. By binding the parameters to the Microsoft Excel spreadsheet, you can also set the values for the parameters from SAP BusinessObjects Dashboards.

SAP BusinessObjects Live Office also allows you to leverage a publication from the SAP BusinessObjects system. If you would like to use a publication as the source for the SAP BusinessObjects Live Office document, you need to open the publication inside SAP BusinessObjects Live Office—not the report itself.

10.3 SAP BusinessObjects Dashboards and BI Web Services

In addition to the direct connectivity to SAP NetWeaver BW, the option to leverage the semantic layer, and the option to use SAP BusinessObjects Live Office, you can also use BI Web Services, which allows you to create a web service based on an SAP BusinessObjects Web Intelligence document. In SAP BusinessObjects 4.x, you can use the universes from the semantic layer directly in SAP BusinessObjects Dashboards. Therefore, the need for a tool such as Query as a Web Service or BI Web Services is reduced. BI Web Services allows you to expose data from an SAP BusinessObjects Web Intelligence report "on-demand," and you can leverage the data from an SAP BusinessObjects Web Intelligence report instance. In addition, BI Web Services allows you to expose blocks from a report; in that way, you can include calculations that are part of the report but not in the semantic layer as part of the web service.

> **Note**
>
> If all the information that you need is part of the semantic layer and you need the data in real-time, there is no need to use BI Web Services. If you may have to include a calculation from a report or leverage a scheduled report instance, that is where BI Web Services can help.

In the next few steps we use BI Web Services to expose the information of an SAP BusinessObjects Web Intelligence report to SAP BusinessObjects Dashboards. We use a report (see Figure 10.14) that uses two separate tables to show net value broken down by country and product, as well as the net value by country, respectively.

Report 1

Country	Product	Net Value
Germany	Notebook Standard 15	703,169,472
	Notebook Standard 17	655,795,216
	PDA Standard	386,231,288
	PDA Professional	358,001,526
	Compact Screen 17	526,710,683
	Large Screen 21	537,045,993
Germany		

Country	Net Value
Germany	3,166,954,178
France	2,459,385,356
United Kingd	2,310,802,482
United States	6,347,269,279

Country	Product	Net Value
France	Notebook Standard 15	599,617,839
	Notebook Standard 17	566,511,465
	PDA Standard	300,017,482
	PDA Professional	302,951,892
	Compact Screen 17	345,028,707

Figure 10.14 SAP BusinessObjects Web Intelligence Report

In the next steps we expose the table showing the net value by country as a web service. With the report open, follow these steps:

1. Select the table showing net value by country in the report. Make sure you select the complete table and not a single cell or column.

2. Right-click the table (see Figure 10.15).

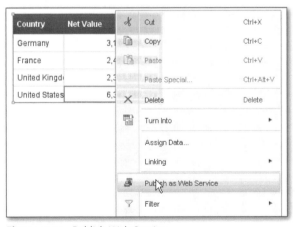

Figure 10.15 Publish Web Service

3. Use the menu item PUBLISH AS WEB SERVICE.

4. The publishing wizard starts. Click NEXT.

5. The wizard checks for any duplicates of web services (see Figure 10.16). Click NEXT.

Figure 10.16   Identify Duplicate Content

6. You can now enter the name for the published content (not the web service); in our example, "Demo" (see Figure 10.17).

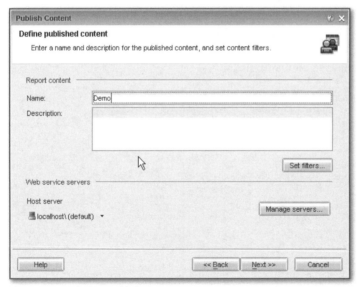

Figure 10.17   Define Publish Content

7. You can also use the MANAGE SERVERS option to decide on which web service server the web service is to be hosted.

8. The SET FILTERS option allows you to select which dimensions and measures will be part of the result set.

9. Click NEXT.

10. Select the new entry (see Figure 10.18).

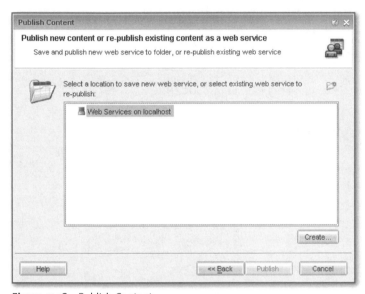

Figure 10.18 Publish Content

11. Click CREATE.

12. Enter a name for the web service (see Figure 10.19). You can also configure the authentication for the web service, which, in our example, is SAP.

13. Click OK. You will receive a status message.

14. Click OK.

15. Click FINISH.

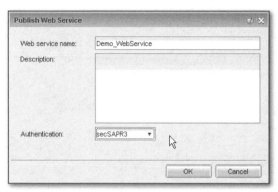

Figure 10.19 Publish Web Service

16. Open the BI WEB SERVICE panel (see Figure 10.20).

Figure 10.20 Web Service Panel

17. Navigate to the newly created web service (see Figure 10.21).

Figure 10.21 Web Service Properties

18. In WEB SERVICE PROPERTIES (see Figure 10.21), you can retrieve the WSDL URL.

19. Copy and paste the URL.

20. Start SAP BusinessObjects Dashboards following the menu START • PROGRAMS • DASHBOARDS • DASHBOARDS.

21. Create a blank SAP BusinessObjects Dashboards model using the FILE • NEW menu.

22. Select the DATA • CONNECTIONS menu.

23. Click ADD.

24. Select the WEB SERVICE QUERY (QUERY AS A WEB SERVICE) entry.

25. Select the newly created connection entry (see Figure 10.22).

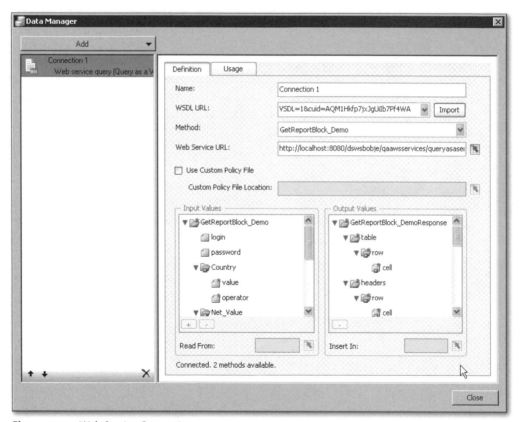

Figure 10.22 Web Service Connection

26. Copy and paste the web service URL into the WSDL URL field.

27. Click IMPORT.

28. Set the method to GETREPORTBLOCK_DEMO. The name of the method also contains the name you configured—in our example, "Demo."

29. The method exposes several parts of the table, such as headers, footers, and the table itself, which allows you to access those parts of the block returned by the web service.

You now have the data retrieved via the BI Web Service in SAP BusinessObjects Dashboards available, and you can use all available components.

BI Web Service Methods

In SAP BusinessObjects Dashboards, BI Web Services does not return information about how many columns will be returned. In our example, the TABLE entry returns the actual data, but you need to ensure that you configure the right number of columns in the spreadsheet based on the definition of the web service.

In this section we reviewed how you can leverage SAP BusinessObjects Live Office and BI Web Services to expose data from the underlying reports to SAP Business-Objects Dashboards.

10.4 Summary

In this chapter we reviewed the option to leverage SAP BusinessObjects Live Office and BI Web Services in combination with SAP BusinessObjects Dashboards, and you learned the steps necessary to use both products as a source for your next dashboard. In the next chapter we set up a publication to create a scheduling process that creates instances for several users but still keeps the data-level security intact in a single step.

Publications provide you with the capability to distribute a report to a large set of users. You can set up your system to run publications with SAP Crystal Reports and SAP BusinessObjects Web Intelligence and still keep security intact.

11 Publications with SAP Data-Level Security

In this chapter we look at how you can use publications on your SAP BusinessObjects system in combination with server-side trust configured on your SAP NetWeaver system to set up a scheduling process that will distribute your report objects to a large number of users. As part of the SAP BusinessObjects 4.x environment, you can establish server-side trust using SNC or you can use the new SSO token service (see Section 2.5.6 of Chapter 2).

11.1 What Is Server-Side Trust?

In your SAP BusinessObjects landscape, you can use server-side trust to set up a publication job for a multi-pass bursting process. This lets you schedule an SAP Crystal Reports or SAP BusinessObjects Web Intelligence object for a large set of SAP roles and users and still keep the SAP data-level security intact.

Server-side trust allows the SAP BusinessObjects system to impersonate other users during the scheduling process without requiring the password for each user account. Impersonation allows the SAP BusinessObjects system to act on behalf of different users or a different security context.

For example, your SAP NetWeaver BW system grants your SAP BusinessObjects system the trust to authenticate with different users in a password-free authentication mode. Your SAP BusinessObjects system can then use the granted trust and the impersonation capability, and can schedule an SAP BusinessObjects Crystal Reports or SAP BusinessObjects Web Intelligence object on behalf of a set of users.

In combination with the publication capabilities of your SAP BusinessObjects system, this means that you can set up a publication process, using the granted trust between your two systems, and create a multi-pass publication process while still ensuring the data-level security that you configured in your SAP system. After the configuration steps, your SAP system grants your SAP BusinessObjects system the trust to execute a report against the SAP system by using impersonation and authenticate with a set of users towards the SAP server without the need for a password.

In order for the SAP BusinessObjects system to perform the above-described process, the actual processing services, such as the SAP Crystal Reports job service and the SAP BusinessObjects Web Intelligence processing service, need to be configured to authenticate with a secure network communication (SNC) account that is also configured to allow impersonation.

In this section, we discuss the components of server-side trust and the steps to configure it.

11.1.1 Server-Side Trust Components

In this section you will learn about the required components to configure server-side trust and the necessary steps involved in configuring the trust your SAP BusinessObjects and SAP systems.

> **Single Sign-On Token Service**
>
> Starting with SAP BusinessObjects 4.0, you can use both the SAP Cryptographic Library and the single sign-on token service in combination with publications. The details of this are explained in Section 2.5.6 and in Section 11.4.

Next we discuss the individual components of server-side trust: the SAP Cryptographic Library and the personal security environment.

SAP Cryptographic Library

SAP delivers the SAP Cryptographic Library, a product used for encryption, as part of your SAP system, and you can use it to configure SNC between server components. After downloading and unpacking the SAP Cryptographic Library software, you receive three main components:

▶ The SAP Cryptographic Library (`sapcrypto.dll` for Windows; `libsapcrypto.<ext>` for UNIX)

▶ A license file `ticket`

▶ The configuration tool `sapgenpse.exe`

SAP Cryptographic Library

You can download the SAP Cryptographic Library from the SAP Service Marketplace (*http://service.sap.com/SWDC*) in the SAP Cryptographic Software area.

For detailed information, see SAP Notes 711093, 597059, and 397175 at *http://service. sap.com/notes.*

You can use the delivered SAP Cryptographic Library for SNC only between server components. If you want to use SNC for frontend components (for example, SAP GUI for Windows), you must purchase an SNC-certified partner product.

Personal Security Environment

A personal security environment (PSE) is a secure location where a user or component's public-key information is stored. The PSE file contains the certificate of the component that created the PSE file and a list of components and parties that are identified as trusted components. It is password-protected to avoid exploits where certificates are added or valid certificates are removed, but operating system credentials can be tied to the PSE file for password-free access.

11.1.2 Steps to Configure Server-Side Trust

Figure 11.1 shows the steps required to deploy and configure server-side trust between your SAP system and your SAP BusinessObjects system. The list below offers an overview of the steps involved; the subsequent sections go into more detail.

1. Deploy and configure the SAP Cryptographic Library on your SAP Business-Objects system.

2. Generate a PSE file and a certificate from your SAP BusinessObjects system.

3. Import the certificate file from your SAP BusinessObjects system to the Trust Manager of your SAP system.

4. Export a certificate file from your SAP system.

5. Import the certificate file from your SAP system to the PSE file from your SAP BusinessObjects system.

6. Grant the credentials used to run the SAP BusinessObjects services access to the PSE file from the SAP BusinessObjects system.

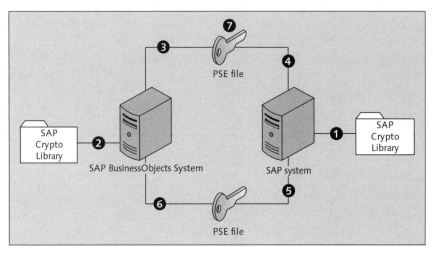

Figure 11.1 Server-Side Trust

11.2   Configuring Your SAP Server for Server-Side Trust

In the following sections we describe how you prepare your SAP system for server-side trust. This involves four main steps:

1. Deploying the SAP Cryptographic Library.

2. Configuring profile parameters for your SAP system.

3. Configuring the Trust Manager for your SAP system.

4. Configuring additional profile parameters.

We go through these steps in detail in Sections 11.2.1 to 11.2.4.

11.2.1 Deploying and Configuring the SAP Cryptographic Library

As the first step, you need to deploy and configure the SAP Cryptographic Library in your SAP system.

1. Download and unpack the SAP Cryptographic Library for your SAP system according to the platform of your SAP system.

2. On your SAP server, copy the SAP Cryptographic Library to the folder *\usr\sap\<SID>\SYS\exe\run*, where the placeholder <SID> represents your System ID—in our example, CIM.

3. On your SAP server, copy the `ticket` file that is part of the SAP Cryptographic Library to the folder *\usr\sap\<SID>\<instance>\sec*, where the placeholder <SID> needs to be replaced with your system ID (in our example, CIM), and the placeholder <instance> needs to be replaced with the instance number (in our example, 00).

4. Create a SECUDIR environment variable pointing to the path for the `ticket` file from the previous step. This environment variable needs to be accessible by the user account that is used to run the dispatcher process for your SAP system.

Folder Structure

The folder structure mentioned above should already exist based on the installation of your SAP system. You might have changed the base folder or some of the naming; therefore, we always refer to the basic installation folders here.

11.2.2 Configuring Profile Parameters

Next, you must configure profile parameters.

1. Log on to your SAP system.

2. Start Transaction RZ10 to go to the server profile parameters (see Figure 11.2).

3. Select the instance profile and select EXTENDED MAINTENANCE.

4. Click the CHANGE button.

Figure 11.2 Profile Parameters

5. Add the profile parameters and values, according to Table 11.1, to the profile settings and value of your SAP system.

Profile Parameter	Value
ssf/name	SAPSECULIB
ssf/ssfapi_lib	Enter the full path, including the file name to the SAP Cryptographic Library on your SAP server.
sec/libsapsecu	Enter the full path, including the file name to the SAP Cryptographic Library on your SAP server.
snc/gssapi_lib	Enter the full path, including the file name to the SAP Cryptographic Library on your SAP server.
snc/identity/as	Enter the distinguished name (DN) for your SAP system.

Table 11.1 SAP Server Profile Parameters and Values

6. Make sure that the distinguished name (DN) of your SAP system follows the *Lightweight Directory Access Protocol* (LDAP) naming convention according to Table 11.2.

In our example, the Distinguished Name could look like this:

```
p:CN=CIM;OU=PM;O=SAP;C=CA
```

In this case, CIM is the system ID of our example SAP server, PM stands for product management, SAP is the name of the organization, and CA stands for "Canada."

Tag	Meaning	Description
CN	Common name	Name of the certificate proprietor
OU	Organizational unit	Name of the organizational unit
O	Organization	Name of the organization
C	Country	Country in which the proprietor resides

Table 11.2 Distinguished Name Values

7. After making these changes, restart your SAP system.

SAP Cryptographic Library and Distinguished Names

When referring to the distinguished name of your SAP system, ensure that you always include the "p:" in front of the name.

11.2.3 Configuring the Trust Manager

Next, configure the Trust Manager.

1. After you restart your SAP server, log on to your SAP system.

2. Start Transaction STRUST to start the Trust Manager for your SAP system. You should now have two additional entries on the left side: one entry for SNC SAPCryptolib and entries for SSL (*Secure Sockets Layer*).

3. Right-click on the SNC SAPCryptolib entry and select CREATE (see Figure 11.3).

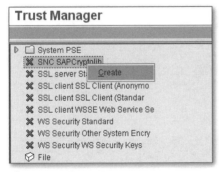

Figure 11.3 Trust Manager

335

4. The distinguished name (SNC ID) of your SAP system should show up now (see Figure 11.4). Click OK.

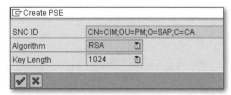

Figure 11.4 Create PSE

5. Open the SNC SAP CRYPTOLIB folder.

6. Double-click the entry shown in the folder.

7. Click the PASSWORD button (see Figure 11.5). Now you need to assign a password to the PSE file. Each time you try to view or edit the content of the PSE file, you are prompted for the password. Click SAVE.

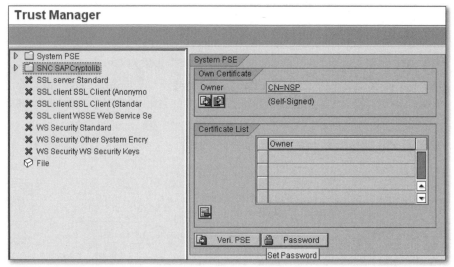

Figure 11.5 Password

Important Note

If you skip the two previous steps (assigning a password and saving the changes), your SAP server won't start after you enable SNC.

11.2.4 Configuring Additional Profile Parameters

Finally, you must configure additional profile parameters.

1. Log on to your SAP system.

2. Start Transaction RZ10 to go to the server profile parameters.

3. Select the instance profile and select EXTENDED MAINTENANCE. Click the CHANGE button.

4. Add the profile parameters and values according to Table 11.3.

Profile Parameter	Value
snc/accept_insecure_rfc	1
snc/accept_insecure_r3int_rfc	1
snc/accept_insecure_gui	1
snc/accept_insecure_cpic	1
snc/permit_insecure_start	1
snc/data_protection/min	1
snc/data_protection/max	3
snc/enable	1

Table 11.3 SAP Server Profile Parameters and Values

5. The snc/accept_insecure_* parameters and values are set to ensure that previous, unsecure communication methods are still permitted. The snc/data_protection parameter is set to the minimum value (1) for authentication and to the maximum value (3) for privacy.

6. Restart your SAP system.

11.3 Configuring Your SAP BusinessObjects System for Server-Side Trust

In the following sections we describe how to prepare your SAP BusinessObjects system for server-side trust. This involves several steps:

1. Deploying the SAP Cryptographic Library in your SAP BusinessObjects system.

2. Generating a PSE file and certificate file for your SAP BusinessObjects system.

3. Importing the certificate file with the Trust Manager of your SAP system.

4. Exporting the SAP server certificate file.

5. Adding an entry to the SNC access control list.

6. Importing the SAP server certificate file to the SAP BusinessObjects PSE file.

7. Granting access to the SAP BusinessObjects PSE file.

8. Configuring the SAP BusinessObjects services.

9. Configuring the SNC options in the Central Management Console.

11.3.1 Deploying and Configuring the SAP Cryptographic Library

As the first step, you need to deploy and configure the SAP Cryptographic Library in your SAP BusinessObjects system.

1. Download and unpack the SAP Cryptographic Library for your SAP Business-Objects system according to the platform of your SAP BusinessObjects system (for example, Microsoft Windows, Sun Solaris, IBM AIX).

2. Log on with an administrative account to the operating system of your SAP BusinessObjects system.

3. Create the folder *<Drive>:\Program files\SAP\CRYPTO*. This is just an example. You can select the location and create your own folder.

4. Add the folder that you created to the PATH environment variable on your SAP BusinessObjects system.

5. Copy the SAP Cryptographic Library (*sapcrypto.dll*) to the folder you just created.

6. Copy the PSE tool (*sapgenpse.exe*) to the same folder.

7. Add a system-wide variable named SNC_LIB with the value pointing to the complete path, including the file name of the SAP Cryptographic Library; in our example, *<Drive>:\Program files\SAP\CRYPTO\sapcrypto.dll*.

8. Add a subfolder called *SEC* to the previously created folder; in our example, *<Drive>:\Program files\SAP\CRYPTO\SEC*.

9. Add a system-wide variable, SECUDIR, with the value pointing to the subfolder.

10. Copy the `ticket` file from the SAP Cryptographic Library to the subfolder.

11.3.2 Generating PSE Files

Now that you've configured the SAP Cryptographic Library, you can generate a PSE file and export it as a certificate so that the trust manager from your SAP system can import it.

1. Log on with an administrative account to the operating system of your SAP BusinessObjects system.

2. Open a command prompt.

3. Navigate to the folder into which you copied the PSE maintenance tool (*sapgenpse.exe*); in our example, *<Drive>:\Program Files\SAP\CRYPTO*.

4. Use the following command to generate a PSE file for your SAP BusinessObjects system:

```
sapgenpse.exe gen_pse -v -p BOE.pse
```

In this command, *BOE.pse* represents the file name for the PSE file.

5. The system asks you to configure a PIN code to secure the PSE file. Provide a PIN code and enter the PIN a second time (see Figure 11.6).

```
C:\Program Files\SAP\CRYPTO>sapgenpse.exe gen_pse -v -p BOE.pse
 Got absolute PSE path "C:\Program Files\SAP\CRYPTO\SEC\BOE.pse".
Please enter PIN:
```

Figure 11.6 Generating a PSE File

6. In the next step, you are asked to provide a distinguished name (DN) for your SAP BusinessObjects system. The distinguished name should follow the LDAP naming convention (see Table 11.2 for details). At this command, you do not have to enter the name with the "p:" prefix.

In our example, this is

```
CN=BOESERVER,OU=PM,O=SAP,C=CA
```

7. Press ⌷Enter⌷ to confirm your distinguished name for the SAP BusinessObjects system.

8. As the final step in generating the PSE file, you should see a window similar to Figure 11.7, and you should have a PSE file located in the folder *<Drive>:\ Program files\SAP\CRYPTO\SEC*.

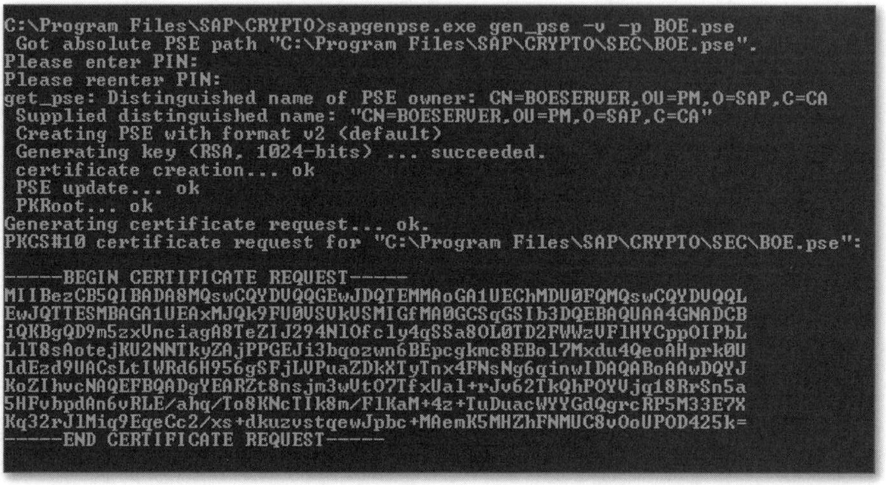

Figure 11.7 Final Step in PSE Generation

9. Next you need to export the PSE file into a certificate so that the Trust Manager from your SAP system can import it. You can use the following command to export the PSE file:

```
sapgenpse.exe export_own_cert -v -p BOE.pse
  -o myBOEcertificate.cert
```

In this command, BOE.pse represents the PSE file you generated for your SAP BusinessObjects system in the previous steps, and myBOEcertificate.cert is the file name for the certificate.

10. You are asked to enter the previously configured PIN. Do so.

You should now have the PSE file for your SAP BusinessObjects system in the folder *<Drive>:\Program files\SAP\CRYPTO\SEC*, and you should have the certificate file in the folder *<Drive>:\Program files\SAP\CRYPTO*.

11.3.3 Importing the Certificate File with Trust Manager

Next you need to import the exported certificate from your SAP BusinessObjects system via the Trust Manager of your SAP system, and then you can export the SAP system PSE to a certificate file.

1. Log on to your SAP system and start Transaction STRUST.

2. Open the SNC SAPCryptolib folder entry.

3. Double-click your server entry and enter the password that you configured previously.

4. Click the Import Certificate button (see Figure 11.8).

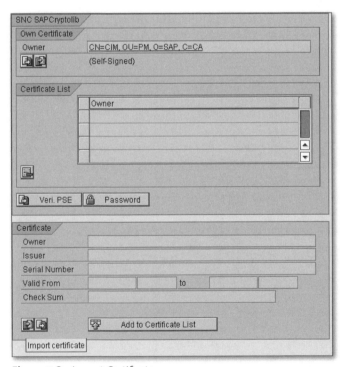

Figure 11.8 Import Certificate

5. Select the certificate file from your SAP BusinessObjects system and then select Base64 (see Figure 11.9). Click OK.

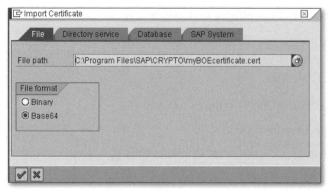

Figure 11.9 File Configuration for Import

6. Return to the screen shown in Figure 11.8. Click the ADD TO CERTIFICATE LIST button. The distinguished name of your SAP BusinessObjects system should now appear in the list on the top screen (see Figure 11.10).

Figure 11.10 Updated Certificate List

7. Click SAVE and close Transaction STRUST.

You have just imported the certificate from your SAP BusinessObjects system to your SAP system. The next step is to export the certificate from your SAP system so that you can import it to the PSE file of your SAP BusinessObjects system.

1. Log on to your SAP system and start Transaction STRUST.

2. Open the folder entry SNC SAPCRYPTOLIB.

3. Double-click your server entry and enter the password that you configured previously.

4. Double-click the top entry of the SAP server, OWN CERTIFICATE (see Figure 11.11).

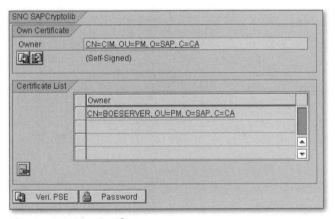

Figure 11.11 Own Certificate

5. The distinguished name of your SAP system should now be listed in the bottom list of certificates (see Figure 11.12). Click the EXPORT CERTIFICATE icon (▣), and you are presented with a screen similar to Figure 11.9.

Figure 11.12 Export Certificate

6. Select a path and file name with the extension *.cert*.

7. Select BASE64 and click OK.

8. Close Transaction STRUST.

11.3.4 SNC Access Control List

Before you import the certificate from your SAP server into the PSE file of your SAP BusinessObjects system, you need to create a system ID as part of the SNC access control list (ACL).

1. Log on to your SAP system and start Transaction SNC0 (see Figure 11.13).

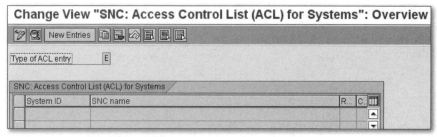

Figure 11.13 SNC Access Control List

2. Click the NEW ENTRIES button, and you'll see the configuration screen for a new entry (see Figure 11.14).

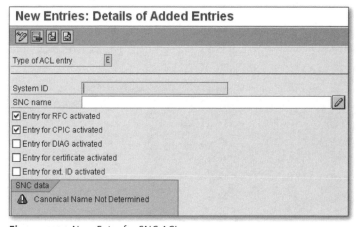

Figure 11.14 New Entry for SNC ACL

3. Enter the name of your SAP BusinessObjects system as the system ID.

4. Enter the distinguished name that you configured previously for your SAP BusinessObjects server in the SNC name field. This time you need to enter the prefix "p:". In our example, this is:

```
p:CN=BOESERVER,OU=PM,O=SAP,C=CA
```

5. Select the ENTRY FOR RFC ACTIVATED and ENTRY FOR EXT. ID ACTIVATED checkboxes (see Figure 11.15) and click SAVE.

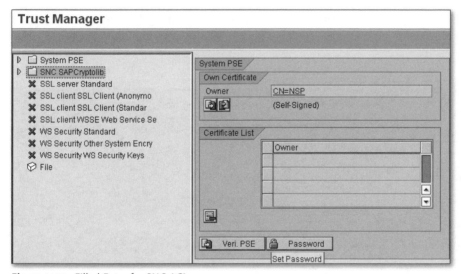

Figure 11.15 Filled Entry for SNC ACL

At this point you've configured your SAP BusinessObjects system as a system ID that can use SNC and impersonation to log on with external IDs.

11.3.5 Importing SAP Server PSE Files

Next, you need to import the SAP server certificate to the PSE file from your SAP BusinessObjects system.

1. Log on with an administrative account to the operating system of your SAP BusinessObjects system.

2. Copy the SAP server certificate to the folder where you copied the PSE maintenance tool; in our example, *<Drive>:\Program Files\SAP\CRYPTO*.

3. Open a command box and navigate to the folder where you copied the PSE maintenance tool; in our example, *<Drive>:\Program Files\SAP\CRYPTO*.

4. Use the following command to add the certificate to the PSE file of your SAP BusinessObjects system:

```
sapgenpse.exe maintain_pk -v -a SAPServer.cert -p BOE.pse
```

In this command, `SAPServer.cert` represents the file name of the SAP server certificate, and `BOE.pse` represents the file name of the PSE file from your SAP BusinessObjects system.

5. When prompted, enter the PIN code that you configured previously. You should then see the distinguished name of your SAP server as an added entry (see Figure 11.16).

```
C:\Program Files\SAP\CRYPTO>sapgenpse.exe maintain_pk -v -a SAPServer.cert -p BO
E.pse
  Opening PSE "C:\Program Files\SAP\CRYPTO\SEC\BOE.pse"...
  No SSO credentials found for this PSE.
Please enter PIN:
  PSE (v2) open ok.
  retrieving PKList
  Adding new certificate from file "SAPServer.cert"

Subject : CN=CIM, OU=PM, O=SAP, C=CA
Issuer  : CN=CIM, OU=PM, O=SAP, C=CA
Serialno: 20:08:12:27:01:59:46
KeyInfo : RSA, 1024-bit
Validity  -  NotBefore:    Sat Dec 27 01:59:46 2008 (081227015946Z)

             NotAfter:     Fri Jan 01 00:00:01 2038 (380101000001Z)

  PKList updated (1 entries total, 1 newly added)
```

Figure 11.16 Added Certificate

11.3.6 Granting Access to the PSE File

Before your SAP BusinessObjects service can use the PSE file that you created for your SAP BusinessObjects system, you need to grant access to a specific user account, which you then can use to run the services. In the following steps we use the administrator account from the system, but you can use any other account, and the steps are identical.

1. Log on with the account for which you want to grant access to the operating system of your SAP BusinessObjects system.

2. Open a command box and navigate to the folder for the PSE maintenance tool; in our example, *<Drive>:\Program Files\SAP\CRYPTO*.

3. Use the following command to grant access to the logged-on user:

```
sapgenpse.exe seclogin -p BOE.pse
```

In this command, `BOE.pse` represents the file name for the PSE file of your SAP BusinessObjects system.

4. Enter your previously configured PIN code. If this is successful, the logged-on user is granted access to the PSE file. Use the following command for verification:

```
sapgenpse.exe maintain_pk -l
```

If the user was granted the access, you can view the content of the PSE file without being asked for the PIN code.

Adding Other User Accounts

If you want to add a user other than the user that is currently logged on, you can use the following command:

```
sapgenpse.exe seclogin -p BOE.pse -O <domain\username>
```

In this command, `BOE.pse` represents the PSE file of your SAP BusinessObjects system, and the placeholder `<domain\username>` represents the domain user to which you can grant access.

11.3.7 Configuring SAP BusinessObjects Services

The next step is to configure your SAP BusinessObjects services to run under the account to which you granted access to the PSE file. The services that require access to the PSE file in this scenario are the processing services for SAP Crystal Reports and SAP BusinessObjects Web Intelligence.

Starting with release XI 3.0 of SAP BusinessObjects, the services are no longer configured in the Central Configuration Manager; instead, you now have an SIA, which acts as a parent process, and the assigned services use the credentials from the SIA.

You now have three options for configuring this step:

▶ You can configure a single SIA for your SAP BusinessObjects system and configure it to run under the credentials that have access to the PSE file. This is the easiest way, but it is also the least secure—because now all of the services of your SAP BusinessObjects system have access to the PSE file, which is not necessary.

▶ You can create a second SIA for your SAP BusinessObjects system and add the processing service for SAP Crystal Reports and SAP BusinessObjects Web Intelligence to this new SIA. You can then remove the original processing services for SAP Crystal Reports and SAP BusinessObjects Web Intelligence. In this way, all of your content is processed on services with access to the PSE file.

▶ You also create a second SIA for your SAP BusinessObjects system, but you don't remove the original entries for the processing services. In this option, you create server groups to differentiate between the two groups of processing services.

We will configure our example system according to the third option. Because the other options follow the same concepts, you should also be able to set up the other options based on the steps outlined here.

1. Start the Central Configuration Manager of your SAP BusinessObjects system (START • PROGRAMS • SAP BUSINESSOBJECTS BI PLATFORM 4 • SAP BUSINESSOBJECTS BI PLATFORM • CENTRAL CONFIGURATION MANAGER).

2. Click the ADD NODE icon (🖘) on the Central Configuration Manager toolbar (see Figure 11.17).

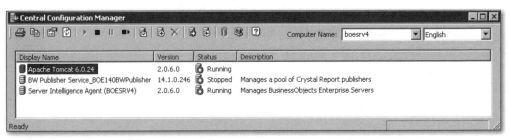

Figure 11.17 Central Configuration Manager

3. Click NEXT.

4. Enter the name of your new SIA and the port number. In our example we'll use "SAPProcessingServices" for the name and "6420" for the port number (see Figure 11.18).

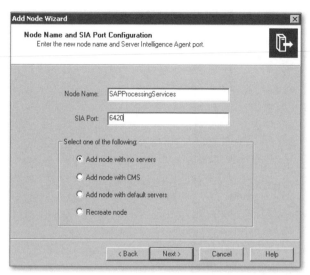

Figure 11.18 Adding the SIA

5. Select the ADD NODE WITH NO SERVERS option.

6. Click NEXT.

7. In the next screen select the USE EXISTING CMS option.

8. Click NEXT.

9. Use the SPECIFY button and point your new SIA to the already existing system database.

10. Click NEXT.

11. After a successful authentication with your SAP BusinessObjects system, you are presented with a summary. Click the FINISH button to add your new SIA (SAPPROCESSINGSERVICE) to the system (see Figure 11.19).

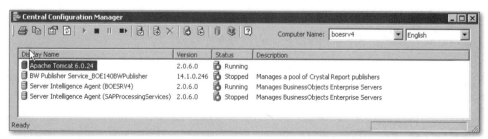

Figure 11.19 Central Configuration Manager

12. Select your new SIA and click the PROPERTIES icon (![]) (see Figure 11.20).

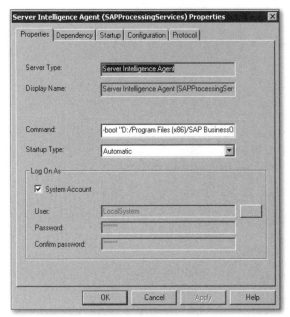

Figure 11.20 SIA Properties

13. De-select the LOG ON AS SYSTEM ACCOUNT checkbox and enter the credentials to which you granted access to the PSE file; in our example, the administrator account.

14. Click OK and start the newly created SIA.

15. Now you need to add the processing services to the newly created SIA. To do so, log on to the Central Management Console of your SAP BusinessObjects system.

16. Navigate to the SERVERS area.

17. Follow the menu path MANAGE • NEW • NEW SERVER (see Figure 11.21).

Figure 11.21 Create New Server

18. In the following pop-up, select CRYSTAL REPORTS SERVICES as SERVICE CATEGORY.

19. Select CRYSTAL REPORTS SCHEDULING SERVICE as SERVICE.

20. Click NEXT twice.

21. Select the newly created SIA as the NODE for the new SAP Crystal Reports service (see Figure 11.22).

Figure 11.22 SIA Assignment

22. Click the CREATE button.

23. Repeat the steps for adding a new server for the additional services according to Table 11.4.

Service Category	Service Entry
Crystal Reports	Crystal Reports Scheduling Service
Crystal Reports	Crystal Reports Processing Service
Crystal Reports	Crystal Reports Cache Service
Web Intelligence	Web Intelligence Processing Service
Web Intelligence	Web Intelligence Scheduling and Publishing Service

Table 11.4 Additional Services

24. After you add all of the additional services, select the SERVERS LIST entry.

25. Follow the menu path ACTIONS • ENABLE SERVERS. After you enable all of the services, select all of the additional services again and follow the menu path ACTIONS • START SERVER.

26. Now navigate to the SERVER GROUPS area on the left-hand side.

27. Follow the menu path MANAGE • NEW • CREATE SERVER GROUP (see Figure 11.23).

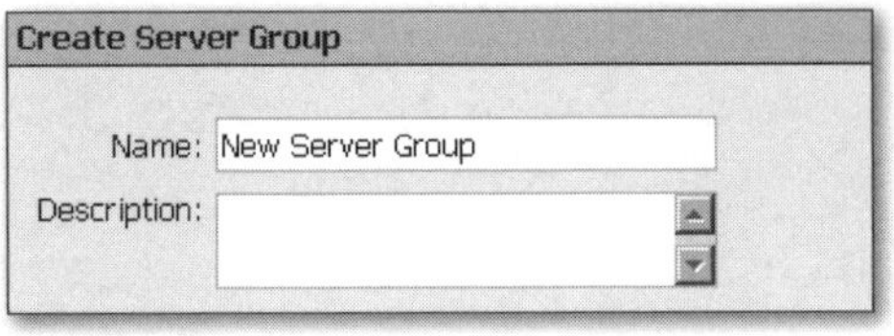

Figure 11.23 Create New Server Group

28. Enter a name for the new server group; in our example, "SAPProcessingGroup". Then click OK.

29. Right-click the newly created SAPPROCESSINGGROUP server group and select the ADD MEMBERS menu.

30. Add the following services to your server group:

   ▶ All six previously created services assigned to your second SIA

   ▶ Adaptive job server

   ▶ Adaptive processing server

   ▶ Destination delivery scheduling server

   ▶ Publication scheduling server

   By adding these services to your server group, you'll be able to use the server group during the scheduling process, and you can ensure that the report is scheduled on the services that have been configured properly.

You've now created an SIA controlling the user account for your processing services, and you've also created a server group with all the necessary services to be able to create a publication for SAP Crystal Reports and SAP BusinessObjects Web Intelligence.

11.3.8 SNC Options in the Central Management Console

To finalize the SNC configuration, you need to provide the details of the SNC options as part of the SAP authentication in the Central Management Console.

1. Log on to the Central Management Console of your SAP BusinessObjects system.

2. Navigate to the AUTHENTICATION area and select the SAP authentication.

3. Navigate to the SNC SETTINGS tab and ensure that your SAP system is selected as LOGICAL SYSTEM NAME (see Figure 11.24).

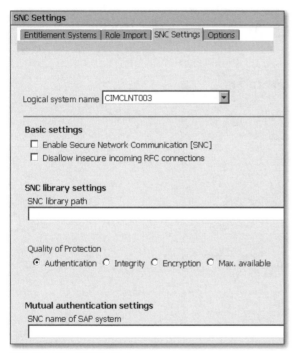

Figure 11.24 SNC Settings

4. Select the ENABLE SECURE NETWORK COMMUNICATION [SNC] checkbox under BASIC SETTINGS.

5. Enter the full path to the SNC library, including the filename in the SNC LIBRARY PATH field under SNC LIBRARY SETTINGS.

6. Select AUTHENTICATION under QUALITY OF PROTECTION.

7. Enter the distinguished name of your SAP system in the SNC NAME OF SAP SYSTEM field under MUTUAL AUTHENTICATION SETTINGS. In this case, you need to add the prefix "p:".

SNC Name of the SAP System

You can verify the SNC name of your SAP system in Transaction RZ10 by viewing the value for the profile parameter snc/identity/as.

---

8. Enter the distinguished name of your SAP BusinessObjects system in the SNC NAME OF ENTERPRISE SYSTEM field under TRUST SETTINGS (see Figure 11.25). In this case, you need to add the prefix "p:".

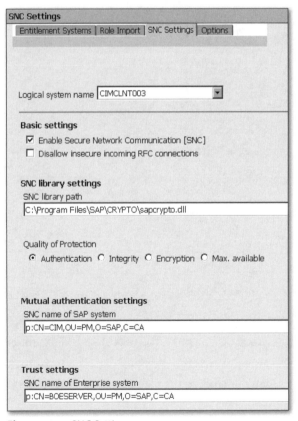

Figure 11.25 SNC Settings

So far, you have learned how to do the following:

▶ Deploy and configure the SAP Cryptographic Library on your SAP system.

▶ Deploy and configure the SAP Cryptographic Library on your SAP Business-Objects system.

▶ Exchange certificates between your SAP and SAP BusinessObjects systems to establish trust between them.

▶ Create a system ID in the SNC ACL to allow password-free impersonation for your SAP BusinessObjects system.

▶ Add a new SIA to your SAP BusinessObjects system, and add the processing tier for SAP Crystal Reports and SAP BusinessObjects Web Intelligence.

▶ Configure the SNC options for your SAP system in the Central Management Console.

You are now ready to create a publication for an SAP Crystal Reports or SAP Business-Objects Web Intelligence object on your SAP BusinessObjects system.

11.4 Creating Publications with SAP Crystal Reports and SAP BusinessObjects Web Intelligence

In this section you'll learn how to create a publication for an SAP Crystal Reports or SAP BusinessObjects Web Intelligence object. A publication allows you to schedule an object for a large set of user groups or users, and define specific rules about the output format and delivery to each of the recipients. In combination with the now-configured server-side trust, you can use a publication to schedule an SAP Crystal Reports or SAP BusinessObjects Web Intelligence object by retaining the data-level security from your SAP system without the need to replicate it. This is because the SAP BusinessObjects system can now act on behalf of the SAP users in a password-free way, and thus schedule the report for each SAP user (*multi-pass bursting*). Those more familiar with the SAP side than the SAP BusinessObjects side can compare a publication with the Information Broadcasting functionality offered as part of SAP NetWeaver BW.

You can use the publication and the configured server-side trust without any data-level security defined in your SAP system, but in the next couple of steps we make the following assumptions:

▶ You configured the characteristic material for the *0D_SD_C03* cube from our BEx query to be authorization-relevant.

▶ You added an authorization variable to the BEx query for the characteristic material.

▶ You created a new SAP Crystal Reports for Enterprise or SAP BusinessObjects Web Intelligence object based on this changed BEx query, and the report is available in SAP BusinessObjects.

▶ You configured two roles with the following data-level security (see Table 11.5).

    ▶ USER_A is assigned to the role BUSINESSOBJECTS_AUTH_ROLE_01.

    ▶ USER_B is assigned to the role BUSINESSOBJECTS_AUTH_ROLE_02.

Role Name	Assigned Values for Material
BUSINESSOBJECTS_AUTH_ROLE_01	CN00S1—Notebook Speedy I CN CN00S2—Notebook Speedy II CN
BUSINESSOBJECTS_AUTH_ROLE_02	CN0400—Terminal P400 CN CN0600—Terminal P600 CN
BUSINESSOBJECTS_CONTENT_ROLE	All values

Table 11.5 Authorization Roles with Values

These are only examples for a configuration of data-level security so that we can use these settings for our publications in the following steps.

1. Log on to the Central Management Console of your SAP BusinessObjects system.

2. Navigate to the Authentication area and select SAP.

3. Navigate to the Options tab and ensure that the user type for the role import matches your licensing model (see Figure 11.26).

4. Navigate to the Role Import tab and ensure that your SAP system is the selected system for the Logical System Name.

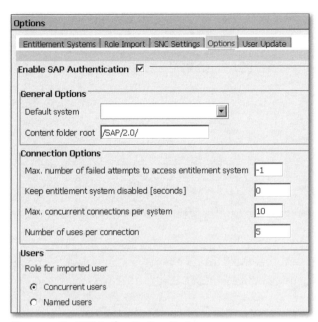

Figure 11.26 SAP Authentication Options

5. Import the roles listed in Table 11.5 into your SAP BusinessObjects system.

Imported SAP Roles and Users and Publications

A publication can be configured to leverage user groups and individual users as recipients. If you use the imported SAP roles, you need to ensure that the users for those roles have also been imported. You can use the USER UPDATE tab as part of the SAP authentication to update the assigned users of the imported SAP roles.

If the users aren't imported, the publication won't process the user group, because the user group does not have any users assigned to it.

6. Now navigate to the FOLDERS area.

7. Navigate to the folder of the report you created for this exercise.

8. Follow the menu path MANAGE • NEW • NEW PUBLICATION (see Figure 11.27).

9. Enter a title and description for your new publication.

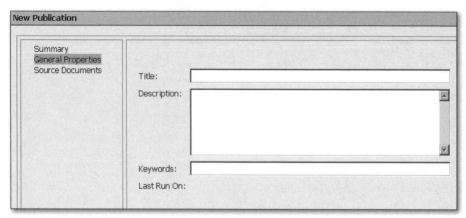

Figure 11.27 New Publication

10. Click SOURCE DOCUMENTS. A screen comes up where you can select the documents that you'll use for your publication (see Figure 11.28).

Figure 11.28 New Publication – Source Documents

11. Click ADD and select the SAP Crystal Reports for Enterprise (or SAP Business-Objects Web Intelligence) document that you created on the changed BW query. After you added the document, the screen will change to provide additional options, as you can see in Figure 11.29.

12. Click ENTERPRISE RECIPIENTS (see Figure 11.29).

13. Click GROUP LIST and add the following user groups as recipients to the SELECTED area:

   ▶ CIM~003@BUSINESSOBJECTS_CONTENT_ROLE

   ▶ CIM~003@BUSINESSOBJECTS_AUTH_ROLE_01

   ▶ CIM~003@BUSINESSOBJECTS_AUTH_ROLE_02

In your SAP BusinessObjects system, the prefix of the roles reflects the logical system name of your SAP system.

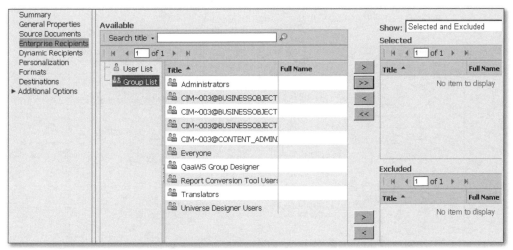

Figure 11.29 New Publication—Enterprise Recipients

14. Click DESTINATIONS in the menu on the left (see Figure 11.30). Here you can define where the output of the process is going to be delivered. The default option is DEFAULT ENTERPRISE LOCATION, which means the output will be delivered to the same location where the source document is being stored. In our example, we also check the BI INBOX checkbox so that each recipient will receive the output directly to the INBOX folder in his SAP BusinessObjects system.

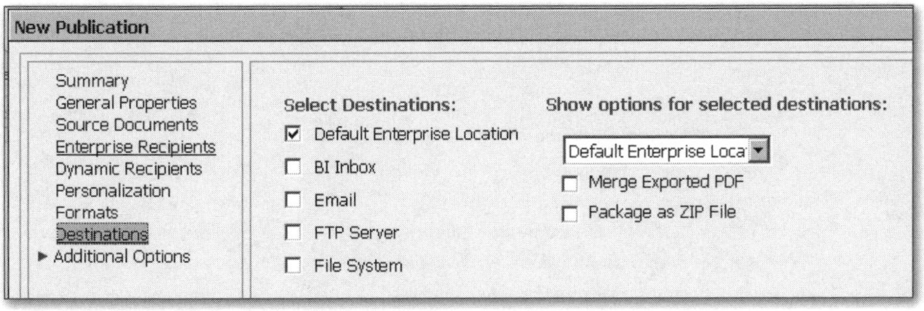

Figure 11.30 New Publication – Destinations

15. Next, open the list of ADDITIONAL OPTIONS in the left-hand menu, and in the dropdown list, select SCHEDULING SERVER GROUP (see Figure 11.31). Select the server group that you created previously under the ONLY USE SERVERS BELONGING TO THE SELECTED GROUP checkbox.

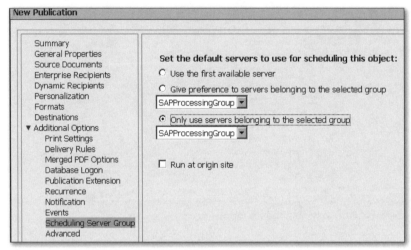

Figure 11.31 New Publication—Scheduling Server Group

16. Select ADVANCED in the list of ADDITIONAL OPTIONS (see Figure 11.32).

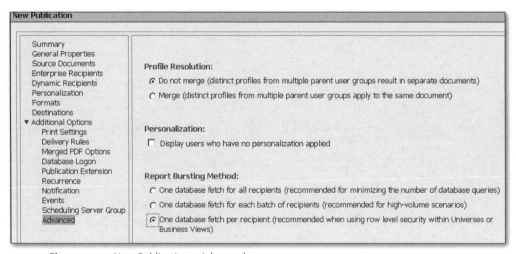

Figure 11.32 New Publication – Advanced

17. Select ONE DATABASE FETCH PER RECIPIENT. In this way, you create a multi-pass bursting process.

18. Click SAVE & CLOSE. Your publication appears in the folder.

19. Next select the publication in the folder and follow the menu path ACTIONS • SCHEDULE.

20. The scheduling screen appears with all of the settings you configured. You can go through them to verify them.

21. Click SCHEDULE to start the process of your publication. When the publication is finished, you should see the message "SUCCESS" and you should be able to log on with the SAP credentials to InfoView and see the output of the process in the inbox of each recipient.

Scheduling SAP BusinessObjects Web Intelligence Documents

When you try to schedule an SAP BusinessObjects Web Intelligence document, you'll see that there is no option for you to enter the user credentials that will be used during the scheduling process. There are two options available to you to successfully schedule a SAP BusinessObjects Web Intelligence document:

▶ The first option is to set up the connection for your SAP BusinessObjects Web Intelligence document to use a set of hard-coded credentials, which results in a scheduling process always using those credentials.

▶ The second option is to configure the connection to use single sign-on, to ensure that the required users are imported via the SAP authentication as proper SAP Business-Objects users. You can then also use the server-side trust as described above for a normal scheduling process. You do not have to create a publication, but the server-side trust configuration needs to be in place so that a user can use his SAP credentials and schedule an SAP BusinessObjects Web Intelligence document.

In this section you learned how to leverage a server-side trust configuration based on SNC in combination with a publication. SAP BusinessObjects 4.x also offers you an alternative for the server-side trust configuration, as shown in Section 2.5.6. You can also use this newly available SSO token service in combination with publications.

11.5 Summary

In this chapter you received an overview of how you can leverage server-side trust between your SAP BusinessObjects system and your SAP landscape to provide the capability to set up a multi-pass bursting process for SAP Crystal Reports and SAP BusinessObjects Web Intelligence. In the next chapter, we discuss SAP Business-Objects integration with SAP NetWeaver Portal.

In this chapter we look at the different options for integrating your SAP BusinessObjects system with SAP NetWeaver Portal in order to show content to your users.

12   Integration with SAP NetWeaver Portal

This chapter gives you an overview of how you can integrate content from your SAP BusinessObjects system into SAP NetWeaver Portal. You'll also learn how you can use iViews to show content to your users and how you can integrate the BI launch pad into the portal system.

12.1   BI Content with SAP NetWeaver Portal iViews

The SAP BusinessObjects 4.x release offers two main options for integrating content from your SAP BusinessObjects system with your portal. You can create iViews and show particular content from your SAP BusinessObjects system as part of your portal, or you can integrate the BI launch pad to provide your end users complete functionality inside the portal environment.

In this section we focus on the option to use iViews as containers for the BI content, and go step-by-step through the process of configuring SAP NetWeaver Portal, your SAP NetWeaver BW system, and your SAP BusinessObjects system.

12.1.1   Technical Prerequisites

Before we look at the specific steps required to configure your system landscape so that you can share BI content via your portal, we look at the technical prerequisites.

To be able to use single sign-on between SAP NetWeaver Portal, your SAP NetWeaver BW system, and your SAP BusinessObjects system, the following is required:

- The SAP NetWeaver Portal and the SAP NetWeaver BW systems are configured as trusted systems (see Section 12.1.2).

- All involved systems (SAP NetWeaver Portal, SAP NetWeaver BW, and SAP BusinessObjects) are in the same domain.

- All involved URLs always use the full qualified domain names of the involved systems.

- The SAP authentication is configured on your SAP BusinessObjects system (see Section 2.5.1) and SAP roles and users have been imported.

- The SAP NetWeaver BW system accepts single sign-on logon tickets (see Section 2.4.4).

These prerequisites need to be configured in addition to all of the steps outlined in the following sections.

12.1.2   SAP NetWeaver Portal—Configuration Steps

The following are configuration steps required to display content from your SAP BusinessObjects system inside SAP NetWeaver Portal with single sign-on.

Configuring Trust

You need to configure trust between your portal system and your SAP NetWeaver BW or SAP ERP system so that single sign-on is possible between those two systems. In the outlined steps we refer to your SAP NetWeaver BW system, but the steps are identical if you use an SAP ERP system.

1. Log on to your SAP NetWeaver Portal system. You need to use a portal user that is part of the system administrator's role of your portal.

2. Follow the menu path SYSTEM ADMINISTRATION • SYSTEM CONFIGURATION (see Figure 12.1) and select KEYSTORE ADMINISTRATION.

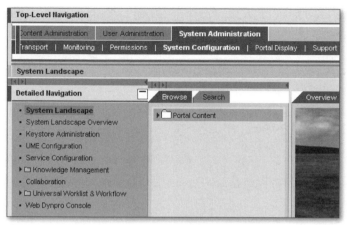

Figure 12.1 SAP NetWeaver Portal—System Configuration

3. Select the CONTENT tab in the next screen (see Figure 12.2).

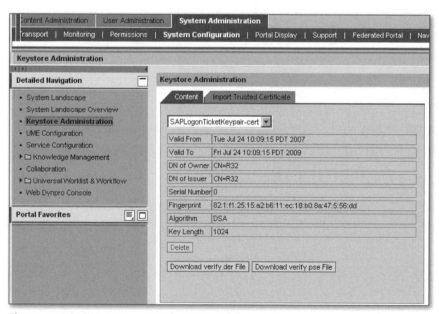

Figure 12.2 SAP NetWeaver Portal—Keystore Administration

4. Click the DOWNLOAD VERIFY.DER FILE button. The *verify.der* file contains the portal certificate that you'll import to your SAP NetWeaver BW system with the Trust Manager.

5. Save the file to your local system and unzip it. If necessary, assign the ZIP file extension to the downloaded file and extract the *verify.der* file from the archive file.

6. Log on to your SAP NetWeaver BW system and start Transaction STRUSTSSO2 (see Figure 12.3).

Figure 12.3 Trust Manager

7. Open the *System PSE* folder.

8. Click the IMPORT CERTIFICATE icon () in the bottom-left corner (see Figure 12.4).

Figure 12.4 Import Certificate

9. When you click the IMPORT CERTIFICATE icon, a new screen pops up and asks for the path and format of the certificate file (see Figure 12.5). Enter the full path to the portal certificate and select BINARY under FILE FORMAT.

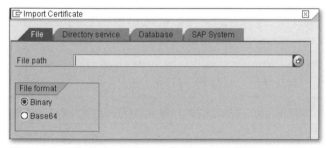

Figure 12.5 File Path and Format for Portal Certificate

10. Click the ADD TO CERTIFICATE LIST button (refer back to Figure 12.3) to add the portal certificate to the SAP NetWeaver BW system.

11. Then click the ADD TO ACL button, and, in the pop-up (see Figure 12.6), enter the system ID from your portal and "000" for the client field. Then click OK.

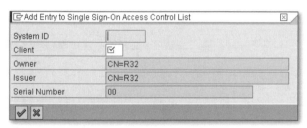

Figure 12.6 Add Entry to Access Control List

12. Use the SAVE icon ( ) to save the changes.

You've now exchanged the portal certificate with your SAP system and established trust between these two systems.

Importing the SAP BusinessObjects iView Template

SAP BusinessObjects 4.x includes an iView template that allows you to create BI-related content from your SAP BusinessObjects system in a very easy and simple way. Technically, the iView template generates a URL for you. You could achieve the same goal by using a standard URL iView template, but then you would have to configure each URL yourself.

The iView template is delivered as an SAP NetWeaver Portal archive file as part of the SAP BusinessObjects installation. The default path is *<Install Directory>\SAP BusinessObjects\SAP BusinessObjects Enterprise XI 4.0\warfiles\portlet\iviews*, and the filename is *com.sap.businessobjects.iviews*.

1. Log on to your SAP NetWeaver Portal system. You need to use a portal user that is part of the system administrator role of your portal.

2. Follow the menu path SYSTEM ADMINISTRATION • SUPPORT (see Figure 12.7).

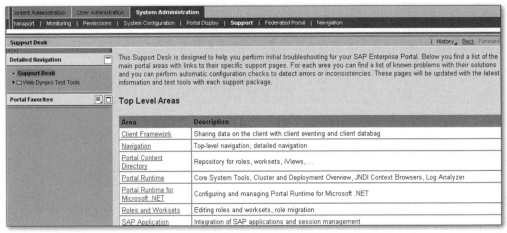

Figure 12.7 SAP NetWeaver Portal—Support

3. Select PORTAL RUNTIME from the TOP LEVEL AREAS list to navigate to the next screen (see Figure 12.8).

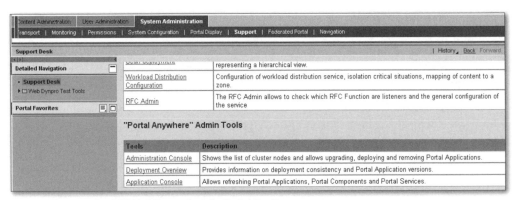

Figure 12.8 SAP NetWeaver Portal—Portal Runtime

4. Click ADMINISTRATION CONSOLE under "PORTAL ANYWHERE" ADMIN TOOLS. You are shown the next screen (see Figure 12.9).

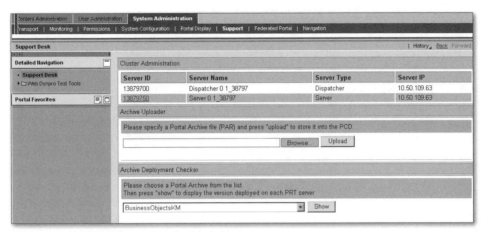

Figure 12.9 SAP NetWeaver Portal—Admin Tools

5. Click on the BROWSE button in the ARCHIVE UPLOADER area and select the SAP BusinessObjects iView template portal archive file. You can find the file in the path *<Install Directory>\SAP BusinessObjects\SAP BusinessObjects Enterprise XI 4.0\ warfiles\portlet\iviews* if you selected the default installation path.

6. Click UPLOAD.

After you successfully upload the portal archive file, the iView template is available to you, and you can create iView content based on your SAP BusinessObjects system.

Configuring the Portal System Landscape

After you upload the portal archive file for the iView template, you need to add your SAP BusinessObjects system to the portal system landscape.

1. Log on to your SAP NetWeaver Portal system. You need to use a portal user that is part of the system administrator role of your portal.

2. Follow the menu path SYSTEM ADMINISTRATION • SYSTEM CONFIGURATION and select SYSTEM LANDSCAPE in the DETAILED NAVIGATION area (see Figure 12.10).

3. Right-click PORTAL CONTENT and select the menu NEW • FOLDER to create a new folder in the portal content directory. You want to create a new folder so that all of the objects will be in the same place.

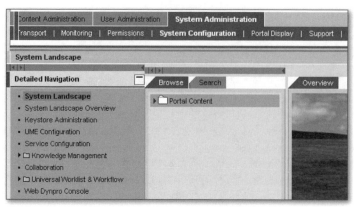

Figure 12.10 SAP NetWeaver Portal—System Configuration

4. Enter a folder name, folder ID, and folder prefix in the next screen. In our example, we enter "SAP BusinessObjects Enterprise" as the folder name and "SAP_BusinessObjects_Enterprise" as the folder ID. We can leave the folder prefix empty for now.

5. Click FINISH to close the system wizard for creating a new folder.

6. Navigate to the newly created folder in the *Portal Content* directory and right-click it.

7. Follow the menu path NEW • SYSTEM (FROM TEMPLATE), and a new screen appears (see Figure 12.11).

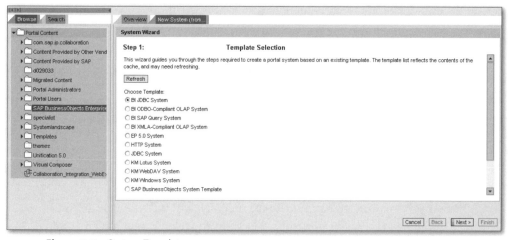

Figure 12.11 System Template

8. Select the SAP BUSINESSOBJECTS SYSTEM TEMPLATE.

9. Click NEXT.

10. Enter a SYSTEM NAME, SYSTEM ID, and SYSTEM ID PREFIX (see Figure 12.12). We use "SAP_BOE_SERVER" as the system name and "SAP_BOE_SERVER" as the system ID. As before, we leave the system ID prefix empty for now.

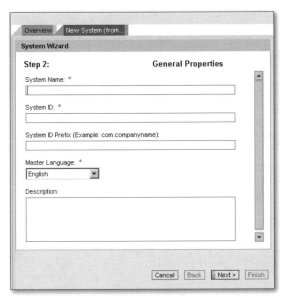

Figure 12.12 System Wizard

11. Click NEXT.

12. Click FINISH.

13. Select OPEN THE OBJECT FOR EDITING when the system wizard closes and click OK. You are presented with a new screen (see Figure 12.13).

Figure 12.13 Open for Editing

14. In the PROPERTY CATEGORY field, select SAP BUSINESSOBJECTS, and the next screen appears (see Figure 12.14).

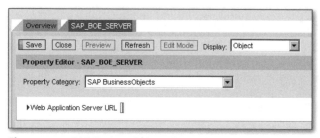

Figure 12.14 SAP BusinessObjects Properties

15. Enter the full qualified name of your application server from your SAP Business-Objects system, including the port; for example, *http://<systemname>.domain.com:8080/BOE/*.

16. Select the USER MANAGEMENT property CATEGORY.

17. Set the AUTHENTICATION TICKET TYPE to SAP LOGON TICKET.

18. Set the LOGON METHOD to SAPLOGONTICKET (see Figure 12.15).

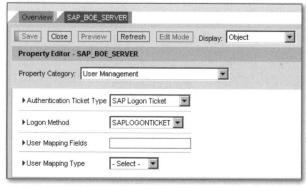

Figure 12.15 User Management Properties

19. Select the CONNECTOR property category.

20. Fill in the details of your SAP system for the fields:

  ▶ GROUP

  ▶ LOGICAL SYSTEM NAME

- ▶ MESSAGE SERVER

- ▶ REMOTE HOST TYPE

- ▶ SAP CLIENT

- ▶ SAP SYSTEM ID

- ▶ SYSTEM TYPE

21. Click SAVE to save all your changes.

22. Select SYSTEM ALIASES in the DISPLAY field (see Figure 12.16).

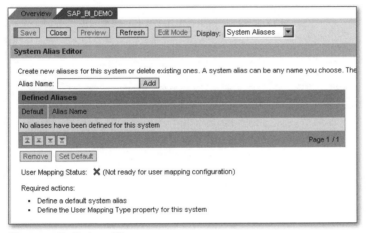

Figure 12.16 System Alias

23. Enter an alias name for your new system. In our example, we use "SAP_BOE_ SERVER".

24. Click the ADD button to add the new alias to the list of available aliases.

25. Save your changes and close the properties of your new system.

You have now created a new system in the portal system landscape with the necessary properties for your SAP BusinessObjects system. The advantage of this configuration is that you can use the system alias for all of your iViews showing SAP BusinessObjects-related content and all of them will read the configuration details from the system definition, instead of entering those details for each iView.

12.1.3   SAP BusinessObjects—Configuration Steps

Configuring BI Launch Pad for Single Sign-On

To integrate SAP BusinessObjects with single sign-on with SAP NetWeaver Portal, you also need to change some configurations in the SAP BusinessObjects system. These steps are performed in addition to the configuration of SAP authentication.

In the following steps we will assume an installation on a Windows operating system using Tomcat as the application server.

1. Navigate to the folder `<Install Directory>\SAP BusinessObjects\Tomcat6\ webapps\BOE\WEB-INF\config\default`.

2. Open the `global.properties` file with an editor.

3. Set the values according to Table 12.1.

Parameter Name	Value
sso.enabled	True
sso.sap.primary	True

Table 12.1   Configuration Values for global.properties

4. Save your changes.

5. Close the file.

6. Open the `BILaunchpad.properties` file in the same folder location with an editor.

7. Set the values according to Table 12.2.

Parameter Name	Value
authentication.default	secSAPR3
authentication.visible	True
logontoken.enabled	True

Table 12.2   Configuration Values for BILaunchpad.properties

8. Save your changes.

9. Close the file.

10. Open the `CmcApp.properties` file in the same folder location with an editor.

11. Set the values according to Table 12.3.

Parameter Name	Value
authentication.visible	True
authentication.default	secSAPR3
logontoken.enabled	True

Table 12.3 Configuration Values for CmcApp.properties

12. Save your changes.

13. Close the file.

14. Open the file `OpenDocument.properties` in the same folder location with an editor.

15. Set the values according to Table 12.4.

Parameter Name	Value
authentication.visible	True
authentication.default	secSAPR3
logontoken.enabled	True
SAPLogonToken.enabled	True

Table 12.4 Configuration Values for OpenDocument.properties

16. Restart the application server from your SAP BusinessObjects system.

With these configurations in place, we can now go ahead and create our first iView showing content from our SAP BusinessObjects system inside the SAP NetWeaver Portal.

> ### Changing the Original Files
>
> The steps above outline how to change the already deployed files on the Java Application Server. In addition, you can make the changes to the original war files so that if you redeploy the files, the changes are still there. You can find those files in the folder *<Install Directory>\SAP BusinessObjects\SAP BusinessObjects Enterprise XI 4.0\warfiles\webapps*.

12.1.4 Create Your First iView

In this section you'll create our first iView showing content from your SAP BusinessObjects system.

1. Log on to your SAP NetWeaver Portal and follow the menu path CONTENT ADMINISTRATION • PORTAL CONTENT.

2. Open the PORTAL CONTENT folder and navigate to the folder you created in the previous section.

3. Right-click the folder and select the NEW IVIEW option (see Figure 12.17).

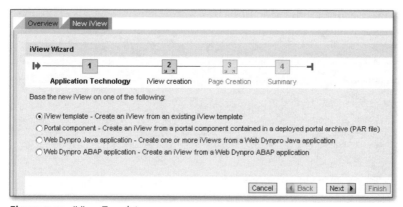

Figure 12.17 iView Template

4. Select IVIEW TEMPLATE.

5. Click NEXT.

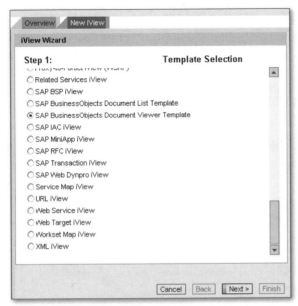

Figure 12.18 Template Selection

6. Select SAP BUSINESSOBJECTS DOCUMENT VIEWER TEMPLATE (see Figure 12.18).

7. Click NEXT.

8. Enter an IVIEW NAME, IVIEW ID, and IVIEW ID PREFIX. We use "SAP_Business-Objects_iView_1" as the iView Name and "SAP_BusinessObjects_iView_1" as the iView ID. We leave the iView ID prefix empty for now.

9. Click NEXT (see Figure 12.19).

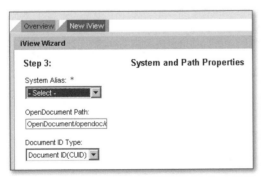

Figure 12.19 System and Path Properties

10. Select the previously configured system alias from the list.

11. Ensure that the relative path pointing to the OpenDocument application matches your deployment.

12. Select the document ID type:

   ▶ Select the DOCUMENT ID (CUID) value if you would like to leverage a report from the SAP BusinessObjects system.

   ▶ Select the BW_ID ONLY value if you would like to show an SAP Crystal Reports 2011 object that was saved to SAP NetWeaver BW and published to SAP BusinessObjects.

13. Click NEXT (see Figure 12.20).

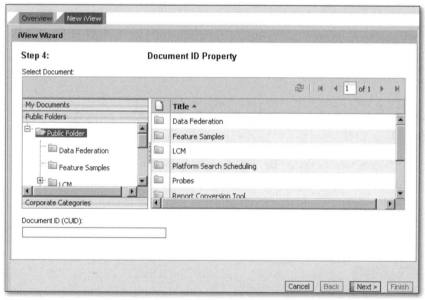

Figure 12.20 Document ID Property

14. In our example, we selected DOCUMENT ID (CUID) in the previous step, and we are now presented with a document browser. We can select our document directly in the browser (see Figure 12.21).

15. Based on our selection, the DOCUMENT ID (CUID) value is set.

16. Click NEXT.

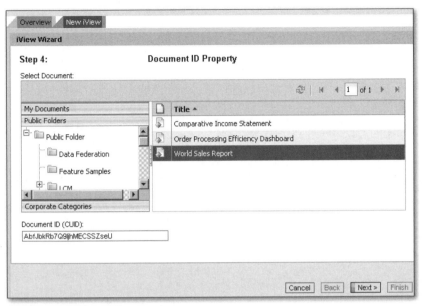

Figure 12.21 Selected Document

17. Click FINISH.

18. Select the CLOSE THE WIZARD option.

19. Click OK.

20. You can now use the iView as part of your portal pages and display the content from the SAP BusinessObjects system.

12.1.5 Integration of the BI Launch Pad and SAP NetWeaver Portal

In addition to the option to integrate a specific report into SAP NetWeaver Portal, you also have the option to integrate the BI launch pad into SAP NetWeaver Portal.

1. Log on to SAP NetWeaver Portal and follow the menu path CONTENT ADMINISTRATION • PORTAL CONTENT.

2. Open the PORTAL CONTENT folder and navigate to the folder you created in the previous section.

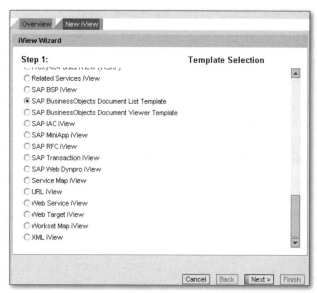

Figure 12.22 Template Selection

3. Right-click the folder and select NEW IVIEW.

4. Select IVIEW TEMPLATE.

5. Click NEXT.

6. Select the SAP BUSINESSOBJECTS DOCUMENT LIST TEMPLATE entry (see Figure 12.22).

7. Click NEXT.

8. Enter an IVIEW NAME, IVIEW ID, and IVIEW ID PREFIX. We use "SAP_Business-Objects_List_iView_1" as the iView Name and "SAP_BusinessObjects_List_iView_1" as the iView ID. We leave the iView ID prefix empty for now.

9. Click NEXT.

10. Specify the previously created alias for the SYSTEM value (see Figure 12.23).

11. Ensure that the default value for the BI launch pad path matches your deployment. If you followed the default installation, the value is BI.

12. Click NEXT.

13. Click FINISH.

You now have an iView that integrates the complete BI launch pad into the SAP NetWeaver Portal.

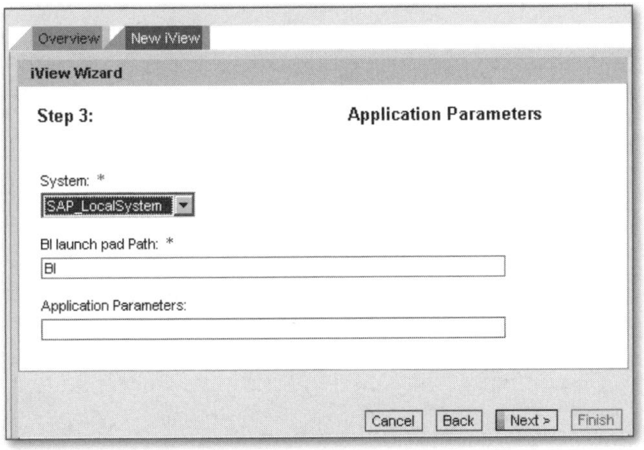

Figure 12.23 Application Parameters

In this section we reviewed the options for integrating content from your SAP BusinessObjects system into SAP NetWeaver Portal. In the next section, you will receive an overview of Knowledge Management in SAP NetWeaver Portal with SAP BusinessObjects.

12.2 BI Content with Knowledge Management

In this section you'll learn how you can use Knowledge Management to integrate your SAP BusinessObjects-based content into the SAP NetWeaver Portal, and then use Knowledge Management features.

> **Note**
>
> The integration between the SAP BusinessObjects system and the Knowledge Management area of SAP NetWeaver Portal is a feature that is available with the XI 3.1 release of SAP BusinessObjects. As it is purely in maintenance mode, it has not been enhanced as part of the 4.x release.

12.2.1 Technical Prerequisites

Similar to the integration of SAP BusinessObjects content via iViews, the integration with the Knowledge Management component of SAP NetWeaver Portal has a list of technical prerequisites.

▶ SAP NetWeaver Portal and the SAP NetWeaver BW system need to be configured as trusted systems.

▶ All involved systems (SAP NetWeaver Portal, SAP NetWeaver BW, and SAP BusinessObjects) need to be in the same domain; otherwise, single sign-on based on a token or ticket will fail.

▶ All involved URLs should always use the full qualified domain names of the involved systems.

▶ SAP authentication must be configured on your SAP BusinessObjects system, and SAP roles and users must be imported for your SAP NetWeaver BW system.

▶ Your SAP NetWeaver BW system should accept single sign-on logon tickets.

▶ Web services need to be deployed for your SAP BusinessObjects system on your application server.

12.2.2 SAP NetWeaver Portal—Configuration Steps

The SAP BusinessObjects installation delivers the Knowledge Management integration as a portal archive file, which you need to upload to your portal server.

1. Log on to your SAP NetWeaver Portal system. You need to use a portal user that is part of the system administrator role of your portal.

2. Follow the menu path SYSTEM ADMINISTRATION • SUPPORT.

3. Select PORTAL RUNTIME from the list of top level areas.

4. Click ADMINISTRATION CONSOLE in "PORTAL ANYWHERE" ADMIN TOOLS.

5. Click the BROWSE button in the ARCHIVE UPLOADER and select the SAP Business-Objects KM portal archive file. In a default installation, the portal archive file is in the path *<Install Directory>\SAP BusinessObjects\SAP BusinessObjects Enterprise XI 4.0\warfiles\KMC* and the file name is *BusinessObjectsKM.par*.

6. Click UPLOAD.

After you upload the portal archive file, proceed with the following steps to verify the installation.

1. Log on to SAP NetWeaver Portal.
2. Follow the menu path SYSTEM ADMINISTRATION • SYSTEM CONFIGURATION (see Figure 12.24).

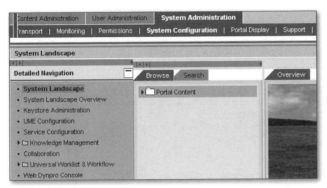

Figure 12.24 SAP NetWeaver Portal System Administration

3. Click KNOWLEDGE MANAGEMENT in the DETAILED NAVIGATION area.
4. Select CONTENT MANAGEMENT from the dropdown menu, and a new screen opens (see Figure 12.25).

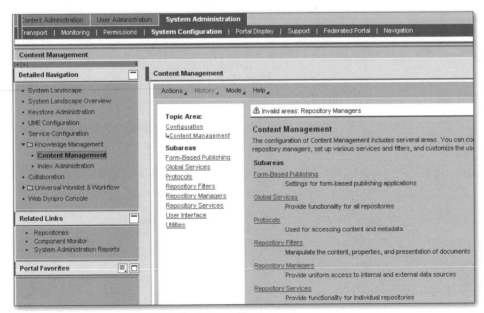

Figure 12.25 SAP NetWeaver Portal—Content Management

5. Select Repository Managers, and, in the following screen, select Business Objects Repository.

6. Click New. You should now see a definition similar to Figure 12.26. We use this template in the next section to configure the repository manager to connect to your SAP BusinessObjects system.

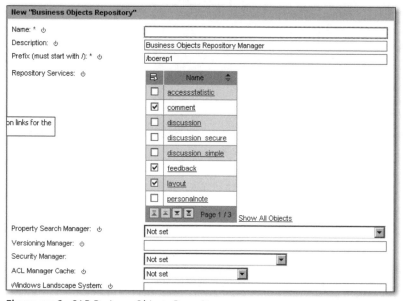

Figure 12.26 SAP Business Objects Repository

12.2.3 Setting Up Your Repository

In this section we use the template that you imported via the portal archive file to set up a Repository Manager that will use your SAP BusinessObjects system.

1. Log on to your SAP NetWeaver Portal system.

2. Follow the menu path System Administration • System configuration.

3. Click Knowledge Management in the Detailed Navigation area.

4. Select Content Management.

5. Select Repository Managers.

6. Select Business Objects Repository.

7. Click NEW to start creating a new entry. The system creates a new repository manager entry with several placeholders for you to fill in (see Figure 12.27).

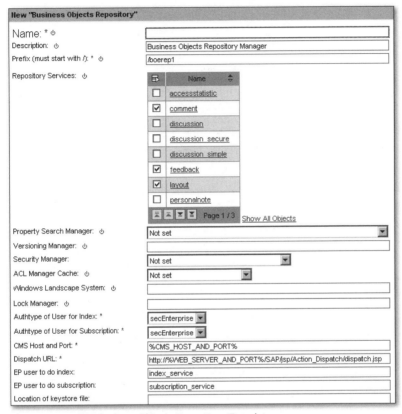

Figure 12.27 SAP BusinessObjects Repository Template

8. Enter a name, description, and prefix for your repository. The prefix is used to identify your repository in the Knowledge Management component when multiple repositories are shown in a browser.

9. Next select REPOSITORY SERVICES. Select at least the repository service layout, but if you're not sure which repository services you want to use, you can select them all.

10. Enter the other values for the existing placeholders according to Table 12.5.

Setting	Value
PROPERTY SEARCH MANAGER	Ensure that the value is set to NOT SET. There have been cases where the property search manager prevents the SAP BusinessObjects Repository Manager from working properly.
CMS HOST AND PORT	The full qualified name of your Central Management Server and the port number. Example: *boesrv.wdf.sap.corp:6400*
DISPATCH URL	Replace the placeholder %WEB_SERVER_AND_PORT% with the value of your application server and port number. Example: *boesrv.wdf.sap.corp:8080*
OPENDOC URL	Replace the placeholder %WEB_SERVER_AND_PORT% with the value of your application server and port number. Example: *boesrv.wdf.sap.corp:8080*
SAP CLIENT	The client number of your SAP system. Example: 003
SAP SYSTEM ID	The system ID of your SAP system. Example: CIM
LOG OFF URL	Replace the placeholder %WEB_SERVER_AND_PORT% with the value of your application server and port number. Example: *boesrv.wdf.sap.corp:8080*
WEB SERVICE URL	Replace the placeholder %WEB_SERVER_AND_PORT% with the value of your application server and port number. Example: *boesrv.wdf.sap.corp:8080*
STARTING FOLDER ID	Enter the ID for the folder in your SAP BusinessObjects system that should be used as the root folder for your repository. You can receive the ID via the properties of the folders in the Central Management Console.

Table 12.5 Repository Manager Properties

11. Save your changes. Your repository should now appear in the list of available repositories.

12. For the SAP BusinessObjects-specific commands to be available for your repository, you need to configure a layout set for your repository.

13. Follow the menu path CONTENT ADMINISTRATION • KM CONTENT and select KM
    CONTENT in the DETAILED NAVIGATION area (see Figure 12.28).

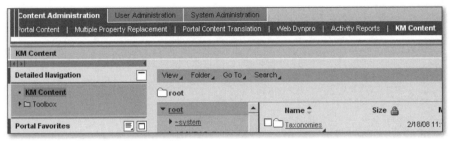

Figure 12.28 Knowledge Management

14. You should, based on the prefix defined, now see your repository in the list in
    the middle of the screen (see Figure 12.29).

15. Click the triangle in the bottom-right corner of your repository folder.

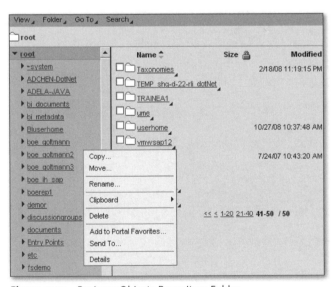

Figure 12.29 Business Objects Repository Folder

16. Select DETAILS. Another screen is presented (see Figure 12.30).

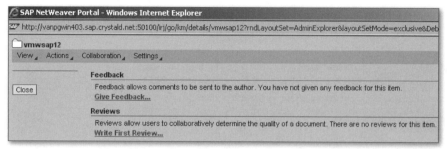

Figure 12.30 Details for the Repository

17. Follow the menu path SETTINGS • PRESENTATION. In the new screen, determine how the folder will be presented for all users and personalize its layout (see Figure 12.31).

18. Click on the SELECT PROFILE button on the SETTINGS FOR ALL USERS tab.

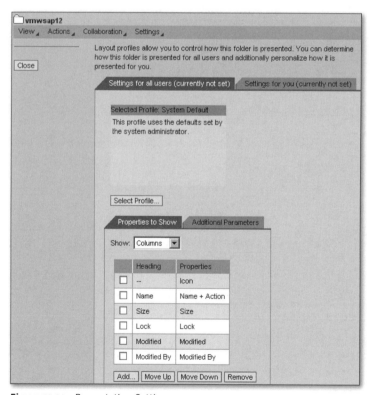

Figure 12.31 Presentation Settings

19. In the next screen (Figure 12.32), you are presented with different profile settings. Select LAYOUT SET and select the BOBJELAYOUT value from the dropdown list. This layout set has been imported as part of the KM portal archive file that you imported previously.

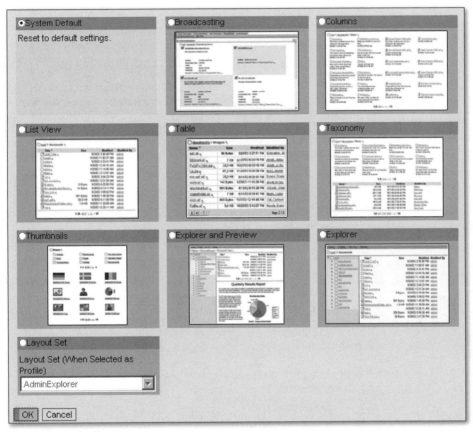

Figure 12.32 Profile Settings

20. Click OK to move to the next screen (see Figure 12.33).

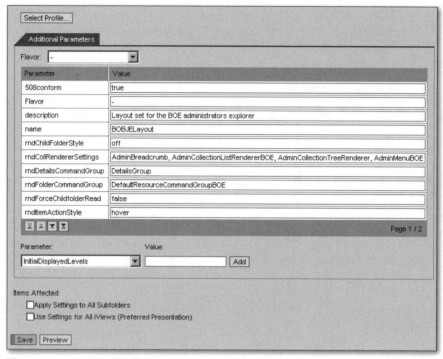

Figure 12.33 Applying Profile Settings

21. Select APPLY SETTINGS TO ALL SUBFOLDERS to ensure that the layout is applied to all folders in the repository. You can also select the USE SETTINGS FOR ALL IVIEWS checkbox to ensure that any iView based on the repository will use the layout.

22. Click SAVE and close the screen.

You have now configured your repository to offer SAP BusinessObjects-specific commands such as VIEW HISTORY, VIEW LATEST INSTANCE, and INFOVIEW.

12.2.4 Using the Repository Manager

This section shows some of the common functions of the newly created repository manager.

1. Follow the menu path CONTENT ADMINISTRATION • KM CONTENT and select KM CONTENT in the DETAILED NAVIGATION area.

2. Your repository should appear in the list, based on the configured prefix.

3. Select the repository you previously configured from the list. Another screen appears (see Figure 12.34).

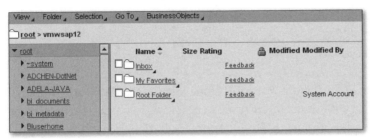

Figure 12.34 KM Repository View

4. The configured starting folder ID (a property you can set as part of the configuration) is used here, and any folder below is shown on the right-hand side. You also can see the SAP BusinessObjects-specific menus.

5. Click VIEW in the menu bar to switch between a view by folders and by category.

6. The menu item FOLDER allows you to create new documents (see Figure 12.35).

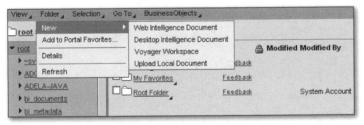

Figure 12.35 Folder Menu

7. Click SELECTION in the menu bar to copy, move, or delete objects in your repository.

8. Click GO TO to directly navigate to InfoView (see Figure 12.36).

9. The BUSINESSOBJECTS menu item allows you to switch to the view by category, navigate to the BI launch pad, and log off from the repository.

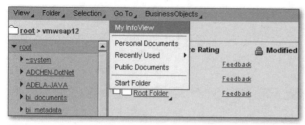

Figure 12.36 Go To Menu

10. Navigate down to the folder for the role from your SAP NetWeaver BW system that you used to publish the SAP Crystal Reports 2011 content. Each object in the repository offers a context menu (bottom-right triangle symbol). Open the context menu of the SAP Crystal Reports 2011 object (see Figure 12.37).

Name	Size	Rating	🔒	Modified	Modified By
☐☐ Consolidated Income Statement	956 KB	Feedback		11/26/08 12:38:37 PM	Administrator,
☐☐ Income Statement	951 KB	Feedback		11/26/08 12:38:37 PM	Administrator,
☐☐ Monthly Variance Cross Tab	952.5 KB	Feedback		11/26/08 12:38:37 PM	Administrator,
☐☐ Rolling Quarter Income Statement	905.5 KB	Feedback		11/26/08 12:38:37 PM	Administrator,
☐☐ Sorted Variance Analysis Report	1.1 MB	Feedback		11/26/08 12:38:37 PM	Administrator,
☐☐ Trial	1.2 MB	Feedback		11/26/08 12:38:37 PM	Administrator,
☐☐ Vari	1.1 MB	Feedback		11/26/08 12:38:37 PM	Administrator,
☐☐ YTD	901.5 KB	Feedback		11/26/08 12:38:37 PM	Administrator,

Context menu:
View
Schedule
History
Copy...
Delete
Add to Portal Favorites...
Send To...
Rating ▶
Give Feedback...
Details
Download

Figure 12.37 Context Menu

As you can see, the context menu offers SAP BusinessObjects-specific menu items such as View, Schedule, and History (see Figure 12.37). It offers Knowledge Management-specific menu items such as Rating and Details.

11. Select Details, and you are presented with a new screen (see Figure 12.38).

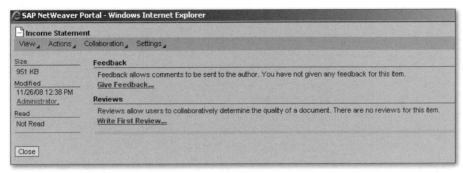

Figure 12.38 Details

12. In the details section you can give feedback, provide reviews, and rank the document. These elements are part of the Knowledge Management component.

In this section you learned how you can integrate SAP BusinessObjects content into the KM part of your SAP NetWeaver Portal environment.

12.3 Summary

In this chapter you learned how you can integrate content from your SAP Business-Objects system into your SAP NetWeaver Portal system. You learned how to integrate the content via iViews and how to configure the integration with the Knowledge Management component. In the next chapter, we discuss tips and tricks for troubleshooting your SAP BusinessObjects and SAP NetWeaver integration.

The ability to troubleshoot common problems in deployment is essential. You can follow the steps discussed in this chapter to collect more details if you face issues with the software.

13   Troubleshooting and Tips

In this chapter we present information and steps you can use to troubleshoot issues you might face, and offer tips on particular topics that will help improve your solutions. Some of the information provided might require you to look for further details in SAP documentation, as the relevant details are beyond the scope of this book.

13.1   Tracing for SAP BusinessObjects Services and Applications

In this section we show how you can activate tracing for services and applications from your SAP BusinessObjects system.

All the logging files from your SAP BusinessObjects system are written to a folder. By default, this folder is *<INSTALLDIR>\SAP BusinessObjects Enterprise XI 4.0\logging* on a Windows platform and *<INSTALLDIR>/sap_bobj/logging* on a UNIX platform.

To configure the tracing for an SAP BusinessObjects service, follow these steps:

1. Log on to the Central Management Console (CMC) of your SAP BusinessObjects system.
2. Navigate to the SERVERS area.
3. Select the server you would like to configure for tracing.
4. Right-click and select the PROPERTIES menu.
5. Scroll down to the TRACELOG SERVICE area.
6. Set the LOGLEVEL to LOW, MEDIUM, or HIGH.

7. Click SAVE AND CLOSE.

8. Restart the configured service and the tracing will start.

To configure the tracing for a particular web application, such as BI launch pad, follow these steps:

1. Log on to the Central Management Console (CMC) of your SAP BusinessObjects system.

2. Navigate to the APPLICATIONS area.

3. Select the application you would like to configure for tracing.

4. Right-click and select the TRACE LOG SETTINGS menu.

5. Set the LOGLEVEL to LOW, MEDIUM, or HIGH (see Table 13.1).

6. Click SAVE AND CLOSE.

You can configure the tracing for the BI launch pad, Central Management Console, Web Services, and Open Document. The location of the trace file for the web application is written to a directory on the system hosting the application in the *$UserHome* location.

Log Level	Description
Low	The trace log filter is set to allow for logging error messages while ignoring warning and most status messages. However, very important status messages will be logged for component startup, shutdown, and start and end request messages.
Medium	The trace log filter is set to include error, warning, and most status messages in the log output. Status messages that are least important or highly verbose will be filtered out. This level is not verbose enough for debugging purposes.
High	The trace log filter does not exclude any messages. This level is recommended for debugging purposes.

Table 13.1 Log Level Details

13.2 Data Connectivity

In this section we focus on how you can verify the connectivity you're using in the SAP BusinessObjects client tools, and which tools are available to you for troubleshooting.

13.2.1 Steps to Validate the Configuration

Before we go into the details of tracing the connectivity and verifying the derived metadata from your underlying SAP system, the following is a list of steps you can take to validate your configuration:

- If you are using SAP Crystal Reports 2011 in combination with SAP NetWeaver BW or SAP ERP, make sure that all ABAP transports have been imported correctly to your SAP system. You can use Transaction STMS to verify the transports. Here it is important to note that sometimes service packs do include updated transport files.

- Make sure the user has enough authorizations to perform the required task. You can use Transaction ST01 to create an authorization trace that will show you any missing authorizations.

- For the InfoSet connectivity, you should verify, with the help of Transactions SQ01, SQ02, and SQ03, that the InfoSet is assigned to the global or local environment and that the InfoSet is assigned to a user group.

- For SAP NetWeaver BW connectivity, you should verify whether the underlying BEx query has been marked for external access in the SAP Business Explorer (BEx) Query Designer by setting the property ALLOW EXTERNAL ACCESS.

- If you experience issues with the data connectivity to SAP NetWeaver BW, you can use Transaction RSRT to execute the BEx query and ensure that it works without the use of any SAP BusinessObjects BI client tools. In addition, Transaction RSRT allows you to execute the BEx query and, at the same time, receive information about specific items such as the use of aggregates or the executed SQL command.

13.2.2 Tracing SAP Crystal Reports 2011 Data Connectivity

To trace the data connectivity of SAP Crystal Reports 2011, you can use the registry (on a Windows environment). All of the SAP Crystal Reports connectivity can be found in the registry key *HKEY_LOCAL_MACHINE\SOFTWARE\SAP Business Objects\ Suite XI 4.0\SAP* on a 32-bit Windows operating system or *HKEY_LOCAL_MACHINE\ SOFTWARE\Wow6432Node\SAP BusinessObjects\Suite XI 4.0\SAP* on a 64 bit-Windows operating system.

Each SAP Crystal Reports 2011 connectivity has a `Trace` registry key, which is a simple "Yes" or "No" value. The location of the trace files can be configured by the `TraceDir` registry key in the registry folder *HKEY_LOCAL_MACHINE\SOFT-WARE\SAP Business Objects\Suite XI 4.0\SAP or HKEY_LOCAL_MACHINE\SOFTWARE\ Wow6432Node\SAP BusinessObjects\Suite XI 4.0\SAP,* which points to the folder for the logfiles.

The resulting traces provide you with a high level of detail, and in the first step you want to look at those traces for common error messages that might not have occurred in the actual software. You can go through the traces and see every step that was performed using the software. In addition, they also contain information about the metadata that has been retrieved, the statement that was used for data retrieval, and, in some cases, the actual data that has been retrieved.

In addition to the traces on the SAP BusinessObjects side, there is a set of tools you can use in your SAP system:

▶ You can use Transaction ST01 to create several kinds of traces. Most importantly, you can use Transaction ST01 to create authorization traces.

▶ You can use Transaction ST05 to create remote function call (RFC) and Structured Query Language (SQL) traces, which are especially helpful for connectivity with the SAP ERP system.

▶ You can use Transactions RSTT and RSRTRACE to generate an OLAP trace, which can be repeated at any time.

13.2.3 Tracing Data Connectivity based on BI Consumer Services

In SAP BusinessObjects 4.x, all the BI client tools rely on BI Consumer Services (BICS) when connecting to BEx queries. The easiest option to trace the data connectivity on the SAP NetWeaver BW backend is to leverage Transaction RSTT. In the next couple of steps, you will learn how to activate the tracing and how to read the logged information.

To activate the tracing, follow the steps below:

1. Log on to your SAP NetWeaver BW system and start Transaction RSTT (see Figure 13.1).

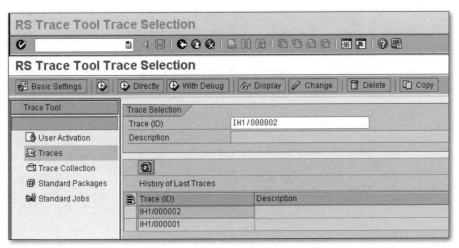

Figure 13.1 RS Trace Tool

2. Click Basic Settings.

3. Ensure that the Application Area is set to BI Reporting, BI Planning, and OLAP Technology (see Figure 13.2).

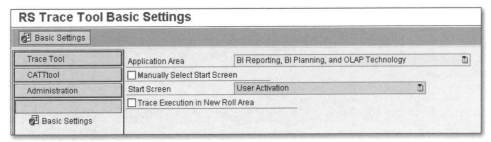

Figure 13.2 Basic Settings

4. Navigate back to the start screen.

5. Select the User Activation item on the left-hand side (see Figure 13.3).

6. Enter the user name that you would like to trace into the Trace User field.

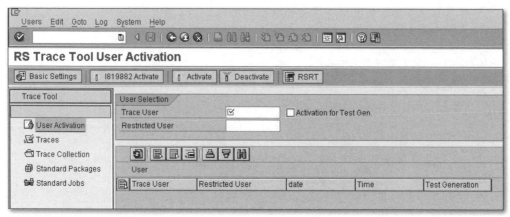

Figure 13.3 User Activation

7. Click ACTIVATE.

The tracing for the selected user has now been activated, and all activities for the selected area in BASIC SETTINGS are now being logged. In our example, we activate the trace for the BI area; therefore, any activity in tools, such as BEx Analyzer, BEx Query Designer, Transaction RSRT, or the SAP BusinessObjects products leveraging the BICS connectivity, is written to the trace.

Before we look at how to read the details from the trace and how to look for the information in the trace, see Table 13.2 for a list of the most important BICS functions.

BICS Function	Description
BICS_PROV_OPEN	This function lets you receive the details on which BEx query was used.
BICS_PROV_VAR_GET_VARIABLES	This function lets you receive a list of variables from the BEx query.
BICS_PROV_VAR_SET_VARIABLES	The entered or selected values for the variables are sent to the backend.
BICS_PROV_GET_INITIAL_STATE	This function configures the initial state of the session. It is important, because it allows you to retrieve IDs for the characteristics and members.

Table 13.2 BICS Functions

BICS Function	Description
BICS_PROV_SET_HIERARCHY	A configured hierarchy is set for a characteristic.
BICS_PROV_SET_STATE	The state of the BEx query is sent to the backend. Retrieve the information about which elements are being set in the rows and columns.
BICS_PROV_GET_RESULTSET	This function allows you to receive information about the result set.
BICS_PROV_GET_MEMBERS	This function is used to receive a list of members from a characteristic.
BICS_PROV_GET_HIERARCHIES	This function is used to receive a list of hierarchies for a characteristic.

Table 13.2 BICS Functions (Cont.)

Each of the functions listed in Table 13.2 uses specific variable names that are relevant. Explaining each of the listed functions in full depth and explaining each of the variables of those functions would go beyond the scope of this book. Therefore we highlight the most important variable of each of the functions in Table 13.3.

BICS Function	Variable Name	Description
BICS_PROV_OPEN	I_DATA_PROVIDER_NAME	This contains the technical name of the BEx query that was used.
BICS_PROV_GET_MEMBERS	I_CHARACTERISTIC_NAME	This contains the technical name of the characteristic that was used.
	E_T_MEMBERS	This variable contains the members that have been retrieved.
BICS_PROV_GET_INITIAL_STATE	E_TH_META_CHARACTERISTICS	This variable contains critical information about which ID has been assigned to which characteristic.

Table 13.3 Details on BICS Functions and Variables

BICS Function	Variable Name	Description
BICS_PROV_SET_STATE	I_T_ROWS_ CHARACTERISTICS	This variable contains information about which elements are part of the rows.
	I_T_COLUMNS_ CHARACTERISTICS	This variable contains information about which elements are part of the columns.
	I_T_FREE_ CHARACTERISTICS	This variable contains information about which elements are part of the free characteristics.
BICS_PROV_GET_ RESULTSET	E_T_ROWS E_T_COLUMNS E_T_DATA_CELLS E_T_MEMBER E_T_MEMBER_ PRESENTATION	These variables contain information that allows you to reconstruct the result set. The details are described in this section.

Table 13.3 Details on BICS Functions and Variables (Cont.)

We will now show you how you can reconstruct the dataset retrieved by a BI client. We realize that there are several ways to reach the same goal in the ABAP Debugger, so consider these steps as one possible option for retrieving the information.

In the following steps we trace a standard SAP BusinessObjects Web Intelligence workflow on top of an OLAP connection using the BICS direct access method connecting to a BEx query with variables. We review the trace and show how to find the information we are looking for.

Follow these steps to review the generated trace:

1. Log on to your SAP NetWeaver BW system and start Transaction RSTT.

2. Select the TRACES entry (see Figure 13.4).

3. The list of available traces is shown. Select one of the available traces in the table and select the DISPLAY option from the toolbar (see Figure 13.5).

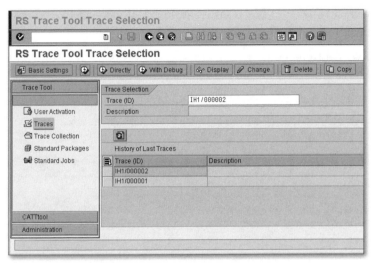

Figure 13.4 Traces Selection

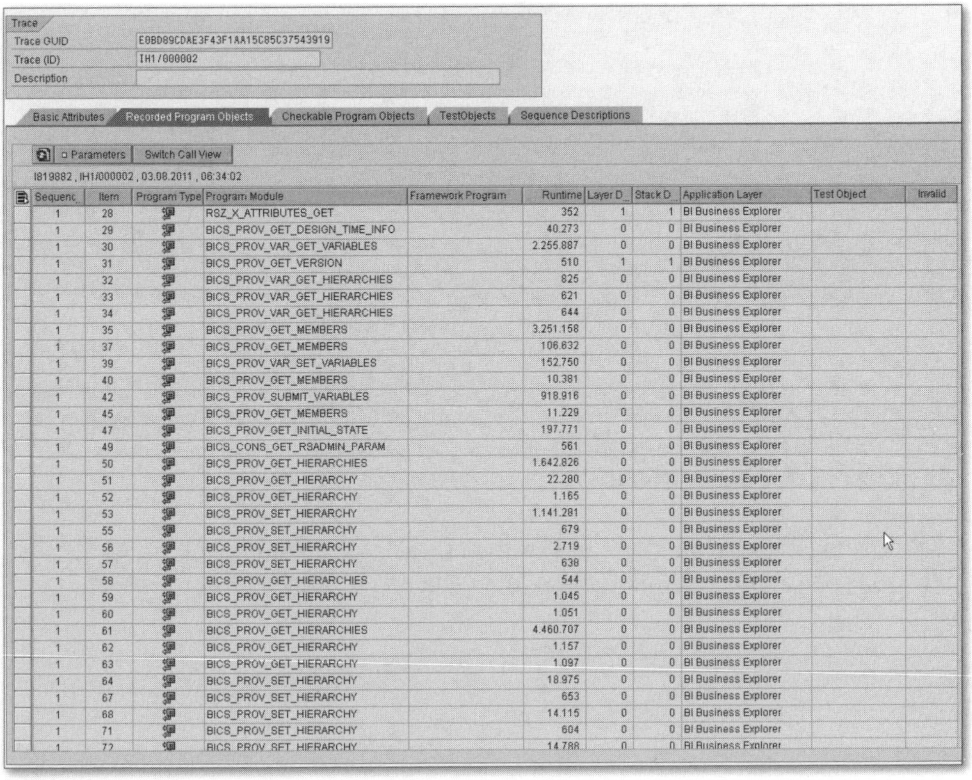

Figure 13.5 Detailed Listing for Trace

4. For the selected trace, the list of functions is displayed. Double-click to go into the actual code of the function.

5. In our example we continue with the function BICS_PROV_GET_MEMBERS as an example to show how you can find the relevant information.

6. Double-click on the BICS_PROV_GET_MEMBERS function entry.

7. You are presented with the ABAP Debugger (see Figure 13.6).

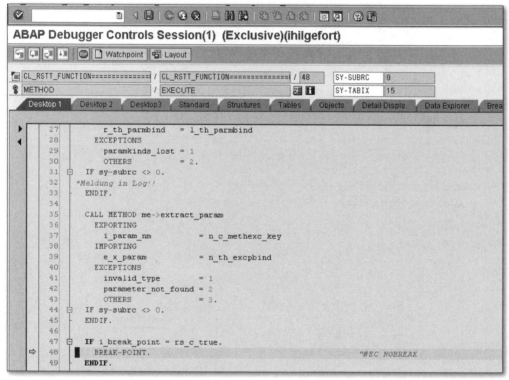

Figure 13.6 ABAP Debugger

8. Use the F6 button (Execute) until you reach the beginning of the ABAP function you entered; in our example, BICS_PROV_GET_MEMBERS (see Figure 13.7).

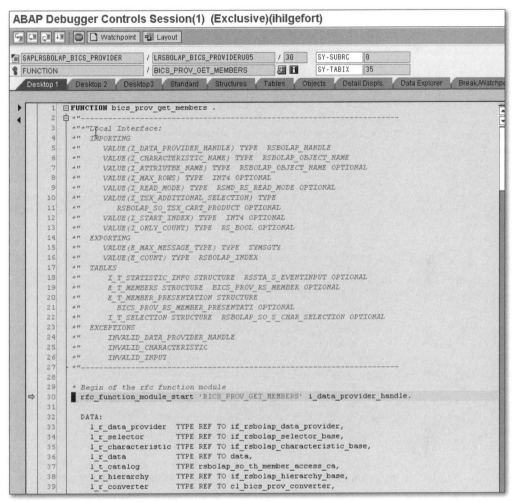

Figure 13.7 Function Header

9. Now scroll down in the ABAP code without executing it until you reach the end of the function (see Figure 13.8).

10. Place the cursor on the last line of code for the function.

11. Right-click and select the CREATE BREAKPOINT option. You have now created a breakpoint in the trace so that you can execute the complete function and it will stop before leaving the function. You can retrieve the information from the relevant variables. Now scroll back up to the beginning of the function. Each of the functions listed in Table 13.2 has an EXPORTING part, and some of

the functions have a TABLES part. These areas list the relevant variables and tables that contain the information.

```
202   LOOP AT l_t_catalog ASSIGNING <l_s_catalog>.
203
204   *      Value access
205          ASSIGN COMPONENT <l_s_catalog>-table_column_index OF STRUCTURE <l_s_data> TO <l_da
206
207   *      Presentations
208          IF <l_s_catalog>-presentation = rsbol_c_presentation-sid AND <l_s_catalog>-attribu
209   *         Sid belongs to the member
210             l_s_member-member_id = <l_data>.
211          ELSE.
212   *         Fill the presentation
213             l_s_member_pres-value = <l_data>.
214
215   *         Check if SID for attribute (case numeric), then condens to avoid bad field move
216             IF <l_s_catalog>-presentation = rsbol_c_presentation-sid.
217                CONDENSE l_s_member_pres-value.
218             ENDIF.
219             l_s_member_pres-presentation = <l_s_catalog>-presentation.
220             ADD 1 TO l_s_member-presentation_index_to.
221   *            Attribute ?
222             IF <l_s_catalog>-attribute IS INITIAL.
223                CLEAR l_s_member_pres-attribute_id.
224             ELSE.
225                l_s_member_pres-attribute_id = <l_s_catalog>-attribute->n_id.
226             ENDIF.
227             APPEND l_s_member_pres TO e_t_member_presentation[].
228          ENDIF.
229       ENDLOOP.
230   *      Fill the member
231       IF l_s_member-presentation_index_from > l_s_member-presentation_index_to.
232          CLEAR l_s_member-presentation_index_from.
233       ENDIF.
234       APPEND l_s_member TO e_t_members[].
235     ENDLOOP.
236    ENDIF.
237   ENDIF.
238  ENDIF.
239
240  * End of the rfc function module
241     rfc_function_module_end l_data_provider_handle.
242
243  ENDFUNCTION.
```

Figure 13.8 End of Function

In Listing 13.1, you can see the header information of the BICS_PROV_GET_ MEMBERS function. In this example, the relevant information is in the TABLES area: E_T_MEMBERS.

```
FUNCTION bics_prov_get_members .
*"----------------------------------------------------------------
*"*"Local Interface:
*"  IMPORTING
*"     VALUE(I_DATA_PROVIDER_HANDLE) TYPE  RSBOLAP_HANDLE
```

```
*"        VALUE(I_CHARACTERISTIC_NAME) TYPE  RSBOLAP_OBJECT_NAME
*"        VALUE(I_ATTRIUTBE_NAME) TYPE  RSBOLAP_OBJECT_NAME OPTIONAL
*"        VALUE(I_MAX_ROWS) TYPE  INT4 OPTIONAL
*"        VALUE(I_READ_MODE) TYPE  RSMD_RS_READ_MODE OPTIONAL
*"        VALUE(I_TSX_ADDITIONAL_SELECTION) TYPE
*"           RSBOLAP_SO_TSX_CART_PRODUCT OPTIONAL
*"        VALUE(I_START_INDEX) TYPE  INT4 OPTIONAL
*"        VALUE(I_ONLY_COUNT) TYPE  RS_BOOL OPTIONAL
*"  EXPORTING
*"        VALUE(E_MAX_MESSAGE_TYPE) TYPE  SYMSGTY
*"        VALUE(E_COUNT) TYPE  RSBOLAP_INDEX
*"  TABLES
*"         I_T_STATISTIC_INFO STRUCTURE  RSSTA_S_EVENTINPUT OPTIONAL
*"         E_T_MEMBERS STRUCTURE  BICS_PROV_RS_MEMBER OPTIONAL
*"         E_T_MEMBER_PRESENTATION STRUCTURE
*"           BICS_PROV_RS_MEMBER_PRESENTATI OPTIONAL
*"         I_T_SELECTION STRUCTURE  RSBOLAP_SO_S_CHAR_SELECTION
OPTIONAL
```

Listing 13.1 BICS Function bics_prov_get_members

12. Double-click on the E_T_MEMBERS variable name in the tables area and the entry is shown on the right-hand side of the ABAP Debugger (see Figure 13.9).

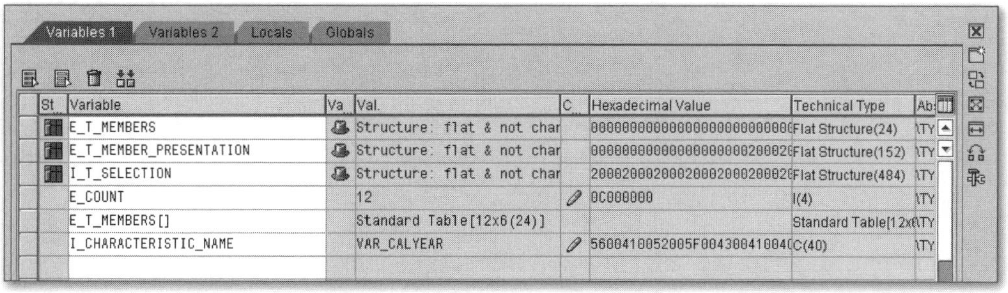

St	Variable	Va	Val.	C	Hexadecimal Value	Technical Type	Ab
	E_T_MEMBERS		Structure: flat & not char		000000000000000000000000	Flat Structure(24)	TY
	E_T_MEMBER_PRESENTATION		Structure: flat & not char		000000000000000000020002	Flat Structure(152)	TY
	I_T_SELECTION		Structure: flat & not char		200020002000200020002002	Flat Structure(484)	TY
	E_COUNT		12		0C000000	I(4)	TY
	E_T_MEMBERS[]		Standard Table[12x6(24)]			Standard Table[12x	TY
	I_CHARACTERISTIC_NAME		VAR_CALYEAR		5600410052005F004300410044	C(40)	TY

Figure 13.9 ABAP Debugger Variables

13. After you add all the elements you need to the right-hand side, you simply execute the trace by using the F8 button. The trace will be executed up to the breakpoint.

14. Now the selected elements should contain the information. Double-click on the selected elements to see the actual values that are part of the trace.

15. In the given example, a double-click on the E_T_MEMBERS structure shows the details of the structure (see Figure 13.10). You can double-click on the TABLE icon (▦) to reach the underlying table (see Figure 13.11).

| Desktop 1 | Desktop 2 | Desktop3 | Standard | Structures | Tables | Objects | Detail Displs. | Data Explorer | Break/Watchpoints | Diff |

Structures | Fld.list

Struct. `E_T_MEMBERS`
Struc. Type `Flat Structure(24)` ▦

Exp.	Component	Val.	Val.	Change	Technical Type	Hexadecimal Value	Absolute Type	Re
	MEMBER_ID	0		✎	I(4)	00000000	\TYPE=RSBOLAP_C	☐
	NODE_PARENT_ID	0		✎	I(4)	00000000	\TYPE=RSBOLAP_C	☐
	NODE_TYPE_ID	0		✎	I(4)	00000000	\TYPE=RSBOLAP_C	☐
	LEVEL	0		✎	INT2(1)	00	\TYPE=BICS_PROV.	☐
	PRESENTATION_INDEX_FRO	0		✎	I(4)	00000000	\TYPE=RSBOLAP_II	☐
	PRESENTATION_INDEX_TO	0		✎	I(4)	00000000	\TYPE=RSBOLAP_II	☐

Figure 13.10 Structure E_T_MEMBERS

| Desktop 1 | Desktop 2 | Desktop3 | Standard | Structures | Tables | Objects | Detail Displs. | Data Explorer | Break/Watchpoints | Diff |

Tables | Table Contents

Table `E_T_MEMBERS[]`
Table Type `Standard Table[12x6(24)]`

Line	MEMBER_ID[I(4)]	NODE_PARENT_ID[I(4)]	NODE_TYPE_ID[I(4)]	LEVEL[INT2(1)]	PRESENTATION_INDEX_FROM[I(4)]	PRESENTATION_INDEX_TO[I(4)]
1	0	0	807	0	1	10
2	2006	0	807	0	11	20
3	2007	0	807	0	21	30
4	2008	0	807	0	31	40
5	2009	0	807	0	41	50
6	2010	0	807	0	51	60
7	2011	0	807	0	61	70
8	2012	0	807	0	71	80
9	2013	0	807	0	81	90
10	2014	0	807	0	91	100
11	2015	0	807	0	101	110
12	2016	0	807	0	111	120

Figure 13.11 Underlying Table for E_T_MEMBERS

In our example, the column MEMBER_ID contains the list of members that was retrieved.

At this point you have learned how to call the traces and how to retrieve the relevant information. You may have noticed that, as part of the trace, not all of the information is shown as "readable" values, but instead leverages IDs. Therefore, you have to resolve those IDs back to characteristics and key figures. As mentioned in Table 13.2 and Table 13.3, one of the critical functions is BICS_PROV_GET_INITIAL_STATE, as this function allows you to retrieve the relationship between the used characteristics and key figures.

In the next step you will learn how to interpret some of the information shown in the trace. In the following example we use an SAP BusinessObjects Web Intelligence report that leverages a BEx query and return the data from two characteristics and one key figure.

Using the previously described steps, we retrieve the details from the BICS_PROV_GET_INITIAL_STATE function in our trace. The most important part of this function is the E_TH_META_CHARACTERISTICS variable (see Figure 13.12).

Line	NAME[C(40)]	ALTERNATIVE_NAME[C(40)]	ID[I(4)]	TEXT[C(60)]	HAS_SHORT_TEXT[C(1)]	HAS_MEDIUM_TEXT[C(1)]
1	OD_NW_SORG		15980	Sales Organization	X	X
2	OD_NW_SOLD		15986	Sold-to Party	X	X
3	OD_NW_PROD__OD_NW_PRDCT		15988	Product Category	X	X
4	OD_NW_PROD__OD_NW_PRDGP		15989	Product Group	X	X
5	OD_NW_PROD		15987	Product	X	X
6	OCALMONTH		804	Calendar Year/Month		
7	OD_NW_CHANN		15978	Distribution Channel	X	X
8	OCALYEAR		807	Calendar Year		
9	OD_NW_SGRP		15993	Sales Group	X	X
10	OD_NW_DIV		15979	Division	X	X
11	D9CRB5IGYM7UPX25CCIKDH7AA		2000000908	Key Figures		
12	OD_NW_CNTRY		15976	Country	X	X
13	OD_NW_REGIO		15977	Region	X	X

Figure 13.12 Variable E_TH_META_CHARACTERISTICS

The E_TH_META_CHARACTERISTICS variable shows all the characteristics from the underlying BEx query in the NAME column. In the ID column, you can see the assigned ID per characteristic.

As the next step, we are interested in seeing the retrieved data from the trace. We start with retrieving the information from the BICS_PROV_SET_STATE function. This function provides information about which rows, columns, and free characteristics have been configured for the result; this is not the actual data but instead the structure of the data set.

Following the above steps, you can look at the variable content for I_T_ROWS_CHARACTERISTICS and I_T_COLUMNS_CHARACTERISTICS, which will provide you with the necessary information. In our example the content is shown in Figure 13.13 and Figure 13.14. In Figure 13.13, you can see the ID 15976 and the ID 15977, which you can now reference back to the information shown in Figure 13.12, and thus resolve it to the Country and Region characteristics. In addition, keep in mind that in this context, the notion of rows goes back to what was put into the rows from a result set point of view. In our example, the function returned COUNTRY and REGION on the rows; think about this like a BEx query that you created with COUNTRY and REGION in the rows.

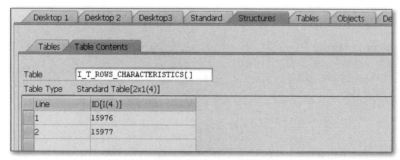

Figure 13.13 Content for I_T_ROWS_CHARACTERISTICS

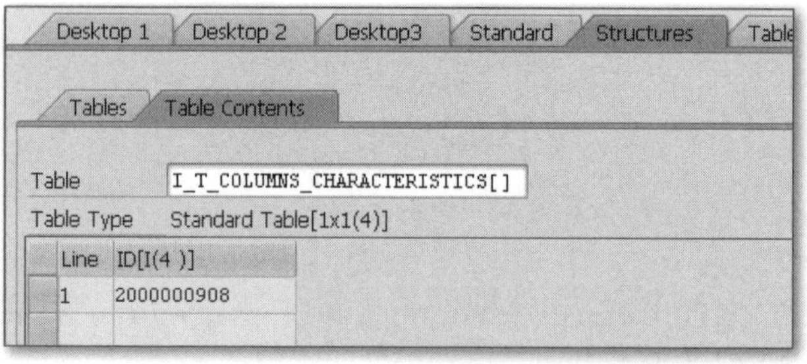

Figure 13.14 Content for I_T_COLUMNS_CHARACTERISTICS

As the final step in retrieving the data that was returned as part of the trace, we look at the information in the trace for the BICS_PROV_GET_RESULTSET function.

As part of the BICS_PROV_GET_RESULTSET function, several variables are relevant to reconstruct the actual data:

▶ E_T_ROWS

▶ E_T_COLUMNS

▶ E_T_DATA_CELLS

▸ E_T_MEMBER

▸ E_T_MEMBER_PRESENTATION

E_T_DATA_CELLS provides you with an overview of the structure for the result set by providing you with a simple matrix for row and column IDs. E_T_ROWS and E_T_COLUMNS allow you to retrieve the members for the rows and columns, and E_T_MEMBER and E_T_MEMBER_PRESENTATION allow you to retrieve the actual data.

In our example we retrieve the information for E_T_DATA_CELLS that is presented in Table 13.4.

Row	Column
1	1
2	1
3	1
4	1
5	1
6	1
7	1
8	1
9	1
10	1

Table 13.4 Result for E_T_DATA_CELLS

In addition to the values for Row and Column, the E_T_DATA_CELLS table also contains a Value column, which shows the actual value for the column. For our example it is important to understand how to reference the information.

In the given examples, we learned that we have two row elements (see Figure 13.13) and one column element (see Figure 13.14). From the E_T_DATA_CELLS table, we learned that the complete result set consists of ten rows and one column, which means that we actually have five rows of data spread across two columns with one column for the key figure.

ELEMENT_INDEX	MEMBER_TABLE_INDEX
1	1
2	2
2	3
1	4
2	5
2	3
1	6
2	7
2	3
1	8
2	9
2	10
2	3
1	11
2	3

Table 13.5 Result for E_T_ROWS

Looking at the result for E_T_ROWS (see Table 13.5), we receive the member table index for each line item of our ten rows. We can use the value from the member table index and continue to look into the values from E_T_MEMBER (see Table 13.6).

Line ID	MEMBER_ID	NODE_TYPE_ID	PRESENTATION_INDEX_FROM	PRESENTATION_INDEX_TO
1	2	15976	1	2
2	2	15977	3	7
3	2000000599	15977	8	12
4	3	15976	13	14

Table 13.6 Result for E_T_MEMBER

Line ID	MEMBER_ID	NODE_TYPE_ID	PRESENTATION_INDEX_FROM	PRESENTATION_INDEX_TO
5	3	15977	15	19
6	4	15976	20	21
7	4	15977	22	26
8	5	15976	27	28
9	5	15977	29	33
10	6	15977	34	38
11	2000000599	15976	39	40
12	2	2000000908	0	0

Table 13.6 Result for E_T_MEMBER (Cont.)

You can use the member table index from E_T_ROWS and look up the value in E_T_MEMBER by matching the value to the LINE ID. In our first row from E_T_ROWS we receive the member table index 1, which is NODE_TYPE_ID 15976. NODE_TYPE_ID 15976 was resolved already (see Figure 13.12) and goes back to the Country characteristic.

In addition we can use the PRESENTATION_INDEX_FROM and PRESENTATION_INDEX_TO now to look into the result for E_T_MEMBER_PRESENTATION (see Table 13.7).

Line ID	PRESENTATION	ATTRIBUTE_ID	CONTINUE	VALUE
1	0	0	0	DE
2	5	0	0	Germany
3	0	0	0	DE 11
4	3	0	0	11
5	5	0	0	Berlin
6	6	0	0	Berlin
7	7	0	0	Berlin
8	0	0	0	SUMME

Table 13.7 Result for E_T_MEMBER_PRESENTATION

Line ID	PRESENTATION	ATTRIBUTE_ID	CONTINUE	VALUE
9	3	0	0	SUMME
10	5	0	0	Result
11	6	0	0	Result
12	7	0	0	Result
13	0	0	0	FR
14	5	0	0	France
15	0	0	0	FR 75

Table 13.7 Result for E_T_MEMBER_PRESENTATION (Cont.)

In our example, we received the values 1 and 2, which are the first two lines, and, in this case, the key (DE) and the description (Germany) for the first cell value of our result set for the Country characteristic.

If we use LINE ID 3 from E_T_MEMBER as a different example, you will notice that LINE ID 8 to 12 is a subtotal description for the NODE_TYPE_ID 15977 Region characteristic in E_T_MEMBER. You will also notice in Table 13.5 that the MEMBER ID with value 3 is listed several times. Based on our example with the Country and Region characteristics in the rows, this shouldn't be surprising.

13.2.4 Validating Metadata

You can validate the metadata that you retrieved in the client tools such as SAP Crystal Reports, SAP BusinessObjects Web Intelligence, and SAP BusinessObjects Dashboards by using a set of SAP tools:

► For the InfoSet connectivity, you can use Transaction SQ02 to validate the metadata that you received with the actual InfoSet in your SAP system.

► For the Open SQL connectivity providing access to tables, views, and ABAP functions, you can use Transaction SE11 and Transaction SE37 to compare the metadata from your SAP system with the metadata in your SAP NetWeaver BW system.

► For SAP NetWeaver BW connectivity, you can use Transaction RSRT to execute the BEx queries and compare the metadata and data set with your report. In addition, you can also use Transaction MDXTEST to see the available metadata for the BEx query.

13.2.5 Validating the Results

If you need to validate the actual data being retrieved, there is a set of tools that you can use.

▶ For SAP ERP InfoSet connectivity, you can easily create a query on top of your InfoSet using Transaction SQ01 and simulate the connectivity without any additional software being involved.

▶ For connectivity with tables for SAP Crystal Reports 2011, you can use the QuickViewer (Transaction SQVI) to create a linkage between the tables and see the actual result set. In addition, you can use Transaction ST05 to enable an RFC and SQL trace on your SAP system to see further details.

▶ For data connectivity towards SAP NetWeaver BW using BEx queries, you can use Transaction RSRT or a simple BEx Analyzer to compare the result set.

13.3 Single Sign-On and Authentication

In this section we focus on steps and tools you can use to verify the steps of the user authentication in your landscape with SAP NetWeaver and SAP BusinessObjects.

13.3.1 Steps to Validate the Configuration

The following is a list of steps to validate your configuration with regards to single sign-on and SAP authentication:

▶ Ensure that the SAP authentication is enabled in the Central Management Console and verify that the SAP entitlement system for your SAP system is not disabled.

▶ Ensure that the SAP system is configured properly and that the necessary SAP roles have been imported to your SAP BusinessObjects system.

▶ Ensure that the underlying SAP system can create and accept logon tickets.

▶ Ensure that all systems are in the same domain and all machine names are always fully qualified.

▶ If you're missing features and functions in your SAP BusinessObjects system, ensure that the imported SAP roles received the necessary authorizations in your SAP BusinessObjects system to perform the task.

▶ Ensure that web applications, such as BI launch pad and OpenDocument, have been configured to use the SAP authentication to leverage the SAP logon token.

▶ Ensure that the roles you want to import into your SAP BusinessObjects system have users assigned to them, because the SAP authentication will list only roles with users assigned to them.

▶ If you're using the SAP NetWeaver Portal as an entry point, ensure that your portal system and your SAP system are configured as trusted systems by exchanging certificates.

13.3.2 Tracing

You can use the Trace registry key in the registry branch *HKEY_LOCAL_MACHINE\ SOFTWARE\Wow6432Node\SAP Business Objects\Suite XI4.0\SAP\Authentication* to enable tracing for SAP authentication. The trace file will be located based on the path of the TraceDir registry key in the branch *HKEY_LOCAL_MACHINE\SOFTWARE\ Wow6432Node\SAP BusinessObjects\Suite XI 4.0\SAP*.

13.4   Publishing SAP Crystal Reports 2011

In this section we focus on the publishing integration of SAP Crystal Reports 2011 with SAP NetWeaver BW, steps you can use to ensure a proper configuration, and steps you can use to troubleshoot this area of the integration of your SAP system with SAP BusinessObjects.

13.4.1   Steps to Validate the Configuration

Similar to the previous sections, the following is a list of items for you to check if you have trouble with the publishing integration of SAP Crystal Reports 2011 with SAP NetWeaver BW.

▶ Ensure that the role you're trying to use on the SAP NetWeaver BW side has been imported into your SAP BusinessObjects system and has been assigned in

Transaction /CRYSTAL/RPTADMIN as the role to your SAP BusinessObjects server definition.

▸ Ensure that the role has a valid description in all languages you want to use. This can be done in Transaction PFCG.

▸ Ensure that your RFC destination in Transaction SM59 is working properly.

▸ Ensure that the user publishing a report has all the necessary rights in the SAP BusinessObjects system.

13.4.2 Tracing

The publishing integration can use either SAP Gateway or the SAP NetWeaver BW publishing service. If you use the publishing service, you can trace the activity of the publishing service by setting the Trace key in the registry branch *HKEY_LOCAL_ MACHINE\SOFTWARE\Wow6432Node\SAP BusinessObjects\Suite XI 4.0\SAP\BW Publisher Service* to the value "Yes". The path for the trace files has been configured by the TraceDir registry key in the registry branch *HKEY_LOCAL_MACHINE\SOFTWARE\ Wow6432Node\SAP BusinessObjects\Suite XI 4.0\SAP* .

The SAP NetWeaver BW publisher itself can be traced by setting the Trace key in the branch *HKEY_LOCAL_MACHINE\SOFTWARE\Wow6432Node\SAP BusinessObjects\ Suite XI 4.0\SAP\BWPublisher* to "Yes".

13.5 Publications

In this section we focus on the publication process and the tools you can use to validate your configuration and to trace the publication process if you face some issues in your system landscape.

13.5.1 Steps to Validate the Configuration

If you face issues with a publication process, there are several areas that you should validate in your configuration. Based on the complexity of the configuration, the best step is to go back to the starting point and ensure that all necessary configuration steps have been taken and have been entered correctly.

However, there are some steps you can use before going through the complete configuration:

- A good starting point is always the automatically generated logfile for the publication itself. If your publication fails, click the FAILED status and you'll receive more details; more importantly, you'll receive a VIEW LOG FILE option that provides you with the logfile of your publication.

- Ensure that you always entered the correct distinguished name for your SAP and SAP BusinessObjects systems as part of the server-side trust configuration. Keep in mind that the values are case sensitive.

- If you use the server-side trust configuration, ensure that the distinguished name is entered with the prefix "p:" in Transaction SNC0 and in the Central Management Console for the SAP authentication.

- If you use the server-side trust configuration, ensure that your SAP BusinessObjects services are running under an account that has access to the PSE files.

- Ensure that you can view the reports that you use for a publication by using the SAP authentication in InfoView without being prompted for your SAP credentials during viewtime.

- Ensure that the user groups you use as recipients have the necessary rights assigned in your SAP BusinessObjects system to view the public folders and to view the reports.

13.5.2 Tracing

Tracing the details of a publication means tracing the underlying data connectivity of the SAP Crystal Reports object or the SAP BusinessObjects Web Intelligence objects that you're using. You can use the details in the previous section for tracing the connectivity.

When you trace the data connectivity for your publication, you should be able to see the text shown in Listing 13.2:

```
Logon string: CLIENT=003 LANG=EN ASHOST="cimtdc00.wdf.sap.corp"
SYSNR=00 SNC_MODE=1 SNC_QOP=1
SNC_LIB="C:\Program Files\SAP\CRYPTO\sapcrypto.dll"
SNC_PARTNERNAME="p:CN=CIM, OU=PM, O=SAP, C=CA"
SNC_MYNAME="p:CN=BOESERVER,OU=PM,O=SAP,C=CA"
EXTIDDATA=USER_A EXTIDTYPE=UN
```

Listing 13.2 Example for Connectivity Trace

The trace needs to include the proper EXTIDTYPE=UN for the user name, and the EXTIDDATA needs to include the user name of the recipient.

13.6 Performance

In this section we outline some common options that you can use to ensure that you're getting the best performance possible from your system. In general, any knowledge you have about performance improvement and performance tuning for your SAP NetWeaver BW system applies to the use of the SAP BusinessObjects software on top of the SAP NetWeaver BW system.

13.6.1 General Performance Considerations

The following are some general recommendations regarding the performance of your SAP NetWeaver BW system. Covering SAP NetWeaver BW performance tuning completely would be beyond the scope of this book, and resources are available on the SAP Developer Network (*http://sdn.sap.com*) and in SAP NetWeaver documentation (*http://help.sap.com*) that explain this topic to a much greater extent. The items listed here are the most common items we have come across so far.

▶ Use your SAP NetWeaver BW statistics to identify the most used but also the slowest-performing BW queries and to identify the reasons for the performance results.

▶ Use Transaction ST03 to evaluate the need for aggregation of the BEx queries that you use for reporting. Pay particular attention to the overall time spent on the database and the ratio between the database selected records and the transferred records. An indicator of missing aggregates is a ratio higher than 10 for the records and a 30% or higher database time compared to the overall time.

▶ You can use Transaction RSRT to execute a single BEx query in debug mode and receive a lot of information about several aspects of performance, such as aggregates and technical information for the selected query.

▶ You can use Transaction RSTT/RSRTRACE to trace and analyze the execution of a BW query or the execution of an SAP BusinessObjects report on top of SAP NetWeaver BW for a single user. You can even go into debug mode for the execution of the trace.

▸ When the needed information is available as a display attribute and as a navigational attribute, you might consider using the display attribute. This is because the usage of navigational attributes leads to additional table joins in the database schema on the SAP NetWeaver BW side.

▸ Especially for SAP BusinessObjects Web Intelligence, you should leverage the query stripping functionality as much as possible. This will ensure that the reports do not ask for all the information based on the SAP BusinessObjects Web Intelligence Query Panel, but instead ask only for the information required for the reports.

13.6.2 BEx Query Design

The following recommendations concern BEx query design:

▸ When your query contains several restricted key figures and calculated key figures, you should select Use Selection of Structure Elements. You can select this option per BEx query in Transaction RSRT by opening the properties of the BEx query. By setting this property, you ensure that the structure elements, such as a restricted key figure, are sent down to the database for processing.

▸ A common approach (and also a common mistake) is to create a single BEx query per InfoProvider, which then is used with SAP Crystal Reports for Enterprise or SAP BusinessObjects Web Intelligence. It is correct that SAP Crystal Reports for Enterprise and SAP BusinessObjects Web Intelligence are able to explicitly ask for specific elements of a BEx query and retrieve the data for those elements. However, the number of elements in your BEx query can have a significant impact on the performance, and there is no need to create a single BEx query for every single SAP Crystal Reports for Enterprise or SAP BusinessObjects Web Intelligence object.

Therefore, it is recommended that you create BEx queries that represent the common denominator. You should try to break down the requirements for your BW environment into groups of characteristics and key figures that represent a high commonality, but also represent a manageable number of BEx queries. If you're not sure whether the BEx queries you create are becoming too large in terms of number of elements, you can easily use the available tools to trace the runtime of your BEx queries and then take the necessary steps to make the required changes.

13.7 Summary

In this chapter you received an overview of the tools available to you to look for further details if you face an issue. In addition, you received tips for BEx query design and report design. In the next and last chapter of the book, we discuss the SAP BusinessObjects BI platform roadmap for the future.

In this chapter you will receive a short overview of upcoming topics that might be of interest for an integrated deployment of SAP BusinessObjects and SAP software.

14 Integration Outlook

When we were close to finishing this book (September 2011), SAP Business-Objects 4.0 was still in ramp-up, enhancement package 01 for the 4.0 release was in the final stages of actual coding and development, and planning for the second enhancement package for the 4.x platform was just beginning. The items listed in this section therefore reflect the status of the product roadmap from that point in time. In regard to overall timing (status as of September 2011), the 4.2 release is planned for the second half of 2012.

> **Product Roadmap Disclaimer**
>
> The above descriptions of future functionality are the author's interpretation of the publicly available product integration roadmap. These items are subject to change at any time without any notice, and the author does not provide any warranty as to these statements.

SAP Crystal Reports for Enterprise

Crystal Reports for Enterprise is positioned as the new SAP Crystal Reports design environment and as a successor to SAP Crystal Reports 2008. Especially for SAP-based solutions, SAP Crystal Reports for Enterprise is the right choice for enterprise reporting. With regards to the future release, the plans include functionality, which will allow the report designer to create common styles and templates. In addition, integration with the SAP BusinessObjects BI platform will be strengthened to increase the capabilities of SAP Crystal Reports for Enterprise for high volume printing.

SAP BusinessObjects Dashboards

For SAP BusinessObjects Dashboards, the team is looking to improve the capabilities around alerting, scorecarding, and exception highlighting, including functionalities such as being able to send alerts based on defined thresholds.

In addition, topics such as generating offline dashboards and integrating geospatial information into the dashboards are part of the planning as well.

Last but not least, the team is also looking into improving integration between SAP BusinessObjects Dashboards and SAP Solution Manger in the areas of tracing and root cause analysis.

SAP BusinessObjects Web Intelligence

For SAP BusinessObjects Web Intelligence, the focus is to further enhance the user experience as part of the on-premise deployment, and also to enhance the new integration of SAP BusinessObjects Web Intelligence for mobile devices. Also on the roadmap are integration with SAP HANA and the capability to leverage to its full extent the functionality of the underlying in-memory engine.

SAP BusinessObjects Analysis Suite

The SAP BusinessObjects Analysis Suite includes SAP BusinessObjects Analysis, edition for Microsoft Office, SAP BusinessObjects Analysis, edition for OLAP, and SAP BusinessObjects Analysis, edition for application design. Here the teams are especially working on the first release of SAP BusinessObjects Analysis, edition for application design as a successor to the Web Application Designer. Topics such as support for report interfaces, support for variable variants, and variable personalization are part of the planning as well. In addition to those functional enhancements, the teams are also working on enhancing integration with SAP HANA and extending the available data connectivity to other sources beyond SAP HANA and SAP NetWeaver BW.

SAP BusinessObjects Explorer

The team for SAP BusinessObjects Explorer plans to deliver an extensive set of APIs allowing management of information spaces via SDK. In addition, the capability to integrate maps as part of the visualizations, the option to add a second dimension to the visualization, and the availability of SAP BusinessObjects Explorer on all type of mobile devices are part of the current planning.

Semantic Layer

With SAP BusinessObjects 4.0, the team delivered the first version of the semantic layer, which allows our customers to combine multiple sources into a single logical view. As part of the planning for the future version, the team is looking to enhance these capabilities and allow the combination of relational data with multidimensional data as well as the combination of data from an on-premise source with data from an on-demand source. In addition, the team intends to increase the SDK so that the semantic layer can be embedded into any application.

14.1 Summary

This chapter has provided you with a short overview of the key products and areas where the teams plan to invest for the future versions.

The Author

 **Ingo Hilgefort** started with Crystal Decisions in Frankfurt, Germany, in 1999 as a trainer and consultant for Crystal Reports and Crystal Enterprise. In 2001, he became the program manager of a small team working in Walldorf at SAP's headquarters for Crystal Decisions. During this time, Ingo worked closely with the SAP BW development group and helped to design and shape the first integration of Crystal Reports with SAP BW, which then became an Original Equipment Manufacturer (OEM) relationship between SAP and Crystal Decisions. With the acquisition of Crystal Decisions by BusinessObjects, he then moved into product management for the integration between BusinessObjects and SAP.

In addition to his experience in product management and engineering, Ingo has been involved in building and delivering BusinessObjects with SAP software for a number of worldwide customers. He has also been recognized by the SDN and BusinessObjects communities as an SDN Mentor for BusinessObjects and SAP integration-related topics. Recently, Ingo has been working on BI end-to-end solution architecture, focusing on the SAP BusinessObjects BI portfolio and helping customers and partners successfully deploy this as part of their overall SAP landscape.

He is also the author of several additional SAP PRESS books: *Reporting and Analytics with SAP BusinessObjects*, *Inside SAP BusinessObjects Explorer*, and *Inside SAP Business-Objects Advanced Analysis*.

Index

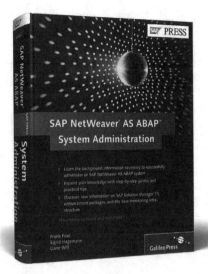

Understand the Basis system's inner workings to quickly address critical situations

Get step-by-step instructions and practical tips about successfully administering an SAP NetWeaver AS ABAP system

Frank Föse, Sigrid Hagemann, Liane Will

SAP NetWeaver AS ABAP
System Administration

As a system administrator, you know that SAP NetWeaver AS ABAP is the core of an SAP system. This book provides essential information on the main concepts and tools of SAP NetWeaver AS ABAP, as well as new information about SAP Solution Manager 7.1 and the new monitoring infrastructure. This all-inclusive resource teaches you a holistic approach to administration, and can also be used to prepare for the Certified Technical Consultant exam.

approx. 700 pp., 4. edition, 79,95 Euro / US$ 79.95
ISBN 978-1-59229-411-4, Nov 2011

>> www.sap-press.com

Interested in reading more?

Please visit our website for all
new book releases from SAP PRESS.

www.sap-press.com